Revolutionary Social Democracy

Revolutionary Social Democracy

The Chilean Socialist Party

Benny Pollack
Hernan Rosenkranz

 Frances Pinter (Publishers) London

© Benny Pollack and Hernan Rosenkranz, 1986

First published in Great Britain in 1986 by
Frances Pinter (Publishers) Limited
25 Floral Street, London WC2E 9DS

British Library Cataloguing in Publication Data

Pollack, Benny
    Revolutionary social democracy: the
    Chilean socialist party.
    1. Partido Socialista de Chile—History
    I. Title   II. Rosenkranz, Hernan
    324.283'074   JN2698.P3
    ISBN 0-86187-579-6

Typeset by Joshua Associates Limited, Oxford
Printed by Biddles of Guildford Limited

Contents

List of Tables

List of Figures

Acknowledgements

We wish to thank all those people in Chile who have helped in some way or another in this research. First, we must thank those party leaders who allowed us to use confidential party documents. Second, we are grateful to our colleagues within the party who made their own documents and records available for research. We would also like to thank the five former leaders of the Chilean Socialist Party who gave us their important opinions on a number of key issues.

In England, we would like to thank Professor Ian Budge, Dr Christian Anglade and Dr Joseph Foweraker from Essex University, whose useful comments on the original manuscript have been invaluable. Dr Anglade's suggestions have been particularly useful, and we are especially grateful to him because of his help and support throughout this research. We should also like to thank the University of Liverpool for giving us the research time needed to complete this book.

All responsibility for errors, omissions and/or inconsistencies is, of course, ours.

Last, but not least, we wish to dedicate this work to the memory of President Salvador Allende. He provided us with great hopes not only for Chile's future but also humanity's. His legacy, and that of his Socialist Party, will very probably be felt for many years to come, more so when the military dictatorship gives way to a new democratic régime in Chile, when both his ideas on democratic socialism and the party's on popular participation, will be put to the test again.

Preface

Before the 1973 military coup it was generally assumed that Chile was the only Latin American country to have strong workers' political parties of the European type.[1] Many reasons have been given to explain this phenomenon, but it is clear that Chile has been the only country in Latin America to allow the development of Marxist parties with strong appeal and following, within the framework of what could be called liberal, democratic processes.

Up to 1970 the electoral force of the Chilean Socialist Party (PSCh) and the Chilean Communist Party (PCCh) oscillated between 20 per cent and 30 per cent of the total national electorate.[2] This increased to more than 40 per cent during 1971.[3]

In addition, the PSCh and PCCh have controlled a number of key areas, including the main trade union organizations. They have also had a strong following within the universities, a notable parliamentary representation and were even successful in the last democratic elections held in 1970, bringing Senator Salvador Allende to the presidency. This gave them, for the first time in Chilean history, the control of the executive power, an achievement which they had never been near to before.

Within this unusual situation, the case of the PSCh itself is even more remarkable.

First, the PSCh had a development of its own, completely independent of that of the PCCh. The existence of a strong Marxist party, apart from the PCCh, able to obtain substantial support from the electorate and with a significant membership drawn from the ranks of the working class, is a unique fact in Latin American political history. These factors help make the Chilean Socialists interesting enough as a subject for study and research.[4]

Second, and with only some exceptions, the PSCh has sustained a continued policy of alliances with the PCCh. This trend has been exclusive to Chile with no equal in Latin America, and only in the case of Guyana, Italy and France can similar features be observed.

Third, it is interesting to study the rather special character of the Chilean Socialists' self-declared Marxism. It should be pointed out that their interpretation of Marxism has been clearly different to that of the Communists.

This is an issue which they have been particularly interested in stressing, and it can be summed up in the assertion that Marxism is for them 'a practical orientation, not a dogma'.[5] This concept has led the Chilean Socialists to adopt a nationalist approach to politics in Chile, Latin America and the world, in order to look for socialist solutions within the framework of a proper Chilean and Latin American context,[6] as against the more inter-nationalist approach of the Communists. There has been, in fact, a consistent attempt by the Socialists to differentiate themselves from the PCCh both in terms of ideology and tactics, although the final strategy to be implemented, the 'model' of socialism to be established in Chilean society, has never emerged from a rather unclear body of ideas.

Fourthly, the PSCh has been to date one of the few Marxist parties,[7] to achieve control of the executive power through democratic, electoral pro-cesses (together with the PCCh and the Chilean Radical Party)—a fact, inci-dentally, that stands in contradiction with the recognized extreme leftist position of the party. It is generally acknowledged that the PSCh has almost invariably been to the left of the Communists in most internal political and social issues, and it has,up to 1973, consistently sustained the idea of the inevitability of violent upheaval to overthrow Chilean legal traditions and the status quo. This, however, has not restrained the Socialists from fully participating in the Chilean democratic processes.

Furthermore, as members of the PSCh, we have known the party from within for almost twenty years, providing us with much information and insight. It was not, then, only the pure scientific curiosity towards a party interesting in itself for any political scientist or political observer; there was also a good deal of personal commitment in the decision to study the PSCh.

As rank and file members, or as officials or advisers within some of the leadership cadres of the party, we were always puzzled by the party's incon-sistencies, and we thought that more accurate research might help to explain them in the context of Chilean politics; for example, in the area of ideology, where the party was proposing violent upheaval as a method to achieve power, while at the same time actively and wholeheartedly participating in each and every election the country had. It was clear enough to us, from our own experiences, that the PSCh in practice was far from following the classic Leninist model in organization and structure. There was a sort of flexibility and freedom which differentiated the party from the rather rigid model to which most, if not all, of the co-called 'Leninist parties' respond: a strong apparatus full of paid officials devoting their time to it; a strict discipline, a clear concentration of power in the highest party echelons, a consequence of power delegated from the membership to the leadership (democratic central-ism); and an internal secrecy which is rarely broken and, if it is, brings firm and sometimes definitive punishments.

The PSCh was, then, a good subject for research. Both the scientific desire to know more about this unique political party and the curiosity arising from our personal experiences made it a logical choice as a research topic. Now that the Chilean Popular Unity's government has been overthrown by force, and the socialist president Salvador Allende is dead, perhaps we should add this tragic point to the list which makes the subject interesting, challenging and, permit us to say so, sad.

This book has been divided into a study in structures and organization (Part I) and the Chilean Socialist Party under military rule (1973–1985) (Part II). There are eight chapters in all. The first chapter is an attempt to present a summarized version of the PSCh's history, in order to provide information that could be useful as a general frame of reference. Here we have used as much as possible original sources which were available in Chile at the time when the field research was done (1971–73). This includes official party documents (acts, declarations, archives, statutes, etc.), periodicals and interviews with people holding, or having held, important positions in the party. Some books written by socialist historians have also proved helpful, as well as other secondary materials available in Chile and in Britain.

The second chapter is a study of the party's overall self-definition as Marxist.

The third chapter studies the related problems of mass and class, the way in which the PSCh has been administered and its method of finance. This chapter is mainly the product of the correlation made between the party's official standing through different kinds of documents and our own experiences within the party's ranks for twenty years. When relevant, some results of an interview with the party's leadership in 1973 are also taken into account.

The fourth chapter studies the practical aspects of organization in an effort to show how the party worked internally.

The fifth chapter is exclusively concentrated on the PSCh's leadership. Apart from the relevant theoretical aspects involved, interviews with some of the party's leadership cadres provide the central focus for the analysis. The interviews were aimed at finding explanations for the leadership's behaviour on a variety of issues related to PSCh politics and the Chilean political situation during the last three months of the Popular Unity government. It consequently shows the conduct of leadership under stress and also the effects on policy of party organization.

The sixth and seventh chapters are mainly an up-to-date study of the party during and after the Popular Unity government, covering such aspects as internal fractionalism, strategies and tactics, policy of alliances, divisions and leadership infighting. These chapters also analyse the difficulties created for the Popular Unity administration by the confrontation between radicals and moderates within the main partner of the coalition, the PSCh, and goes on to examine the nature of the party's opposition to the military government which took power in 1973, and the somehow insurmountable problems of perennial fractionalism and divisions which seemingly weakened the party's stand against the dictatorship. As such, they provide a comprehensive study of political organization and behaviour under their repressive political circumstances.

For the historical introduction, sources were reasonably good—mainly books covering the period before the PSCh was established. It was, therefore, just a matter of selecting the appropriate texts to allow for a short incursion into the historical background that enabled the appearance and development of a socialist party in Chile. The analysis of certain books—dealing with Chile's development at the turn of this century and including the first few decades—provided the main insights into this area.

As has been said, the first chapter was based on an examination of two main sources: the few books that have so far been written on the PSCh's history, and the collection of archive material chaotically stored on shelves and in corners of private libraries and the party's old offices. Amongst the most important were Party Congresses' resolutions, and various unofficial records, letters and internal reports, many of them confidential and of restricted access.

Sources for the second, third and fourth chapters were both theoretical and empirical. The relevant literature covering the subject of political parties was used when pertinent to create a framework for the analysis. The authors have utilized certain theories developed in this literature to facilitate analysis of the PSCh.

Empirical data was provided mainly by primary sources (archives, letters, internal reports), made available especially for this research. Party and non-party journals and periodicals also proved useful.

The fifth chapter contains the survey summarizing the position of the PSCh's leadership structure as it stood in 1973.

The sixth and seventh chapters have been written using almost exclusively primary sources (internal party bulletins and periodicals, both in Chile and in exile; official statements; speeches; and other documents), covering the 1973–85 period. Many of these materials were produced under very difficult circumstances in Chile, where the repression of all forms of political activity after 1973 sent party leaders and cadres into underground politics. Other sources were provided by the several socialist groups which have appeared and disappeared outside Chile since 1973, some in fact having been important vehicles of solidarity with the opposition and resistance movement inside the country.

NOTES

1. Ernst Halperin, in *Proletarian Class Parties in Europe and Latin America: A Comparison*, MIT Press, Cambridge, Mass., 1967, makes a strong argument on this issue.

2. Official statistics of the Dirección Nacional del Registro Electoral, Santiago, Chile.

3. If the percentage received that year by the centre-left Radical Party, which integrated the governmental Popular Unity coalition, is added, the figure amounts to more than 50 per cent.

4. Hereafter, by *working class* we mean manual workers of all sorts (mainly industrial workers, peasants, salary-paid technicians). By *middle class* we mean what in general are called the 'petite bourgeoisie' (mainly employers, small entrepreneurs, small farmers, professionals and intellectuals). By *bourgeoisie* we mean big entrepreneurs and landowners, mainly employing a labour force of more than fifty. By *oligarchy* we mean a socio-economic group monopolizing the use of political power, no matter whether it is industry-orientated, land-orientated or both. By *dominant class or sector* we mean those socio-economic groups which own the main means of production in a given society, and whose political, moral, religious and cultural aims filtrate through that society. By *dominated class or sector* we mean those socio-economic groups which provide the labour force in a given society, and whose political, moral, religious and cultural aims normally do not prevail in that society.

5. From the *Manifiesto Socialista*, p. 3 (first concrete available public document on the foundation of the party); issued in 1934, the concept has been repeated if not in form, at least in substance. From hereon, all quotations from sources in Spanish will be presented in English. The translations have been made by us.

6. Again this idea has been present in almost every socialist document available, since the *Manifiesto Socialista* on.

7. Cheddi Jagan's accession to power in Guyana had similar features.

PART I

A Study in Structures and Organization

Historical Introduction

Dependency theory is perhaps one of the most appropriate models to explain some of Latin America's historical peculiarities. Latin America became a part of the international division of labour with the most advanced commercial and industrial countries (mainly Great Britain in the nineteenth century and the United States afterwards). International trade can be characterized as 'asymmetric', as it is generally agreed that the industrialized countries have been those who have benefited most from it. In the long run this asymmetry has resulted in the Latin American countries being subjected to forms of domination by the superior military, economic and political powers of the centre.

There existed economic domination when the powers of the centre imposed on Latin America a model of subordinate development, generally adjusted to the industrialized countries' own economic needs. The best example is provided by the fact that Latin America has long been one of the main world producers of raw materials and food at cheap prices, while at the same time acting as a major market for manufactures produced in the industrialized world. Political domination is always more difficult to describe, but it is clear that political élites in Latin American countries were normally recruited from the agro- and mining-export sectors, somehow in combination with the traditional *latifundista*, and commercial sectors. This model is what Cardoso has called *the compromiso oligarquico*, (or oligarchical agreement).[1]

The above scheme could be said to apply generally to Chile. In the last quarter of the nineteenth century Chile became a solid member of the international market as one of the world's top nitrate producers, satisfying most of the growing agrarian needs of Britain. Towards 1875 exports to Britain had reached almost $22 million, and were equivalent to approximately 60 per cent of the total value of exports by Chile. At the same time, Chile performed well as one of Britain's clients for her industrial products, as around US$16 million were being spent in imports from that country, or 41 per cent of the total amount.[2] Between 1845 and 1875 the increase in commerce between the two countries was larger than the total increase of Chilean international commerce as a whole.[3]

The nitrate enclave provided the socio-economic basis to support the oligarchic system of domination in Chile. However, the native oligarchy lacked the necessary resources to keep under his control the primary export apparatus which was handed over to foreign interests, and was soon reduced to subordinate roles: commerce, financing and agriculture for the internal market. Furthermore, it is generally accepted that the nitrate enclave did not generate the dynamic effects which would have enabled a diversification of the local economy. This was not only because it never originated new technological requirements to improve methods and/or standards but also because the economic surplus was kept by the dominant economies, therefore blocking a national process of capital accumulation. In 1888, for example, the nitrate exported to Europe was valued at more than $79 million, but only $28.7 million remained in Chile as salaries and taxes, while the rest was transferred abroad.[4]

While this picture is a fair reproduction of similar enclave economies in the area, there are certain peculiarities which help to explain some aspects of the political and economic development of Chile. Perhaps the most important of these features is the existence, at a very early stage, of a centralized state. This in turn naturally gave birth to a politico-administrative apparatus in constant process of development and growth. In other words, the local oligarchical groups, their economic power being debilitated by their marginalization *vis-à-vis* the mining-export sector (nitrate, first, and copper afterwards), managed to present themselves as the 'political class'. This gave them a considerable negotiating power with the dominant metropolitan economies. The state claimed for itself, therefore, the right to share the fruits of the nitrate and copper exports. 'It is the government and not the native owners of the export sector, which administers, spends and distributes a considerable part of the national income generated by international trade.'[5]

The creation of a centralized state is partly the consequence of particular historical peculiarities of the nineteenth century.[6] This development had important repercussions with long-lasting effects on the shape of the Chilean economy as a mining enclave. In the first place it meant that within the political system the institutionalization levels became more important than the mobilization levels.[7] Second, it encouraged the virtual legitimization of a form of clientelistic politics, by which the state co-opted groups and classes through the redistribution of the income provided by the mining enclave. These phenomena help us understand the relative solidarity and stability of liberal democratic institutions in Chile. Briefly, the end of the nineteenth century witnessed a political model in which Chile is governed by a strong parliamentarian machine co-existing with a weak executive. The various agro-export factions emerge as dominant, while an incipient industrial faction begins to appear.

During the last years of the nineteenth century and the first of the twentieth century, some important social and ecological changes took place. Between 1885 and 1907 there were massive migrations from the rural areas to the north and centre. A mainly rural economy was thus gradually being transformed into an urban economy.[8] The mining enclaves, commerce and services, together with a still incipient but already notorious industrial development, were being matched by the growing political presence of new social groups, particularly bureaucrats, businessmen and even some pro-letariat. Most of these new groups came to add variety and sophistication to the traditional middle class of mine-owners, while the working-class groups came to enlarge the artisan associations that had been active as far as in the 1860s.[9]

In 1904, when copper mines became important, nitrate fields provided work for almost 25,000 workers.[10] This had its obvious social effects: strikes and other kinds of protest movements gradually became common, mainly in Valparaíso, Santiago, Antofagasta and Iquique, places with the main concen-tration of miners and artisans. *El Mercurio*, a Santiago conservative daily, and traditionally the mouthpiece for the native oligarchy, estimated that between 25,000 and 30,000 people attended a public meeting held in October 1905.[11] This certainly reveals that already by the turn of the century important social and political phenomena were taking place, including some forms of mobili-zation.

The incorporation of Chile into the minerals' international market at the end of the last century contributed, therefore, to a process of social diversifi-cation and to the gradual development of both the middle and the working classes. Their importance was soon to become apparent. However, a situation existed by which the levels of mobilization resulting from economic modernization could in fact be subjected to effective social control. The centralized state and its politico-administrative apparatus would normally succeed in shaping the levels of institutionalization required to cope with the increasingly complex social situation. Traditional oligarchical parties began then to show concern about the 'social problem'. The Conservative Party,[12] traditionally the articulator of agrarian interests, produced a somehow theological interpretation of social unrest, attributing it to a 'growing de-christianization' of the country. For the Conservatives this phenomenon was responsible for the now debilitated links between *terratenientes* and peasants and the resulting effect, the abandoning of old loyalties and allegiances.

A faction of the Liberal Party,[13] in turn, representing urban orientated, commercial and industrial sectors, showed itself far more realistic in its assessment of social unrest. In the 1907 Party Congress two clear tendencies came into the open: one that recognized the existence of a 'social problem' and made a dramatic call for harmony between capital and labour; and the other that simply ignored the existence of such a problem at all. More to the left, the Radical Party was active mobilizing the independent-minded small and medium-sized mine-owners and workers of the *Norte chico* (the little north, mainly the Atacama and Coquimbo provinces). Furthermore, this party was being seen as a progressive instrument to challenge the power of Conservatives and Liberals, by the new emerging professional and bureau-cratic groups. In their National Congress of 1909 the 'pro-socialist' faction of Valentín Letelier defeated the 'pro-liberal' wing of Enrique Mac Iver.[14]

Between 1911 and 1920 almost 300 official strikes took place, including approximately 150,000 workers. In 1919, the Federación Obrera de Chile decided to replace its co-operativist programme for one with strong socialist overtones, proposing the replacement of the existing social system. Several organizations with socialist ideas were being established in the main Chilean cities,[15] with the Mexican and Soviet revolutions increasingly playing an influential ideological rôle. In addition, Anarchism, alive and well in Argen-tina as a consequence of the massive Italian migrations to that country, was also proving an important ideological current in Chile, particularly among artisans' associations.

The end of the First World War caused a drastic recession in the nitrate world market, a situation made worse by the incorporation of synthetic nitrate as a cheaper substitute. Successive governments tried to solve the increasing crisis by the only expedient they had—massive loans, which quickly made the public debt soar to levels unknown up to then.[16] In 1920 the Partido Obrero Socialista, originally a faction of the small Partido Demó-cratico, affiliated itself to the Third International and came later to be the basis of the Chilean Communist Party (PCCh).[17]

The new working class was by then a fact within the Chilean political system. This precipitated a readjustment of the rules of the game, as the Liberal Party showed in its National Congress of 1920, when Arturo Alessandri was chosen as its presidential candidate:

There exists an urgent need for new social legislation, for a new governmental entity to carry out housing programmes, for laws to put man and woman at the same legal level, for laws to establish direct and progressive taxes on incomes, for a central bank able to control monetary problems, including money supply, for special secretaries at ministerial level, with enough powers to deal with agricultural, and labour and social problems.[18]

The declaration also emphasized the need of a constitutional reform: 'the separation between church and state should be clearly established, to put an end to the so-called 'theological problems' that have been dividing the Chilean people for so many years.'[19]

Eventually, Alessandri was elected, counting on the support of both working- and middle-class groups, including important industrial sectors. His government was characterized by confrontation with the traditional agrarian oligarchy, a processs which culminated in his ousting by the Army on 5 September 1924. The military junta that succeeded Alessandri enacted a series of decrees aimed at removing oligarchical power. Many of the measures adopted had been strenuously fought against by the most powerful oligarchical groups during Alessandri's administration. However, a group of young officers, viewing the performance of the junta as too weak, reinstated Alessandri as president on 23 January 1925. By then the trend within the Chilean Armed Forces, as a consequence of its Prussian instructors' influence, was for professionalization. Furthermore, this brought about various modernizing measures (i.e. more middle-class recruitment into the officers' ranks), which eventually reflected upon the political system in a similar way.[20]

Alessandri's government got the new Constitution of 1925 approved, putting an end to formal oligarchical power, until then exercised through Parliament. The new Constitution established a strong executive, whose powers were largely taken from Parliament. In 1927, however, a new military coup deposed Alessandri yet again. An unstable period followed, and only the installation as president of General Carlos Ibáñez put an end to the growing and sometimes uncontrollable anarchy.

Ibáñez set about a number of measures aimed at modernizing the role of the state. Among these, the creation of the Corporación del Salitre (COSACH) stood as perhaps the most important as it came to replace the Asociación de Productores de Salitre, under British control. Ibáñez also pushed public works programmes to diminish unemployment, but in order to do so he had to increase still further the foreign debt, mainly through North American loans. The bureaucratic apparatus was significantly enlarged so as to be able to manage the increased and more complex roles of the state.

The measures adopted by Ibáñez could not in fact alter the consequences of the world's nitrate crisis. His government could not reverse significantly the negative trends of the social situation, and he was deposed in 1931. His successor, Juan Esteban Montero was, as expected, also unable to do anything spectacular to ease social tensions, now gravely augmented by the impact of the world recession on Chile which was in turn still fighting to save something out of the nitrate disaster. The lack of industrial diversification, and the monoproductive and dependent nature of the Chilean economy, were already causing widespread misery to important sectors of the Chilean people. On 4 June 1932 a new military coup, headed by Air Commodore Marmaduke Grove, expelled Montero and seized power bloodlessly. Their ideology could better be described by repeating their main political slogan: "Pan, Techo y Abrigo para el Pueblo' (Bread, a roof and shelter for the people).

NOTES

1. The *compromiso oligárquico* refers to a fundamental political 'agreement' between the primary export sector of the economy, the commercial and financing groups, and latifundia proprietors producing for the internal market. For details, see F. H. Cardoso, 'Des élites: les entrepreneurs d'Amérique Latine', *Sociologie du Travail*, 3 July–September, 167. Dependency literature is abundant. Perhaps the most useful works are: Aníbal Quijano, *Dependencia, cambio social y urbanización en Latinoamérica* (ILPES, mimeo, 1967); F. H. Cardoso y Enzo Faletto, *Dependencia y Desarrollo en América Latina*, (Siglo XXI, México 1972); Theotonio Dos Santos, 'El nuevo carácter de la dependencia', in José Matos Mar (ed.), *La crísis del desarrollismo y la Nueva Dependencia*, Amorrortu, Argentina, 1972); A. G. Frank, *Capitalismo Y Desarrollo en América Latina*, (Siglo XXI, Argentina, 1973).
2. Hernán Ramírez Necochea, *Historia del imperialismo en Chile* (Austral, Santiago, 1970), pp. 46, 58.
3. Ibid., p. 58.
4. Ibid., p. 62.
5. Aníbal Pinto, 'Desarrollo y relaciones sociales', in *Chile Hoy*, (Siglo XXI, Mexico, 1971), p. 10.
6. See the perceptive analysis by Robert R. Kaufman, *Transitions to Stable Authoritarian-Corporate Regimes: The Chilean Case* (USA, Comparative Series Number 5, SAGE, 1976).
7. To assess the anomaly of this situation, and the common pattern of mobilization trends having pre-eminence over institutionalization trends, in countries struggling for modernization, see S. P. Huntington, *Political Order in Changing Societies* (Yale University Press, New Haven, 1968), pp. 1–92.
8. In 1865 approximately 28.6 per cent of the population was urban, as compared with 71.6 per cent living in rural areas. In 1907 the percentages had varied to 43.2 per cent and 56.8 per cent respectively. See Raúl Atria, 'Tensiones políticas y crísis económica: el caso chileno (1920–1938), *Revista de Estudios Sociales* 1 (Marzo 1973); and Ricardo Lagos, 'La Industria en Chile: antecedentes estructurales' (Santiago Instituto de Economía, 1966).
9. In 1858 the *Sociedad de Artesanos de Valparaíso* and the *Unión de Artesanos de Chile* were established. In 1885 the first barbers' strike caused much public concern, while the printing workers' 1888 strike revealed that the 'social problem' could no longer be ignored.
10. Julio César Jobet, *Ensayo Crítico del Desarrollo Economico-Social de Chile* (Ed. Universitaria, Santiago, 1959), p. 137.
11. Fernando Pinto Lagarrigue, *Crónica Política del Siglo XX* (Orbe, Santiago, 1972), p. 41.
12. The Conservative and Liberal parties were established in the nineteenth century, as part of the political infightings that followed Bernardo O'Higgins' abdication in 1823.

13. Fernando Pinto Lagarrigue (*op. cit.*), p. 41.
14. The Radical Party was founded in 1861 by Pedro León Gallo and the Matta brothers (Manuel Antonio and Guillermo), wealthy northern miners.
15. In 1897 the Unión Socialista was created, while the Partido Obrero Francisco Bilbao and the first Partido Socialista were founded in 1898 and 1901, respectively.
16. The public debt increased from $850 million between 1900 and 1904, to $1,776 million between 1915 and 1919. See *Statistical Abstracts of the Republic of Chile*, p. 65.
17. Jorge Barría, *El movimiento obrero en Chile* (Universidad Técnica del Estado, Santiago, 1971), p. 44.
18. Fernando Pinto Lagarrigue (*op. cit.*), p. 88.
19. Ibid.
20. See Alan Joxe, *Las Fuerzas Armadas en el sistema político de Chile* (Ed. Universitaria, Santiago, 1970).

1 A brief history of the Chilean Socialist Party[1]

INTRODUCTION

Between 1931 and 1932 there was a proliferation of leftist movements in Chile. The most important were Nueva Acción Socialista (NAP), Acción Revolucionaria Socialista (ARS), Partido Socialista Marxista, Partido Socialista Unificado and Orden Socialista, none of which had been able to obtain any degree of popular following. However, unemployment was already severe, exports had diminished abruptly, inflation reached extremely high levels and foreign credits were exhausted.[2] Julio César Jobet gives the following statistical indicators of the social and economical situation during 1930 and the ten years that followed:

Latifundia–87,790 properties of less than 5 hectares, with a total of 139,445 hectares (an average of $1\frac{1}{2}$ hectares per person); 41,437 properties from 5 to 20 hectares, with a total of 469,339 hectares (an average of 11 Has. per person); 21,341 properties 20 to 50 Has. with a total of 691,581 Has. (an average of 32 Has. per person); 6,000 properties of 100 to 200 Has; 5,323 properties of 200 to 500 Has; 3,560 properties of 500 to 2,000 Has. With a total of $2\frac{1}{2}$ million Has.

Against the statistics just given, there were 626 big latifundia proprietors who owned farms of more than 5,000 Has. with a total of 14.5 million Has. and an average of 23,000 Has. per landowner. So 626 landowners owned more land than 180,000 small and medium landowners including those owning farms of 5,000 Has.[3]

Needless to say, latifundia blocked the organization of a rational agrarian economy, worked against increasing production and productivity, and were the main cause of peasant miseries and oppression.[4]

Foreign capital influence: The following are the approximate figures for foreign investment. Investment in:

	US$ (millions)	%
Copper	402	59.3
Manufacturing industry	18	2.6
Electricity and transport	56	8.2
Insurance and banking	13	1.9
Commerce	37	5.4
Communications	151	22.3

$677[5]

Almost all foreign properties belonged to North American concerns, but there also existed some medium and small British, German and French companies.

All raw materials such as nitrate, copper, iron and manganese, were exploited by foreign companies. Monopolies in other areas (coal industry, gas, cattle, cement, beet, sugar, tobacco, alcohol, rice, among the main ones) were widespread. Foreign domination was true also of the banks.

Social injustice: The social situation of the country, it could be said, paralleled the economic climate, as can be inferred from the following indicators:

Mortality rate:	262 per 1,000 (1934)
Illiteracy:	28 per cent (400,000 children were excluded from schooling each year).
Life expectancy:	23 years
Housing shortage:	500,000
TB index:	in 1936 almost 12,000 people died of TB and in 1937 that number actually increased.[6]

At this time the PCCh was rather weak and preoccupied with the struggle between Trotsky and Stalin,[7] mostly irrelevant for the Chilean people. With no strong working-class representative party in the country conditions were right for a new party of that kind to develop, and five small left-wing groups, with no real relevance in the Chilean political scene, decided to fuse in order to create a single, united organization. On 19 April 1933, Acción Revolucionaria Socialista, Partido Socialista Marxista, Nueva Acción Pública, Orden Socialista and Partido Socialista Unificado, founded the Partido Socialista de Chile (PSCh). The immediate origins of the party can be traced to 4 June 1932, when Eugenio Matte Hurtado and Marmaduke Grove overthrew Juan Esteban Montero's government and proclaimed a twelve days long 'Socialist Republic'. The social conditions of the country were such as to allow the foundation and eventual development of a new, alternative party to the Communists on the left, and to the traditional parties. As Eugenio González said:

When the Socialist Party was founded, there was no party (traditional or otherwise), which could properly represent the economic and social interests of the working class. So, there existed objective conditions for the creation of a new party.

On the other hand, the Communist Party was affected by a rigidity in ideology and a world-wide strategy which led to dogmatism. These elements could not serve the interests of the proletariat.[8]

Thus the reasons for founding a new left-wing, Marxist-orientated party to compete with the new PCCh for working-class allegiance can be summarized as follows:

1. Failure of traditional political parties to alleviate the Chilean people's social and economic problems.

2. Failure of the PCCh to gain the support of the working class.
3. PCCh doctrinal rigidity, world-wide strategy and, consequently, dogmatism.
4. The lack of populist movements, as it was the case in Peru (APRA), for example.

This fact has been even recognized by the communist historian Hernan Ramirez, who stated that in the 1930s PCCh tactics were wrong insofar as they isolated the working-class and consequently strengthened its enemies. He added that the line of the party was 'extreme-leftist', 'infantilist' and 'sectarian'.[9]

With the country deeply affected by a social, economic and political crisis, and a communist party which was both inefficient and ideologically divided, the new working-class party had a potential for strong development.

An analysis of the PSCh can be made clearer by dividing its history into three distinct stages of its development:

1. The stage of consolidation (1933–39).
2. The stage of internal division and governmental responsibilities (1939–53).
3. The stage of ideology (1953–70).

1. THE STAGE OF CONSOLIDATION (1933–39)

The first period clearly corresponds to the party's need to establish itself within the Chilean political arena. The party was characterized by its firmly anti-fascist position, reflected in bloody street fighting with the Movimiento Nacional-Socialista (the nazi movement) during the period when PCCh policies were handicapped by the Molotov-Von Ribbentrop pact. Moreover, the party strongly supported the creation of CTCh (Confederación de Trabajadores de Chile) and placed itself in a clear, unambiguous anti-oligarchic position.[10] Pursuing its leftist programme the party withdrew its own presidential candidate, Marmaduke Grove, from the 1938 elections, in order to provide support for the Popular Front candidate, radical Senator Pedro Aguirre Cerda.

In its first 'Declaración de Principios', the PSCh adopted a clear nationalist position on most internal and external issues. This stance has distinguished it to the present.

'We want to know Chilean reality'—said Marmaduke Grove—'and make a comprehensive analysis of the social and economic features which characterize it. We want to mobilize the Chilean people to get our second independence. We want to consider all the acceptable aspects of our traditions ... my party is anti-imperialist and would like, first, to organize all Latin American working-class people to fight against the agents of foreign penetration and exploitation, but we are not going to reproduce here an abject copy of the methods and procedures which have been applied in other countries.'[11]

Latin American nationalism, then, was the most important feature in the PSCh, as can be seen from the following: 'The Socialist Party will fight for the economic and political unity of all Latin American peoples. We want thus to reach a Federation of Socialist Republics of this Continent and an anti-imperialist economy.'[12] Marxism was recognized as 'a method for the inter-pretation of reality, which has been enriched by all scientific inputs arising from social development', and class struggle was recognized as the expression of antagonistic interests: 'One class has appropriated for itself the means of production which are exploited to its own profit and the other class works, produces and earns its living with a wage'.[13]

However, its support of Marxism did not lead the Chilean Socialists to adhere to the Internationals of the moment. On the contrary, the first 'Declaración de Principios' was highly critical of them in every respect.

Besides the general issues of nationalism and Marxism, more specific themes were important in the Socialist ideology of the 1930s.

1. A proletarian dictatorship as a necessary step in the construction of a socialist society.
2. The claim to represent 'manual and intellectual workers' against 'bour-geois interests'.
3. The claim of a 'natural proletarization' of the middle strata, especially those of the *pequeña burguesia* (petty bourgeoisie), which included artisans, small merchants, public employees, teachers, small farmers, small indus-trialists and intellectuals. The party aimed to represent the interests of these groups as well as the interests of the proletarian sectors.[4]
4. Class struggle as inevitable in the Chilean situation, as a result of social injustice, the political failure of the bourgeoisie and economic policies.
5. Anti-imperialism with particular reference to the United States.
6. Anti-capitalism.
7. Anti-communism.

Each of these points will be developed in greater detail below:

1 Proletarian dictatorship has been one of the principles most consistently sustained by the Chilean Socialists throughout the years. This aspect of Socialist ideology was clearly established in official documents and the speeches of Socialist leaders from the party's foundation as an organized entity. The first declaration of principles says that:

during the process of total transformation of the system a workers' dictatorship is needed. Evolution to progress is not possible through the democratic system, because the dominant class is organized in armed civil corps and it has established its own dictatorship in order to keep workers in misery and ignorance. This, in turn, prevents the emancipation of workers.[15]

2. The assumption that the PSCh represents both 'worker' and 'petty bourgeois' interests is rather explicit in party documents of the 1930s.[16] As already established, the impact of world depression on the Chilean economy was considerable. This, together with the perennial instability of the oligarchic régime, the mismanagement of the new social situation caused by the development of new social strata, and the obstacles to the ever increasing demands of new groups, led sectors of the middle classes dependent on state activities to support parties on the left and centre-left, especially the Radicals and Socialists. The extreme conservatism of the traditional Chilean dominant class enabled the anti-establishment parties to co-opt groups that otherwise might have supported the oligarchy. Their situation in capitalist society is so unstable and dependent that often they support the parties of the dominant class.

This trend culminated in 1938 with the election of Pedro Aguirre Cerda, a radical Senator, as president, with the support of Socialists, Communists and Radicals, a reoccurrence of the Popular Front phenomena in France under Léon Blum and very similar to the republican Spanish alliances system in the 1930s.

Jobet says of the social composition of the party during the 1930s that there were 'nitrate coal and copper miners; wood, industrial, transport, and maritime workers; printers, public, municipal and private employees; small industrialists and farmers; artisans, teachers and technicians; professionals and intellectuals'.[17]

3. Of the top leaders in the 1930s (Central Committee level) 75 per cent were of petty bourgeois origin (intellectual and professionals, mainly), while only 25 per cent were of working-class origin (mainly artisans, miners, and industrial workers). A proletarization of the middle sectors was viewed as inevitable.[18]

It is evident that the new groups rallied with the Socialists rather than with the Communists, whose 'rigidity', 'sectarianism' and 'infantilist extremism' has already been described. The social classes closely linked to industrial and governmental activity and notably to an educational system in rapid expansion, would not rely on a communist party unprepared to recognize them as a special social group, different from the traditional manual working class. One party leader of the 1930s told us that:

the Communist Party was then viewed by middle-class people as a group of fanatics, a type of sect dedicated to the cult of the Soviet Union. They were so wrong that they only reacted to Soviet policies and almost always tried to copy Soviet solutions in

Chile. This led them to alienate middle-class sectors from becoming members, as they were suspicious of that kind of behaviour. On the other hand they were unable, either, to gain significant support from working-class people because their foreign ideology was absolutely incomprehensible to them.

4. The idea of a class struggle was present in the Socialist ideology of the 1930s, as indeed it remained after that period. Perhaps the clearest definition of the concept of class struggle as understood by the Socialists in the 1930s is that given by Jobet when analysing the official documents issued by the leadership during the first ten years of the party:

The stage of capitalist economic organization divided humanity into two classes, which are being more clearly defined every day: one class is that which has appropriated for itself the means of production and exploits them for its own profit; the other class is that which really works and has to produce in order to be able to make its living, receiving a wage. The working class needs to fight for its well-being while the class which owns the means of production tries to preserve its privileges. Thus the struggle between the two emerges. The capitalist class is represented by the state, which is an entity for the oppression of one class by another. Once classes are eliminated, the oppressive character of the state will also disappear. Then it will only perform as guide, arbiter and protector of society.[19]

5. Anti-imperialism has been a permanent Socialist issue, since the founding of the party, but what is most remarkable is the distinctive latin-americanist view of this concept. During the 1930s the party stressed the need for a united Latin American continent in a way that would be clearer than that view expressed later. Speeches, reports and declarations suggest that the strong anti-imperialist trend of the Socialist ideology during the 1930s was not only aimed at fighting what was called 'North American imperialism' but the position also had a strong positive content. This is reflected in the repeated belief in the usefulness and necessity of a powerful, supra-national organization to promote a united Latin America. The Federación de Repúblicas Socialistas del Continente would also create the basis for an anti-imperialist regional economy which would eventually compete with North American economic expansion and its political arm, imperialism.[20]

6. Linked to this anti-imperialism, the Socialists maintained strong anti-capitalist views. The first declaration of principles stated that:

the system of capitalist production based on the private ownership of land, the means of production, of trade, of credit, and transport, should necessarily be replaced by an economic and social system in which that property be collective property. Socialized production is organized by previous rational plans, scientifically systematized, and always in accordance with the needs of the people.[21]

The concept, which definitely condemns the capitalist system as a means to organize social and political life, has remained untouched as a primary Socialist principle throughout the party's history. The party continually stressed its anti-capitalism, reinforcing its aim to represent the interests of 'manual and intellectual workers' against 'bourgeois interests'.[22]

7. The Chilean Socialists' distinct anti-communism of the 1930s was strongly influenced by a ferocious nationalism.[23]

What happened was that the Communist Party was then fighting for a revolution which would establish a worker-peasants government, with a view to setting up the dictatorship of the proletariat. They were guided by the Soviet Revolution without worrying about the fact that Chile's conditions were quite different from those of Czarist Russia. They did not consider, either, the fact that in Russia a war was necessary to allow for the break-up of the old system and the incipient democracy that was already being implemented.[24]

Thus the PSCh tried to put itself in a sort of independent third position between what was considered the 'corruption' of social democracy and the 'sectarianism' of communism. The circumstances before the Second World War deepened the differences with the Communists, because whilst the Socialists adopted a clear anti-fascist and anti-nazi position from the beginning, the Communists in Chile and elsewhere were constrained by the Soviet–German pact.[25]

The Socialist position led them to defend Mazzini's theories on the importance of nationalism and to attack Soviet Russia's contention to be 'the Motherhood of the proletariat'. The Socialist historian Jobet wrote that 'Soviet Communism did not act as an ideological, political or emotional substitute for nationalism, but as an instrument to serve a nation or an empire, the USSR. This is why contemporary antagonism between capitalism and communism took the way of a fight between the USSR and the United States.'[26]

This independent position was maintained by the Socialists throughout most of the 1930s and was only partially alleviated once the Communists had already disengaged themselves from their previous stand on the nazi issue, and particularly when the Popular Front was formed in Chile, including both Communists and Socialists.

Summary

During the period of consolidation, the PSCh established a nation-wide organization and developed a consistent policy in favour of democratic and progressive changes in Chile (Fig. 1.1). Its leaders suffered persecutions under the governments of the decade, especially under Alessandri, who deported

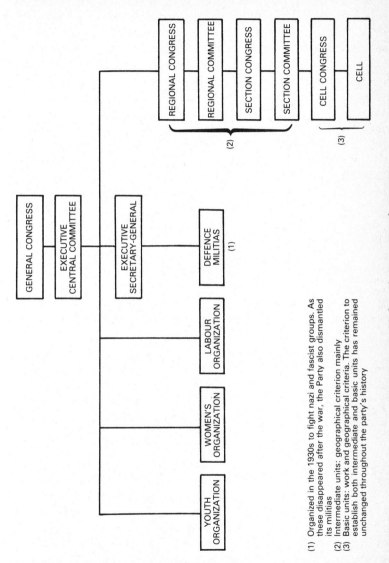

Figure 1.1 PSCh formal structure in the 1930s

(1) Organized in the 1930s to fight nazi and fascist groups. As these disappeared after the war, the Party also dismantled its militias

(2) Intermediate units: geographical criterion mainly

(3) Basic units: work and geographical criteria. The criterion to establish both intermediate and basic units has remained unchanged throughout the party's history

party-founder Marmaduke Grove and other important leaders as a result of party views on a number of key political issues.

It is important to note that during the 1930s the party did not form part of any government, neither did they intend to do so. On the contrary, the Socialists maintained strong opposition to the conservative governments which were in office in the country throughout the 1930s. This situation ended with the Popular Front's alliance which brought Senator Pedro Aguirre Cerda to the presidency in 1938.

The executive power was in the hands of a new coalition, formed by the middle-class, centre-left Radical Party, the Communists and the Socialists, giving the latter an opportunity to enter into governmental responsibilities. Thus the first period of the PSCh's history was one of organization.[27] The party remained united, concrete policies were consistent with its ideology and the internal organization became stronger. Already by 1938 the party had succeeded in spreading its working units (*núcleos*) throughout many areas of the country. The small group of disenchanted intellectuals and workers of the late 1920s had become a political party with strong foundations in Chilean society.

2. THE STAGE OF INTERNAL DIVISION (1939–1953)

The second period in the history of the PSCh begins in 1939, with the party's role in the Popular Front government, and ends in 1953, with the party's withdrawal from Carlos Ibáñez' government.

During this period of its history, the party had the opportunity of participating in government and consequently of discovering the temptations and risks of power-sharing.

Besides participating in government, the party suffered divisions which in some ways affected its unity and strength. For these reasons this period could be considered as one of 'collaboration with the government and internal divisions'.

Even though it actively participated in the creation, during Aguirre Cerda's administration, of the Corporación de Fomento de la Producción (CORFO)—Chilean National Development Corporation—it was clear from the very beginning of the Popular Front that the centre-left Radical Party was the strongest in the alliance. Communists and Socialists provided electoral support and a number of party cadres in public administration and ministries, but government policies were distinctly moderate. The political and social aims of the Radical Party, with its large middle-class support, were aimed primarily at producing industrial growth and a redistribution of the GNP through progressive taxes, state participation in the economy and protectionist policies. The more extreme stand of the two Marxist parties of the coalition, aimed at changing the type of power structure and the socio-economic system then prevailing in Chile, was rapidly overcome by the Radicals' able political manoeuvring.[28]

The participation of the PSCh in the Popular Front caused major internal dissensions and signalled the beginning of a period in which the party exhibited several divisions, with its internal structure suffering various organizational setbacks.

Jobet says that 'the Socialist Party began to divide itself and to weaken as a consequence of its engagement with the Popular Front's government and the hopes it put upon parliamentary-type fights'.[29]

During the first days of 1940, and after the tumultuous Sixth Ordinary Congress held in Santiago from December 20 to 23, a group of five deputies decided to leave the party, accusing it of being 'corrupted by the appeals of a well-supplied bureaucracy, while the rank-and-file, honest member is still waiting for the implementation of true socialistic measures'.[30]

The first recorded division in the party's history was prompted, according to Chelén, by 'the policy of collaborationism with the Popular Front, aimed at suppressing the fighting impulses of the masses'.[31] This view is supported by the fact that the Popular Front's strategy was intended to provide mild reforms, but without altering the basis of the existing social and political system. The strategy was obviously related to the world-wide strategy established by the Communist International for popular fronts elsewhere (specially the triumphant ones in Spain and France) and was a rather difficult, if not impossible, task for any party to change that course of events.[32]

The critical attitude adopted by the nonconformists who left the party in 1940 came as a shock to the rank-and-file membership and prompted a new, extraordinary congress in Curicó in May 1940. As a result, the party left the Popular Front coalition and ran alone in the parliamentary elections of 1941, polling 17.9 per cent of the vote, a 3.2 per cent increase with respect to the results of the 1937 elections, before the party had entered the Popular Front.

The Curicó Congress marked what Jobet considers the starting point of Socialist decadence. 'From then on', he says, 'the Socialist Party lost the support and confidence of the masses and was caught by a rampant and ferocious bureaucratization. For the following five years the party suffered one division after another and was near total disintegration'.[33]

Why was all this happening? We would suggest, among others, the following reasons:

1. *Bureaucratization*: The party suffered from an artificial internal administrative structure which did not always respond to its needs. This in turn

developed a broad set of external relationships with the government bureaucracy and other institutions on an official and unofficial basis.

2. *Co-option of officials*: The process of bureaucratization resulted in an unnecessary number of people occupying all kinds of posts, from the top Central Committee apparatus to the irrelevant *jefes de núcleos*. These officials became frequently linked with governmental activities through patronage and contracts in which they provided services on a private basis. This process led to a significant weakening of the theoretical party positions on a variety of issues.

3. *Corruption*: The line between what could be considered legitimate and what could not is a very thin one, and although there exists no evidence to suggest that a large number of people holding party posts were actually involved in illegal business transactions, there is evidence in a number of individual cases.

Besides, various party leaders of all sorts accepted public and private appointments of all kinds. From the very moment that it entered the Popular Front government in 1938 up to the National Congress of 1946, the PSCh attracted a considerable number of government and, to some extent, private business favours, independent of the fact of party presence in the government. The withdrawal of the party from the Popular Front did not, in fact, cause a subsequent withdrawal of Socialist officials from governmental responsibilities.[34]

Internal structure in the second period

The internal structure of the party somewhat favoured that course of events and the party's ideological radicalization to the left was matched by a rigidity in both its internal structure and working behaviour.

The scheme for organization was officially sanctioned by the party in its Sixth Ordinary Congress in 1940 (Fig. 1.2). It established at the top a Central Committee, headed by a secretary-general, who in turn was supposed to work under the guidance of the Political Commission, consisting of five members.[35] The centralized structure of both the Central Committee and the Political Commission could lead to a wrong conclusion about the real power of these bodies. In fact, the real power of the Central Committee and the Political Commission was rather small. Internal relationships from the top down to the Regional and Section Committees and the *núcleos* were entirely the responsibility of the Department of Organization and Control. In turn,

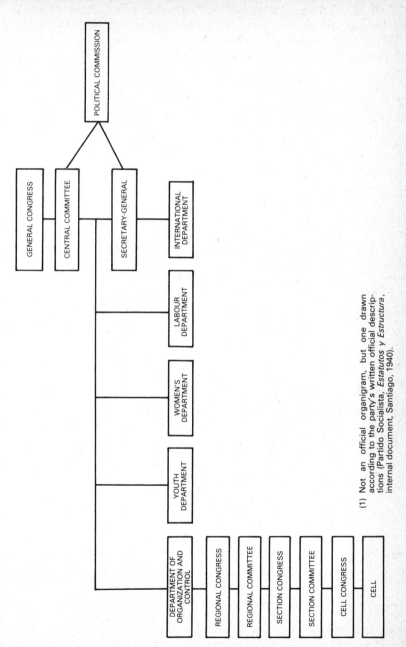

Figure 1.2 PSCh formal structure 1940–53

(1) Not an official organigram, but one drawn according to the party's written official descriptions (Partido Socialista, *Estatutos y Estructura*, internal document, Santiago, 1940).

this depended on the Central Committee (as a body) and not simply on the secretary-general. He, of course, was responsible to both the Central Committee and the Political Commission, but his duties did not include direct responsibility for handling internal party matters.[36]

The Regional Committees were composed of a variable number of people, depending on the actual size of each administrative unit (number of *Seccionales*, or sections, and geographical limits).

The Section Committees varied in a number of their components. These units were to be established in industries, geographical zones and even universities. The criterion for establishing Section Committees was one of *necessity*. When a reasonable number of *núcleos* had proved difficult to manage then a Section Committee was formed to control those *núcleos* and served as intermediary between the *núcleos* and the Regional Committee.

The *núcleos* were maintained as the basic working units of the party as before. These were formed whenever six members of the party worked together in the same place. At least thirty *núcleos* were considered enough to set up a new Section Committee.

To form a Regional Committee, at least eight Sections were considered necessary.

This type of organization enabled two developments in internal party relationships: the creation of *caciquista*[37] relations between members of the Central Committee and the lower administrative structures; and second, the development of factionalism. As the Regional and Section Committees were not in fact directly linked to the secretary-general but to the Central Committee, individual members were able to develop spheres of influence within the party. It was the case that certain members were *strong* in certain party provincial apparatuses while others were strong in others. This greatly encouraged the creation and development of factions with informal although practical structures. The existence of *Congresses* at different levels reinforced these tendencies instead of weakening them.[38]

Already by 1942, an internal party document was stating the uneasiness of the secretary-general on the 'repeated tendency of Central Committee members to use their hierarchies to build bases for their own, political power, with a blatant disregard for Marxist principles'.[39]

But if in internal matters the organization of the party showed weaknesses, it was on external issues that its shortcomings proved even more significant. The 'mechanisms of control' which Carl Beck observed in the Czechoslovakian Communist Party were much the same as in the PSCh whenever the party held governmental responsibilities during this second period.[40] Beck says that those mechanisms take many forms. 'One effective method is that of dual office holdings', another is the fact that 'each individual ministry is subject to various controls', and a third mechanism consists of the existence of 'party organizations and check-points staffed by the party designed to supervise the operation of the ministry'.[41]

The Socialists in Chile clearly corresponded to that model but were nevertheless unable to exercise influence on the policies that Socialist officials were supposed to carry out, whether they were top-level bureaucratic cadres (ministers and under-secretaries), politically appointed medium-level civil servants or even unimportant employees in some remote provincial offices. On the contrary, they continually disregarded party principles and instructions. If one top leader proved to be too insistent on doctrinal matters, he would be rapidly co-opted by the bureaucratic structure so that he could be neutralized.[42]

Perhaps the most important factor in determining this non-obedience pattern observed between 1939 and 1953 (but especially between 1939 and 1947), is the fact that, unlike the Czechoslovakian Communist Party, the Chilean Socialists were part of an open political system in which they shared power with other political parties, as well as there being a well-organized opposition. Political controls of the Czechoslovakian type to supervise the political and private behaviour of party cadres were and are possible in the context of the overall control of power by a single political party. Cadres have in this case much to lose personally if they venture to disobey instructions. Multi-party systems, on the other hand, provide the basis for continuous bargaining and flexibility in both internal and external party relationships. These two features can lead to excesses if and when a given party is not able to create a party structure which can ensure a reasonable degree of discipline on the part of its members.

The image of the party as deeply affected by 'corruption and decadence' was at its peak in 1946, when the Eleventh Ordinary Congress took place in Concepcion.[43] There a group of young members, headed by Raúl Ampuero, succeeded in obtaining a majority in the newly elected Central Committee and promoted the scheme for a Conferencia Nacional de Programa (National Programme Conference) to be held in November 1947.

The conference of 1947 was unable to agree on sensible, major reforms as conflicting groups tried to impose themselves on the new secretary-general. However, it was the starting point of a concerted effort aimed at reorganizing the party structures, raising confidence and purging the bureaucratic apparatus of dishonest elements at all levels.[44] The party was no longer sharing government office, but some of its members were still holding positions in the administration. Even though the Central Committee led by Raúl Ampuero had to use the old, inadequate party organization, Ampuero's personality as secretary-general filled the vacuum. He was a man with a firm character, and his knowledge of Marxist theory was much greater than that of his predecessors. Besides this, he came to lead the party untainted. He had not previously held any governmental post and consequently had had no opportunity to be co-opted by either the public or the private sectors of the Chilean system.

However, according to Jobet, 'the Socialist attempt to rebuild party discipline and morale found opposition from the group defeated at the Concepción Congress'.[45] That group was very much to the left of the official position of the party which had succeeded in provoking the Socialists' engagement in the Popular Front's strategies and policies. They found Ampuero's revitalizing measures rather *weak* and *insufficient*.[46] On the other hand, Ampuero was also under heavy attack by the internal right-wing groups, which wanted to revitalize the already disintegrating Popular Front and to rally the party's support for González Videla.

The First Significant Division

The situation reached a climax in 1948, when the González Videla decided to outlaw the PCCh and asked for Socialist support to do so. Some leading socialists headed by Juan Bautista Rosetti and Bernardo Ibáñez accepted González Videla's appeal and entered a governmental coalition of Radicals, Liberals and Conservatives (known as the Gabinete de Concentración Nacional). They were immediately expelled from the party, together with three Regional Committees which out of a total of twenty-seven had supported Rosetti and Ibáñez.

The expelled group managed to obtain the official recognition of the Dirección de Registro Electoral (Electoral Registry) and consequently were entitled to use the name of Partido Socialista. Furthermore, they voted in favour of the *Ley de Defensa de la Democracia* (Law for the Defence of Democracy), which outlawed the PCCh and culminated in the imprisonment in the concentration camp of Pisagua, in the extreme north of Chile, of all known Communist militants, irrespective of their status in the PCCh.

The majority socialist group led by Raúl Ampuero voted against the anticommunist law (through its six MPs.) and continued a virogous opposition against González Videla's régime. However, in view of the ruling by the Electoral Registry, they had to change the official name of the party, which from then until 1957, when a Unity Congress was organized to unite both groups, came to be known as the Partido Socialista Popular (PSP).

The Partido Socialista Popular was undoubtedly the most representative of the two socialist groups. The other group, notwithstanding its governmental recognition and the official name, Partido Socialista de Chile, was nevertheless unable to win significant popular support.[47] In 1949 the Partido Socialista Popular enlisted the support of the other opposition parties (Falange Nacional, Radical, Democratico and Agrario Laborista) to elect its secretary-general, Eugenio González, as senator for Santiago. Santiago was the main province of the country, both in terms of population and political weight. While this was happening, the dissident group of Rosetti and Ibáñez was being ousted from the presidential cabinet, after the president decided to replace the Gabinete de Concentración Nacional. The new cabinet included the Social Christians, the Falangists (later on, the Christian Democratic Party), the Democrats and the Radicals, and became known as the Gabinete de Sensibilidad Social.

During González Videla's administration, the Partido Socialista consistently maintained its opposition stance. In ideology, it began to shape the doctrine of the Frente de Trabajadores (Workers Front), as opposed to the Frente de Liberación Nacional (National Liberation Front) proposed by the Communists.[48] The Frente de Trabajadores proposed to focus the struggle for socialism in Chile in the formation of an exclusive working-class front, which would exclude the middle class from participation. This position meant in practice excluding the Radical Party from participating in any alliance, as it was considered to be the main representative of the Chilean middle class. This proposal was, of course, rejected by the Communists, in line with the international stand consistently supported by them since the Popular Front strategy began in the 1930s.

Socialist ideology in the second period

The most important aspects of Socialist ideology during this second period were the following:

1. *Titoism*: The Chilean Socialists strongly opposed the Stalinist pressures on Yugoslavia and viewed the Soviet claim to be the main irradiating centre of world socialism as completely unacceptable. When Yugoslavia was isolated by the East European countries, the PSCh firmly endorsed Tito's position. This led them to endorse the Yugoslav system as a form of proletarian control of power, as opposed to the bureaucratic, extremely centralized Soviet system.

2. *Third World strategy*: The creation of several national liberation movements in Asia and Africa, and in newly independent countries later, provided the Chilean Socialists with an opportunity to stress their independence from any 'capital of socialism'. They began in the late 1940s to elaborate the thesis of the need for independent, new forms of socialism to be created, in accordance with the national conditions of each country concerned. Later,

this thesis evolved into the concept of a *Third World Front*, independent of both the capitalist and the communist blocks. The idea acquired a distinct anti-Soviet and anti-American character in the 1950s and 1960s, a fact that erroneously led to the conclusion, by some authors, that the Chilean Socialists were holding 'pro-Chinese' views.[49]

3. *Peronism*: During the late 1950s, the Socialists felt strongly attracted by Justicialismo, the populist political movement led by General Juan Domingo Perón, in Argentina. Justicialismo was in some way a form of neutralist party, which strove to differentiate itself from both capitalism and Marxist-socialism. Its appeal to the Chilean Socialists at that time cannot be considered surprising, given party attitudes towards what they termed the 'block politics' of the United States and the Soviet Union, the aggressive course of Stalin's policies towards Yugoslavia and the continued North American intervention in Latin American politics.

4. *Nationalism*: The titoist, neutralist, somewhat justicialist approaches to Chilean problems meant it was only natural that the Socialists' position of straight, uncompromising nationalism continued unchanged throughout this second period. The Chilean Socialists had never joined any of the Internationals, either Communist or Socialist, and this trend did not change then, nor has it changed up to the present. The Socialists have always been 'ferocious' nationalists.[50] This meant that they were suspicious of any international political groupings which attempted to set out strategies and tactics according to what were considered foreign needs and not those of each nation.[51]

5. *Chilean socialism as opposed to 'communist socialism'*: All the peculiarities of the Socialist ideology of this period helped create a truly nationalist, exclusively Chilean brand of socialism. The task of shaping a sort of independent, native socialist ideology which could interpret Chilean social, economic and political realities would have been perhaps impossible without the leadership of the former party secretary-general and senator Raúl Ampuero. Halperin describes him as a:

highly competent professional, a machine politician of great experience and toughness, who has managed to maintain control over a turbulent and rebellious party ever since he pushed aside the old-guard leadership in 1946. Besides being a skilful and determined machine politician, Ampuero is one of the leading intellectual lights of the Socialist Party and one of its most interesting ideologists.[52]

It is a generally accepted fact that Ampuero helped to shape the very special character of Chilean Socialist ideology, mainly after 1946 through the setting up of channels for internal discussion and, at the same time, the practice of a severe 'watchdog' activity on the part of the centralized party

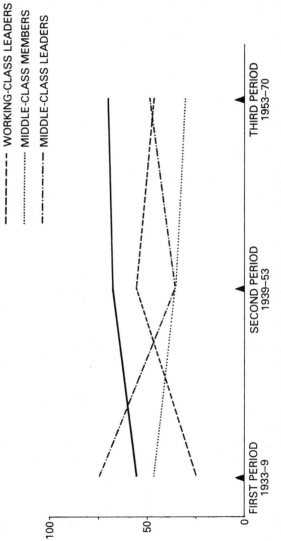

Figure 1.3 Average class origin of members and leaders 1933–70

leadership on any attempt to undermine party discipline in both ideological and organizational matters.

All that was possible because new, though informal, patterns of internal party organization allowed for full control of all and every activity of party cadres from the Political Commission of the Central Committee down to the *núcleos*.[53] Thus, while the two types of internal structure which had prevailed before 1957 permitted the development of almost 'legal' factionalist policies on the part of individual members of Central Committees, the type of internal structure formally adopted in 1953 increased the power of the secretary-general and leaders under his command.

The class background in the second period

The toughness of the Socialist position during part of this period was certainly reflected in the social character of the party's membership and leadership. As much as 55 per cent of the leaders of this period were of working-class origin, while only 45 per cent could be described as petty bourgeois (Fig. 1.3).

That trend, which clearly showed a tendency towards working-class predominance within the top echelons of the party's bureaucratic structure, was reflected in the rank-and-file membership of the party. The percentages for this second period were 65 per cent for working-class members and 35 per cent for petty bourgeois members. But it should be noted that this tendency began to increase steadily only during the last five years of this period, once Raúl Ampuero had been able to reshape party discipline and morale, so low during the party's association with the Popular Front.

Ibáñez and the second division of the party

The removal of the dissident Rosetti group from González Videla's cabinet and the election of Eugenio González, one of the party's secretary-generals, as senator for the Santiago province, practically destroyed the importance of the small rightist faction which had supported the Radical administration. This in turn strengthened the Partido Socialists Popular and encouraged it to undertake a new political venture. It decided to support the presidential candidature of Carlos Ibáñez in the 1952 election.

The decision of the party to support Ibáñez caused a new major division when Senator Salvador Allende decided not to accept that decision and proceeded to leave the party. He was followed by deputy Astolfo Tapia and a small group of party intellectuals and cadres. Shortly afterwards they joined the already weak and politically discredited Partido Socialista de Chile.[54]

The issue of supporting or not supporting Ibáñez was one of the most controversial topics in the party during that period. The personality of Ibáñez was very much the central issue: he had been a staunch militarist engaged not in one but in several anti-constitutional attempts from the 1920s on, having even succeeded in the 1930s and being deposed by a violent popular upheaval not long afterwards. He also had clear pro-nazi sympathies during the 1930s and 1940s and had even been nominated as a candidate to the presidency for the 1938 election by the Chilean Nazi Party.[55]

He was not a member of the PSCh nor of any other party, and it could be said that this fact was, without doubt, his most popular political asset in a country where political manoeuvring and excesses had reached a point where almost any political activity was bound to be considered illegitimate and perhaps dishonest.[56]

The policies of the Radical Party in government had encountered a strong resistance in the PSCh. It considered the Radical administration as:

wholly orientated towards satisfying the demands of the ever-increasing monopolistic national and foreign financial groups with complete disregard of the people's needs. The administration had also engaged the country in the Military Pact with the United States, which many viewed as undermining the traditional sovereign stand of the Chilean people. It had also persisted in its policy of persecuting progressive thought and activity by maintaining the illegal ban on the Communist Party, imprisoning its members and prohibiting any literature construed as subversive.[57]

The political situation as viewed by the Chilean Socialists was clear. The Radicals were counting almost exclusively on the support of the right-wing Liberal and Conservative parties. The banning of any progressive activity or thought in trade unions, universities and even high schools was a daily occurrence. The Military Pact signed with the United States had aroused widespread and conflicting reactions within the ranks of the Chilean press and, in general, within Chilean public opinion.

The Radicals' eagerness in financial dealings which were sometimes dishonest, added to the general feeling of uneasiness and dissatisfaction within the country, not only with those that were supposedly to blame but with all other political associations as well.

Thus Ibàñez appeared as a saviour, a man not linked to the traditional party politics, independent of any known financial group; a type of 'anti-politician' who would lead the country out of its moral crises:[58] 'the support given to Ibàñez was due to the fact that the popular support he was promoting for himself was out of control. The character of this support overwhelms any partisan attempt to contradict it. The party is thus unable to stop the tumultuous, vociferous, enormous support Ibàñez is getting.'[59]

The triumph of Carlos Ibàñez in the 1952 presidential elections helped reflect the general dissatisfaction with party politics. Posing as an independent with the support of the Partido Socialista Popular and the Partido Agrario Laborista (a centrist party with a large middle-class allegiance taken from the Radical Party, mainly from the bureaucracy, small merchants, industrialists and small farmers), he managed to poll an impressive 446,000 votes, against 265,000 for the right-wing Arturo Matte (supported by the Liberal and Conservative parties), and compared with a mere 190,000 for the official candidate, the Radical Pedro Enrique Alfonso. Fourth came Salvador Allende, who had run with the support of the small PSCh and of the PCCh, the latter still officially banned.

The impressive vote for Ibàñez prompted the formation of a government with Socialist and Agrario-Laborista support which included the Socialist Minister of Labour Clodomiro Almeyda (later in Mining) and Under-Secretary Fernando Morales from the same ministry.

The participation of the Socialists in the Ibàñez government had a completely different character from their role in the Popular Front's administration. The party, under the leadership of Raul Ampuero, together with the distinct intellectual lucidity of Clodomiro Almeyda, tried to give the new administration a seal of progressiveness and political sanity, a task that after only one year proved difficult and almost impossible to achieve. From June to October 1953, the Socialist party obtained two further ministerial posts at cabinet level, those of Mining and Finance. There was an attempt to press for the implementation of a Socialist-orientated programme, with the following characteristics:

1. Industrial reform, aimed at nationalizing certain strategic enterprises and workers' participation in their administration.
2. Land reform, aimed at redistributing land and reducing social injustice in rural areas.
3. Denunciation of the Military Pact with the United States.
4. Repeal of the anti-communist legislation.
5. General economic reform, aimed at producing anti-trust legislation, progressive taxes and the control of inflation.[60]

However, 'all initiatives which attempted to promote these measures, were being obstructed in some way or other by cabinet ministers who joined the cabinet as "personal friends" of the President. These maintained links with the defeated parties, mainly those of the right. Every day the influence of "personal friends" was increasing, almost always with the support of the ambiguous behaviour of the president. The party decided, therefore, to quit the government'.[61] In the 1953 parliamentary elections, the first to be held

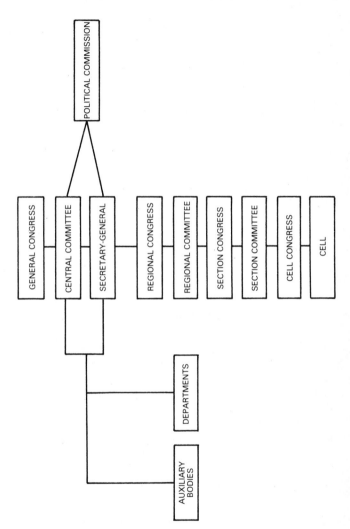

Figure 1.4 PSCh formal structure from 1953–67

(1) Partido Socialista Popular, 'Organigrama de Organización', internal document, Santiago, 1953.

under the new administration, the Socialists polled 70,000 votes, obtaining four senators and nineteen deputies, a reasonable showing for a party just emerging from a period of depression, popular distrust and moral crisis. This fact was no doubt decisive in prompting the party's decision to leave the government coalition in October.

At the end of 1953, the party had again obtained a momentum that its leaders did not want to put at risk by succumbing to the temptations of power. After a period of internal disorganization, the party had adopted a more realistic structure producing greater discipline and higher morale; (see figure 1.4). The prestige of its leaders was now high, thanks to their clear, principled position on most issues, and their undisputable lack of connection with any known financial dealing. Most of all, the party was now being seen as a true socialist alternative to capitalist tendencies in Chilean politics, and that certainly was an asset not to be disregarded.

The ban on the Communists further contributed to give the Socialists respectability as a viable political alternative (a fact that was encouraged by the Socialist decision to struggle to put the PCCh once again in the arena, as a legal political association, notwithstanding the known, if certainly not reactionary, anti-communism of the PSCh).

The justification for the party's decision to leave the Ibàñez administration had perhaps its clearest defence in the political Declaration issued by the Fifteenth General Ordinary Congress of October 1953. There the Socialists stated that 'during the period of co-operation with the government, the party made a loyal decision to support the president, even at the risk of being misunderstood'. Because of this position, the party had to suffer on several occasions, criticism from popular sectors to policies for which it was not directly responsible.[62] The party was then guided by the overall necessity of maintaining its position of safeguarding the whole of the programme to which it was committed:

That policy was possible only if the party could effectively implement its programme, mainly aimed at destroying the unjust privileges of the oligarchy and liberating the country from imperialist pressures. We have insistently requested the government to proceed directly with the programme, but we have encountered not only inexcusable vacillations but also open transactions with those groups traditionally enemies of the working class.

The Partido Socialista Popular has never accepted, nor will ever accept, transactions with the enemies of Chile, and it prefers to recover its independence. We shall not be tempted to appear in dubious positions.

In retiring from the government, the party wishes to express the hopes of the majority of the people, who want a firm anti-oligarchical and anti-imperialist policy and is sure its position will be understood by the other parties that have supported Mr Ibàñez and which expressed the same desire during the elections. These ultimate goals will never be forgotten by the party and that was the only reason why we co-operated with the government. We call upon all the forces who in some way or another supported the election of this administration to close ranks in order to implement the policies for whose achievement it was originally elected. We are sure that the natural course of events will prove that the social processes now in movement will lead to the creation of a Democratic Republic of Workers, which will form the basis for a socialist system. Through it, all hopes of workers, peasants, employees and, in general, the poorer sectors of our society, will find the satisfaction of all their needs.[63]

3. THE STAGE OF IDEOLOGY (1953–1970)

The last of the three periods summarizing the development of the PSCh in Chile could be called 'the stage of ideology'. It provides one of the richest periods of both internal and external ideological discussion. During this period, which began with the party's withdrawal from the Ibàñez administration in late 1953 and ended with the party having governmental responsibilities in President Allende Popular Unity's government in 1970, the Socialists had the opportunity to prove themselves as a truly alive political association, able to exhibit both political experience and internal democracy. The PCCh had already been reinstated as a full, legal political association, by a law enacted during the Ibàñez government, and the period in which the PSCh was the sole, and somehow unique representative of certain sectors of Chilean society had ended. From the late 1950s competition between these two popular parties developed for the support of the Chilean working class.

During that struggle, however, the differences on general strategy as well as tactics inevitably emerged into the open, as also did internal differences.

Until 1953 the Socialists retained their old organizational structure, with some minor statutory adjustments made from time to time. The average composition of membership according to unofficial party statistical figures was as follows: working class, 70 per cent; middle class, 30 per cent. These percentages reflect a tendency from the foundation of the party in the 1930s. An examination of the leadership shows that an average of 50 per cent of the members were of petty bourgeois origin, and as much as 48 per cent were of working-class origin. The remaining 2 per cent were of 'other origin', mainly belonging to the bourgeoisie, a new and interesting fact in the composition of the Socialist leadership.

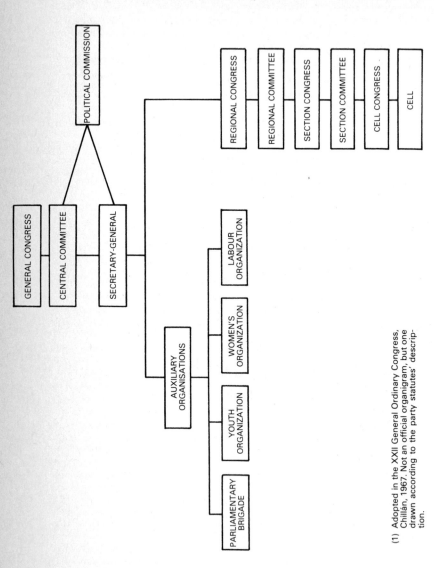

Figure 1.5 PSCh formal structure from 1967 on

(1) Adopted in the XXII General Ordinary Congress, Chillán, 1967. Not an official organigram, but one drawn according to the party statutes' description.

The Conference on Organization held in December 1953 reformed the existing organizational scheme, aimed at giving the secretary-general stronger powers over the party apparatus, in order to avoid as far as possible the development of *caciquista* policies. The new scheme proved once again inadequate, and in 1967 the Twenty-Second General Ordinary Congress held in Chillan adopted a new structure, illustrated in Figure 1.5.

The internal structure in the third period

The new internal structure adopted in 1967 provided the organizational answer for most of the questions arising from the political situation in Chile. This situation had brought about increasing difficulties in dealing with internal and external affairs for any political party. It concentrated the exercise of decision-making in the highest party echelons, namely the Central Committee and its Political Commission, but clearly emphasized respect for internal discussion in order to allow for the full implementation of the party's stand on such an important doctrinal issue as *internal democracy*.

At every level of party activity, congresses were established, providing an opportunity for discussion and avoiding excessive or abusive exercise of power on the part of the national leadership.[64] But when decisions had to be taken these could only be processed through normal internal procedures, up to the highest level. Here, all decisions were binding, unless a congress changed them.

It is true that generally those aspects of party organization were present in practical party behaviour before the Chillán Congress of 1967 sanctioned them as official, written party policies. But it was only then that they were clearly adopted as party policy.[65]

In ideology, the party developed support and allegiance to various *isms* from 1953 on, a trend that, according to Halperin, 'denotes an open-mindedness, a curiosity, and an inclination towards intellectual adventure that to this European observer at least are a great relief after the stuffiness, narrow-mindedness, and obstinate anti-intellectualism of European Social Democracy'.[66] Without subscribing to Halperin's opinion on European socialism, we would generally agree with that part which refers to Chilean Socialism. As he says, 'it is easy to sneer at the amazing transition of the Chilean Socialists from anti-Communism to Popular-Frontism to Peronism to Titoism to Castroism and, later, at least partially, to Maoism. This seems to be the behaviour of a political chameleon'. However, these characteristics appear to have been more of a positive approach to the social realities of

Chilean society than the dispassionate behaviour of an uncompromising political party.

Halperin adds more to this view by saying that 'the susceptibility of the Chilean Socialists to intellectual fashions does not mean that they are lacking in basic principles. If that were so, it would be impossible to explain the remarkable vitality of their party, its ability to recover from the schisms that have plagued it throughout its troubled history, and from the serious decline it suffered during the 1940s'.[67]

While agreeing on the whole with Halperin's view, one should also point out the handicaps of this strange, unique socialist party, for if those were aspects to be regarded as positive, they were also the very reasons for its weaknesses. A communist party that firmly adhered to its international character, with a rigid revolutionary ideology and a strong, well-trained party apparatus had a distinct advantage over the Socialists.

On the whole, the Socialist organization appeared rational and logical. But it lacked the necessary practical support to achieve real success. While the Communist machinery relied on paid workers, 'full-time revolutionaries' as Lenin called them—the PSCh counted on dedicated rank-and-file members who devoted their leisure time to the party. Thus it can be said that while the PCCh was a *full-time party*, the PSCh was only a *part-time* one. It may sound amusing, but it was a reality that strongly affected overall party behaviour, especially during the last ten or fifteen years of its development, when open competition for working-class support was at stake. Trade unions, universities, even high-school student bodies were used in the daily political fight for supremacy. And to a very well organized and determined PCCh, the Socialists were opposing an unrealistic model of organization, an uncompromising stand for socialism in a Chilean fashion, and fluctuating adherence to the *ism* of the moment. It was a strength, but it was also a weakness.[68]

Ideology in the third period

A wide range of ideologies became fashionable:

Peronism:

The Socialist adherence to the 'intellectual fashions' to which Halperin refers, affects this last period more than any other. It began with the successful development in Argentina of the Justicialist movement headed by General Juan Domingo Perón in the 1940s, until his overthrow which took place in 1955. Halperin says 'they admired him for his struggle against the democratic political parties, which were regarded by them as instruments of the oligarchy, and also, with some justification, for his labour legislation and encouragement of the labour movement'.[69]

The Socialists viewed it as a kind of liberation movement, at a time when Latin America was plagued by North American interventions and big-business interference. The nationalism of Peronism, its vociferous anti-imperialism—albeit not always carried out in practice—appealed to the independent-minded PSCh.

The eclipse of Peronism in Argentina uncovered knowledge of corruption in the movement and brought about a more dispassionate analysis of the true character of Peronism by the Chilean Socialists. It was accepted that the ambiguities of Peronism embodied the germ of its own destruction, as it never really tried to achieve clear, firm stands against capitalism, but rather compromising, middle-of-the-road anti-oligarchical measures that only weakened the oligarchic power without destroying it.

Titoism:

In 1955 Khruschev's denunciation of Soviet errors in handling the Yugoslav dissenters strengthened the position of those within the party trying to follow a Titoist line. Ampuero himself, Oscar Waiss and Aniceto Rodriguez were among the leading members of this tendency, which was later adopted more openly. The Titoist idea of a socialist state heavily dependent on workers' councils at every level of the social fabric, captured the imagination of Chilean Socialists, as did the neutralist approach of Yugoslav foreign policy. After a trip to Belgrade, Central Committee member Oscar Waiss wrote: 'I had learned a great lesson. A lesson of quiet heroism, of efficiency and of modesty, of titanic effort and thrift. I had learned a lesson, the importance of which I could not yet fully appreciate but which would bear fruit in time in my own activity as a fighter for socialism.'[70]

The fascination of the PSCh with Titoism caused discomfort in the PCCh. 'It is very much in evidence', stated the PCCh General Secretary Luis Corvalán:

that in the Socialist Party there are influential people who do not hide their sympathy for Yugoslav revisionism. In every case where topical theoretical and political problems, and specifically Yugoslav revisionism, have a practical significance, it becomes necessary to point to the danger involved in differences of opinion about these matters, and to the need for the most determined efforts to overcome them.[71]

The pro-Yugoslav approach to both Chilean and international affairs prompted an occasionally bitter open debate with the Communists. This was only moderated when, on the one hand, the Communists gradually began to accept the existence of Titoism as a fact of life and, on the other hand, the Socialists began to move further to the left in the political spectrum, a move mainly inspired by the new challenges arising from the Cuban experience.[72]

Castroism

From 1960 the influence of the Cuban Revolution overshadowed Titoism within the Socialist ranks, although it still retained significant intellectual support. Just as Peronism had symbolized the Latin American struggle against North American and big-business interference, so Castroism then appeared as the catalyst for all revolutions in that part of the world.

Senator Salvador Allende, who had been reinstated as a full party member in 1957 in a special congress aimed at reuniting the Partido Socialista Popular and the PSCh, stated in 1960 that:

the Chilean people have been aroused and deeply moved by the Cuban Revolution: they understand it and defend it as their own . . . the parties of the people, and, with some reticence, even centre parties, have declared their support for the revolution. This means that the immense majority of Chileans are for the revolution. It is time to realize that the lesson of Guatemala has been learnt. The United States must understand that today Latin America is revitalized by the Cuban Revolution. With different methods and strategies, in accordance with the characteristics of each one of our countries, we are marching towards a common goal that shall give dignity to our lives and assure the economic independence of our countries.[74]

The Communists, although at first reluctant, gave their support to the Cuban Revolution, and this helped a movement towards the Socialists. By 1956, encouraged by the shortcomings and corruption of the Ibàñez administration, both parties had formed the Frente de Acción Popular (FRAP), the historical precursor of the Popular Unity. This also included the Socialistas de Chile and other small leftist groupings.

Relations with the PCCh

The formation of FRAP was the culminating point of a tendency towards political co-operation gradually developing among party cadres. Even though the leadership still sustained attitudes that could be easily considered anti-Communist or anti-Socialist, the rank-and-file members felt that to achieve real success in the fight against right-wing parties, a united front was necessary.

From 1962 onwards the Socialists adopted the general strategy the tactics known as the Frente de Trabajadores (Workers Front), while the Communists adopted an overall commitment to the Frente de Liberación Nacional (National Liberation Front). The differences proved increasingly difficult to hide.

The Frente de Trabajadores sustained the idea in the Chilean road to socialism, of a class front composed exclusively of working-class parties, as opposed to any other political association and/or grouping. This automatically excluded centrist parties, and especially the middle-of-the-road, left-centre and predominantly middle-class Radical Party, together with the Falangists (later Christian Democrats).

The Communists' Frente de Liberación Nacional, on the contrary, stressed the importance of the support of the middle-class and used every opportunity to stress this point. This clearly meant that in any fight to get political influence and eventually viewed as to govern, collaboration with the Radicals and the Christian Democrats was indispensable.

As early as August 1956, only four months after the FRAP alliance had been formed, the Socialist secretary-general, Raúl Ampuero, stated:

> the PCCh always adjusted its policies to the needs of Moscow. They suffer a sort of progressive deformation of their political role, which is common to all their fellow parties throughout the world ... they think that there is a dogma which states that no revolutionary process is genuine if it is not under Soviet inspiration, or adjusted to general Soviet strategies in world politics. Where the Soviet Union was, there the truth, democracy and peace were. If the old Bolshevik guard was sent to death, it was because they were spies and traitors. If they allied themselves with Hitler, it was because the war was an inhumane crime of the imperialists. If they decided to crush Tito, it was because he and his partisans were all fascists. Such a party ends by considering watchwords as a more reliable truth than the objective examination of reality, it puts its prejudices before its class duties.[74]

This view of Communist strategy and tactics on the part of the Socialist leadership became most intensive in the well-known Communist-Socialist debate of 1962, six years after FRAP had been formed and while both parties were working alongside each other to gain political influence.

The continuous reference of the Socialist leadership to Communist *weaknesses*, namely its tendency to repeatedly invite centrist parties to form coalitions and to supposedly adjust its policies to Soviet needs, forced a strong reply from the Communist Central Committee Member, Orlando Millas, in the daily party newspaper *El Siglo*. He accused Ampuero of being *intransigent* and, without saying it directly but through a courteous suggestion, anti-Communist as well.[75]

Ampuero counter-attacked in a long article in *El Siglo*, which the Communist leadership courteously allowed to be published. There, he not only maintained the original traditional stand on Soviet behaviour and Communist *adjustment* but stressed very strongly the weakening effect this behaviour had, and would have in the future, on the Chilean and Latin American fight for socialism.

The Emergence of Ideological Consensus

The main points made by Ampuero form the basis of the theoretical stand of the PSCh in the 1960s:

1. Rejection of the principle of unified world leadership of the revolutionary movement under Soviet (or Chinese) control.
2. Rejection of the policy of military blocks and of the theory of the two camps.
3. Rejection of the Communists' claim to be an ideological monopoly.
4. Criticism of the Chilean Communists' policy for the 'Peaceful road'. Ampuero criticized this policy *from the left*.

The last point merits a more detailed explanation as it concerns the main Socialist ideological stand. 'The Frente de Trabajadores', a party declaration issued in 1954 stated, 'meant and means that we have to recognize that the working class and its allies the peasants are the only vehicle able to produce the great transformations which are needed'.[76]

In practice, the strong Socialist opposition to accepting the collaboration of middle-class parties was helped by the ambiguous, rather pro-rightist behaviour, of those parties, particularly the Radical Party. Only in the presidential elections of 1970 did the formation of the Popular Unity overturn the traditional Socialist stand. Then, for the first time in Chilean history, a coalition of predominantly Marxist parties took government.

It is important to note that during this period ideological discussions flourished at all levels. At the top Raúl Ampuero and Clodomiro Almeyda (both Central Committee members for many years), developed vigorous interpretations of the party's role in the Chilean struggle for socialism—the role of the great powers *vis-à-vis* the underdeveloped world, the confrontation between China and the Soviet Union, the Yugoslav way to socialism and many other topics of political relevance.[77]

The main points developed were:

1. *Economic model*: Workers self-management was recommended by Ampuero as a deterrent to Stalinist practices.

It is debatable whether we have already arrived at the highest form of socialism by making the state the sole property owner and regarding it as the natural representative of the working class. Judging by recent experience it would seem that state property is still a long way from really being the property of the community, of society. This the self-management of the means of production and the development of democracy in the industrial and economic field constitute important approaches that today are being implemented, in varying degrees, in some states that have succeeded in abolishing capitalism.[78]

2. *Party model*: 'The notion of a party as center, nucleus, and spinal column of a broader organization of institutions, and individuals faithful to the revolutionary creed' appeared to him as highly desirable. He added 'that the notion of the Bolshevik party as the exclusive and unique representative of the political opinion of the masses and certain new experiments now in process of formation or implementation' were not the same thing. The 'Socialist Alliance of the Working People' appeared mainly as Ampuero viewed it in Yugoslavia, as 'an ample political and social platform which at the very least gives it the means for an exact appraisal of the tendencies, inclinations, and aspirations of public opinion'. The party, then, would be much more of an interpreter than a guide.[79]

3. *Soviet–Chinese dispute*: Ampuero criticized the Chinese for their manifest underestimation of the consequences of an atomic holocaust and for their assertion of an 'alleged antagonism between socialism and peace', while Almeyda tended to reinforce that stand, which he considered favoured a Third World position with which to confront the developed world. 'Indiscriminating peace can only serve the purposes of those wishing to perpetuate social injustice and political oppression in the underdeveloped world'.[80] Both men rejected the Soviet pretensions to be considered as the revolutionary hegemonic centre and sustained the view that any socialist party or movement in any place should be considered on its own merits. Accordingly, the strategy and the tactics for implementation should be chosen according to the special circumstances—historical, social, cultural, religious—of each separate case and not by adjusting them to the political goals of the Soviet Union or any other socialist or capitalist country.

4. *Anti-Terrorism*: Ampuero developed a strong anti-guerrilla stand. This did not mean that he condemned guerrilla activity in other countries, but he considered them irresponsible and unsuitable for Chile.

5. *Factional activities*: 'In practice, the real threat to unity is constituted by factional activities, that is, when several member units work together, creating a clandestine machine within the official organization. The mere fact of promoting such a group indicates contempt for normal procedures and institutions, and, in essence, for the party itself.'[81]

The repudiation of what he considered Trotskyist activities within the party was very strong.

The party has been extremely open-minded in accepting individuals and groups with a Trotskyist background. Such elements—heretics to the Communist mind— objectionable to us are because of their sectarian inclination, and above all because of their doubtful loyalty to the organization ... some of them sought refuge here [in the party] in order to exploit our bases as a recruiting field for their own ends.[82]

6. *Revolution and Peace*: The Soviet exaggerated stand on peace 'is that of a country that is already on a relatively advanced level of socialist construction. But this reasoning does not apply to the black nations of Africa and the exploited nations of Asia ... these are nations that have nothing to lose and everything to gain by revolution', according to Almeyda.[83]

7. *Socialism according to Chilean needs*: Both Ampuero and Almeyda laid great stress on the importance of building socialism according to Chilean circumstances. 'We Chilean Socialists must draw out conclusions from our experience and learn to find the authentic and real inspiration our actions and our political philosophy in the harsh and unavoidable facts that shape our country and our people and determine our future,'[84] Ampuero suggested. This was certainly the policy of the party throughout its history.

NOTES

1. The bulk of the data used for this chapter was mainly gathered from primary sources made available to us by several internal party instances, as well as party members. We are indebted to Clodomiro Almeyda, Alejandro Chelén, Manuel Mandujano, Tito Stefoni, Manuel Eduardo Hübner, Mario Planet and other PSCh members who asked to remain anonymous, for their continuous co-operation and stimulus. They put at our disposal their private collections of documents and other valuable original materials. However, we committed ourselves not to specifically reveal (as much as this was possible) concrete sources of information in specific cases. The climate of suspicion surrounding all social research at the time our work was being carried out, more than justified this unfortunate limitation.

2. *Las grandes luchas revolucionarias del proletariado chileno*, Tesis del Buró Sudamericano de la Internacional Comunista (Editorial Marx–Lenin, Santiago, Chile, 1932) gives a dramatic account of the crisis affecting Chile's popular sectors in the 1930s. More than 50,000 miners were then at the point of being sacked.

3. *El Partido Socialista de Chile* (PLA, 2 vols., Santiago, 1971), Vol. 1, p. 35.

4. For details of these aspects of Latin American societies, see: Peter Calvert, *Latin America: Internal Conflict and International Peace* (Macmillan, London, 1969); Jacques Lambert, *Latin America: Social Structures and Political Institutions* (University of California Press, Berkeley, 1971); Stanley J. Stein and Barbara H. Stein, *The Colonial Heritage of Latin America* (Oxford University Press, New York, 1970); David Lehmann (ed.), *Agrarian Reform and Agrarian Reformism*, *Studies of Peru*, *Chile*, *China and India* (Faber & Faber, London, 1973).

5. Jobet, *op. cit.*

6. Official national statistics. Cited by Jobet, *op. cit.*, pp. 35–7.

7. In January 1922 the Partido Obrero Socialista had ceased to exist, to give way to the Communist Party of Chile. It immediately affiliated itself to the Third International.

8. Eugenio González Rojas, socialist senator, speech in the Chilean Senate, cited by Alejandro Chelén, *Trayectoria del Socialismo* (Austral, Buenos Aires, 1966).

9. Hernán Ramírez Necochea, *Orígenes y fundación del Partido Comunista de Chile* (Austral, Santiago, Chile, 1962), pp. 283–4.

10. See *Nosotros, los trabajadores* (mimeo, *Editorial Pueblo*, Santiago, 1936).

11. Marmaduke Grove, *Senado de la República de Chile*, 23 May 1934, (Annals of the Chilean Senate).

12. 'Declaración de Principios', party document, 1933. This paragraph was inserted in the first known public document of the new party.

13. Ibid., p. 3.

14. This contention would somehow suffer modifications later on, when the party would stress its proletariat-orientated ideology and goals.

15. First 'Declaración de Principios', *op. cit.*, p. 3.

16. Especially relevant to assess this aspect of the PSCh's ideology are: *Acta de Deposición del señor Juan Esteban Montero*, mimeographed document, Santiago, Chile, June, 1932; *Acta de la sesión de fundación del Partido Socialista*, mimeographed document, Santiago, Chile, April 1933; I Congreso General Ordinario (resolutions), internal document, Santiago, Chile, 1933; II Congreso General Ordinario (resolutions), internal document, Santiago, Chile, 1934; III Congreso General Ordinario (resolutions), internal document, Santiago, Chile, 1936; IV Congreso General Ordinario (resolutions), internal document, Santiago, Chile, 1937; I Congreso General Extraordinario (resolutions), internal document, Santiago, Chile, 1937; V Congreso General Ordinario (resolutions), internal document, Santiago, Chile, 1938.

17. Jobet, *op. cit.*, p. 82.

18. Unofficial party statistics give the following average type of membership during the 1930s: working class (peasants, workers, miners)—55 per cent; middle class (professionals, employees, small industrialists and farmers)—45 per cent; official statistics are not available and the estimated percentages were given to the authors by reliable old party leaders. The situation then looked different from the situation as it looked from 1940 on, when a distinct proletarization of the party membership began to take place. Last statistics (official 1973), put membership as follows: working class—75 per cent; middle-class—24 per cent; bourgeoisie—1 per cent. As no official reports exist, the information should be accepted with caution.

19. Jobet, *op. cit.*, p. 79.

20. 'Declaración de Principios', internal document, *op. cit.* This idea remained up to the late 50's and early 60's, and was further strengthened afterwards by the emergence of the Cuban revolution as a major ideological influence in the Continent. Only in the 30's was the concept of latinomericanism so well developed and fought for.

21. 'Declaración de Principios', *op. cit.*, p. 1.

22. This contention must be understood to include both working and middle classes at least in the 1930 decade.
23. They publicly repudiated the Second International as 'conciliatory and reformist' and the Third International as 'sectarian'.
24. Chelén, *op. cit*., pp. 69–70.
25. Later the change in the PCCh's position alleviated the tense relationship between the two parties in Chile.
26. Jobet, *op. cit*., p. 95.
27. See Figure 1.1.
28. In 1937, two years before the accession to government of the Popular Front Alliance, Socialists, Communists and Radicals together polled 37.4 per cent in the parliamentary elections, while the right (Liberals, Conservatives, Nationalists and others) polled 47.9 per cent. In the first parliamentary elections held after the Popular Front was formed (1941), the Left received an impressive 56.9 per cent, a fact which should have enabled the governmental coalition to move further and faster with its reforms. The Radical Party's overall control of the administrative structure, a clever co-option policy on the part of the traditional Chilean oligarchy and the right's own 36.9 per cent in the 1941 elections, combined to persuade the Socialists not to push their allies too much and to accept their middle-of-the-road, mildly socialistic approach to political and social reforms. This trend was favoured by the stand of the International Communist, aimed at supporting class alliances for rather mild social reforms.

    In Chile, these policies were intended primarily to encourage industrialization and a mild redistribution of GNP, but were deliberately aimed at leaving the agrarian structure untouched and were intended not to disturb the development of private ownership. The Socialist and, to a certain extent, Communist attempts to produce reforms in those areas were decisively overcome by the Radicals, which relied on these issues on the unconditional support of the right-wing Liberal and Conservative parties.
29. Jobet, *op. cit*., p. 53.
30. Godoy Urrutia, Berman, Waiss, Herrera, Morales and Pérez, *Porqué fundamos el Partido Socialista de Trabajadores*, mimeographed document, Santiago, Chile, 1940, p. 3.
31. Chelén, *op. cit*., p. 103. But, as it will be seen later in this work, bureaucratic problems were also determinant in prompting the division.
32. The Partido Socialista de Trabajadores soon became fully integrated into the PCCh a rather surprising end for a party that had come into existence criticizing the Communist-orientated Popular Front policies.
33. Jobet, *op. cit*., p. 54. In the 1945 parliamentary elections the PSCh polled a poor 7.2 per cent of the votes, which nearly destroyed their parliamentary representation.
34. Some important aspects of the contradictions of Socialist behaviour during this stage can illustrate the reasons for the lowering of morale among party members.

    — When in December 1940 the Popular Front Alliance was broken, the Socialists continued holding ministerial posts. Thus, they were out of the Popular Front but within the Government.

— The Socialists were very much against what Chelén calls the 'class collaboration' theory sustained by Stalin and which determined the formation of the Popular Fronts, including that in Chile, but nevertheless they accepted to form part of the Popular Front, together with the Communists and the left-centre Radicals.

— The Socialists repeatedly proclaimed their intention of promoting peasant organization in order to enable that sector of the working class to improve its living conditions. However, they accepted the Popular Front policies of 'not touching' agrarian matters to avoid possible landowner uprising.

35. The new scheme had already been approved by the *Special Conference on Organization* of 1939.

36. For a discussion on party organization, see Chapters 2, 3 and 4.

37. *Caciquista*, comes from the Chilean *araucano* and the term *cacique* (also used by the Peruvian *Incas*), and means *bossism*. The expression is very common in Chilean and Latin American politics to indicate absolute, undisputed exercise of power by one man, amid straight arbitrarianism and abuse.

38. The congresses were held in an informal way. Their powers were unclear and, therefore, their mere existence contributed to further confusions.

39. Secretary-General, *Sobre el uso y abuso del poder político*, internal mimeographed document, Santiago, April 1942, p. 4.

40. Specially during Aguirre Cerda's and Ibáñez' administrations, in 1938–40 and 1952–3, respectively.

41. Carl Beck, 'Party Control and Bureaucratization in Czechoslovakia', *The Journal of Politics*, Vol. 23, 1961, pp. 289–90.

42. A common practice was to offer him a senior civil service post, or even a position at ministerial level (according to his rank in the party apparatus).

43. Jobet reports that during this period, the party 'lost its massive support' (an assertion which is supported by the poor 7.2 per cent polled in 1945 against the 23.2 per cent of 1941, even though this last percentage includes the small vote got by several unrepresentative leftist groups). Jobet, *op. cit*., p. 54.

44. Formally, however, the new reforms to the organizational scheme were not implemented until 1953.

45. Jobet, *op. cit*., p. 55.

46. *Vanguardia*, an internal Socialist newspaper which existed only for two months of 1946, stated that he was doing well, but that something more should be done to stop the party being pushed into collaboration with González Videla's presidential candidature that year. González Videla was supported by his own party, the Radical Party, and by the Communists.

47. As can be inferred from the 1949 and 1953 parliamentary election results, in which they nearly disappeared from the political scene. In the extraordinary senatorial election of 1949, in which the PSP managed to get its candidate elected, the Partido Socialista de Chile did not dare present a candidate. The election of Eugenio González as senator for Santiago and the ousting of Rosetti's

socialists from González Videla's cabinet, contributed, on the one hand, to strengthen the Partido Socialista Popular and to weaken the Partido Socialista de Chile, on the other.

48. The Frente de Trabajadores was officially adopted as party policy during the Sixteenth Ordinary Congress, in October 1955.

49. Ernst Halperin, in *Nationalism and Communism in Chile*, MIT Press, Cambridge, Mass., 1965, somehow sustains this belief. In fact, the Chilean Socialists were not as pro-Chinese as they were anti-Soviet. A dramatic need for distinguishing itself from the PCCh provides much, if not all, of the explanation for adopting this stand. They have always had very friendly relations with both the Soviet and the Chinese Communist parties. After the intervention of the Warsaw Pact countries in Czechoslovakia, Chilean Socialist relations were strained with the Czechoslovak Communist Party but not with the Soviet Communist Party.

50. Ibid., p. 131.

51. This stand would lead them, later on, to engage in a controversy with the PCCh over a variety of issues, including the Soviet Union's stand on proletarian revolution, the problem of class alliances or class confrontation in Chilean politics, the question of the Chinese and Yugoslav communism, among other important issues. Those matters are presented and analysed in this work when describing the last of the three periods of socialist history.

52. Halperin, *op. cit.*, p. 145.

53. The model was officially adopted in 1953, but the firm, disciplined personality of Ampuero enabled its use from the very moment he took office (see Fig. 13.).

54. But the Ibáñez candidature was by no means the only cause of the division, even though it was certainly the most notorious one. As it will be seen later on, old bureaucratic problems were also determinant.

55. He decided to abandon his candidacy and support the Popular Front candidate, Pedro Aguirre, after President Arturo Alessandri violently squashed a nazi attempt to disrupt the legal life of the country, an incident known as the *masacre del Seguro Obrero* (the massacre of the Social Security Building, after the place where the incident took place).

56. 'My candidature represents the violent antithesis of all that the actual régime represents. It is a protest of public character against the scandals in the administration, the illegal dealings, the stealings. It is a vigorous reaction of the national ego against political corruption' (René Montero, *Confesiones Políticas*, Orbe, Santiago, 1958, p. 127, quoting an Ibáñez' speech.)

57. *González Videla ante la Historia*, party document, mimeographed, p. 4, 1951.

58. This interpretation is widely accepted by the Socialist Chilean historians. Among those who have stated this view more clearly are: Chelén, *op. cit.*; Jobet, *El socialismo chileno a través de sus congresos* (PLA, Santiago, 1965). We fully agree with this view of Ibáñez' personality, as seen by the Chilean public. Clodomiro Almeyda, the former Chilean vice-president, foreign minister and member of several Socialist Central Committees and Political Commissions, once told us that 'the General [as Ibáñez was called by his intimates] appealed to the irrational that everyone of us has. He was the man who was going to purge the country of

corrupted politicians, through the practice of firm, non-transactional policies. The man in the street viewed him as a true sage, a man that stood well apart from party interests and one who was even prepared to stop big-business abuses. He was 'anti-Radical' (referring to the Radical Party), at a time when they were absolutely discredited, and that had a liberating sound.'

59. Chelén, *op. cit*., p. 129.
60. Among the documents of that time which clearly provide the data on the Socialist programme for the Ibáñez administration, the following can be quoted: *El Mercurio*, Santiago daily newspaper from January to October 1953; *Un Programa para Ibáñez*, party document, mimeographed, February 1953; *Un Parlamento para Ibáñez*, party document, mimeographed, January 1953.
61. Chelén, *op. cit*., p. 153.
62. A veteran socialist leader, then a member of the Central Committee, told me that a majority of the leadership favoured a 'firm intransigent stand against Ibáñez because he was beginning to show himself as the very sort of politician we, under his guidance, were supposed to eradicate from Chilean politics'.
63. *XV Ordinary Congress*, Partido Socialista Popular, mimeographed document, December, 1953, p. 3.
64. *Congresses* were in fact held before, but a clear recognition of their rôle came to the open only in 1967.
65. The composition of Regional and Section Committees as well as those of the *núcleos* remained the same as that adopted in the Sixth Ordinary Congress of 1940.
66. Halperin, *op. cit*., p. 142.
67. Ibid.
68. The most tragic consequence of all, this could be observed with the overthrow of President Allende's government in September 1973. The PSCh organization was quickly dismantled by the military, many of its leaders killed or arrested and its membership persecuted. On the other hand, it is generally believed that most of the PCCh apparatus remained intact. Most of its leadership, at the national, regional and even cellular level, apparently stayed in hiding without suffering any major setbacks.
69. Halperin, *op. cit*., p. 136.
70. Oscar Waiss, *Amanecer en Belgrado* (PLA, Santiago, 1956), p. 158.
71. *Principios* (Official review of the Chilean Communist Party), July–August, 1958.
72. For a further understanding of this issue, see: Partido Comunista de Chile, *Documentos del XI Congreso Nacional realizado en Noviembre de 1958* (Lautaro, Santiago, 1959); Oscar Waiss, *op. cit*.; *Principios, op. cit*.; Luis Corvalán, *Chile y el nuevo panorama mundial* (speeches) (Lautaro, Santiago, 1959); Edvard Kardelj, *La Democracia Socialista en la práctica Yugoeslava* (PLA, Santiago, 1960).
73. Salvador Allende, *Cuba, un camino* (PLA, Santiago, 1960), p. 55.
74. Raúl Ampuero, *Boletín del Comite Central del Partido Socialista Popular* (mimeographed, Santiago, August, 1956).
75. See Orlando Millas, 'El Senador Raúl Ampuero y los tópicos anti-comunistas', in *La Polémica Socialista-Comunista*, (PLA, Santiago, 1962).

76. *Informe político del Comité Cental del Partido Socialista al Pleno Nacional de Diciembre de 1964*, mimeographed, p. 2.
77. A good and comprehensive description of the theoretical aspects of the PSCh's ideology during the 1960s is provided by Ernst Halperin, *Nationalism and Communism in Chile*, op. cit.
78. Halperin, *op. cit*., pp. 154–9, quoting *ARAUCO Review*, article of 1964.
79. Ibid.
80. Clodomiro Almeyda, *Caso por el tercer mundo*, internal, mimeographed, 1964 p. 8. Almeyda was continuously stressing this point. He personally did so to Benny Pollack on many occasions. His idea of a 'Third World revolution' aroused suspicions from Communist quarters, as they tended to consider it a way to hide anti-communist tendencies. In our opinion, those suspicions were absolutely unjustified. The sophisticated political and theoretical thinking of Almeyda contributed in fact to strengthen within the PSCh the position of those promoting the cause of unity between both parties.
81. Ampuero, *op. cit.*, p. 173.
82. Ibid., p. 176.
83. Almeyda, *op. cit.*, p. 11.
84. Ibid., p. 107.

2 A Study in Party Structures

INTRODUCTION

'In the course of the last two decades, party structures have been studied, often in great detail, particularly in Western countries. They have also given rise to a substantial amount of general theory, some of which began to be developed at the end of the nineteenth century.'[1] Blondel's assertion clearly indicates two general problems arising from the analysis of political parties. On the one hand, there exists a considerable number of studies arising from different theoretical perspectives. On the other, the study of party structures covers a whole range of issues, some of which the researcher, through lack of information, must reluctantly ignore in his analysis.

The study of a particular political party raises a number of theoretical and practical problems: which theoretical orientation, if any, is to be considered as a frame of reference? Which details are worthy of observation and analysis and which are going to be abandoned for the sake of precision? Which typology is the most suitable for studying a particular political party?

Confronted with these questions, the researchers have necessarily to make choices. These amount to the following:

1. The selection, when considered appropriate, of a given theoretical framework and, consequently, a given typology.
2. The selection of a given set of structural aspects to be observed and analysed.

In practical terms, both decisions imply one important *a priori* assumption: that the choices are taken as a methodological need rather as a categorical support for given ideas and theories. It is the need to use operational definitions that causes the researcher to select a given theory. It is the need to select the important aspects of a given political party that causes the researcher to analyse some aspects of its organization without devoting too much time to others. The choice is obviously difficult and may be subject to controversy, but it is something that has to be done if the party is to be analysed within the framework of a particular model.

The assumption of given theoretical perspectives imply almost necessarily the avoiding, as much as possible, of discussions of theories, because these are not necessarily relevant to this work. This work intends by no means to exhaust or even produce discussions of given theories and/or typologies, but a general discussion is nevertheless presented when relevant.

Furthermore, there are at least two specific problems which the researcher faces when he tries to determine and analyse the organization of a given political party: what we may term the *political aspects* of organization and the *technical aspects* of organization.[2] By *political aspects* of organization are understood all those issues that in one way or another are connected with what constitutes the political and social components of a party, such as class and mass, membership and leadership, internal mobility, bureaucracies and oligarchies, and the internal finance system. By *technical aspects* of organization we mean those issues that in one way or another are connected with the working day-to-day habits of the party: the type of relationship among the various bodies, both vertical and horizontal; the type of internal relationships among members of the various bodies and among members of other bodies; the type of disciplinary control; centralization *versus* decentralization of the power-sharing and decision-making processes; the type of bodies, from the highest party echelons to the lowest levels of organization (see Figure 2.1).

Both political and technical aspects are by no means independent of one another. On the contrary, at least in the case of the PSCh, they appear linked through the existence of an ideological precondition: the 'Marxist–Leninist' character of its ideology.

There is, of course, an extensive literature which has tackled these problems from one of these two perspectives. Generally, Marxist social scientists have emphasized the political aspects involved, while others have tended to emphasize the technical aspects. There are those, however, that have dealt with the matter utilizing a comprehensive approach. This method atempts to produce studies of political parties which take into consideration as much as possible all the aspects involved. It is clear that one-sided, unilateral approaches have failed to fully explain the phenomenon of party organization in its widest context.[3]

It is relatively clear that the technical aspects of party organization cannot be completely separated from the political aspects. There is a close link between both, caused by the central issue from which no approach can escape: ideology. This does not explain by itself the type of organization of a given political party, nor does it explain the complex set of internal and external relationships within the various bodies which give formal structure to a party. However, from an observation of the PSCh we came to the conclusion that the role of ideology was more important than we would have expected. In fact, the very special character of what we have called the political, social and technical components of the party determined to an important extent the character of its organization and, moreover, its working habits; but the ultimate, overall influence behind it was its self-proclaimed Marxist-Leninist ideology (Fig. 2.1).

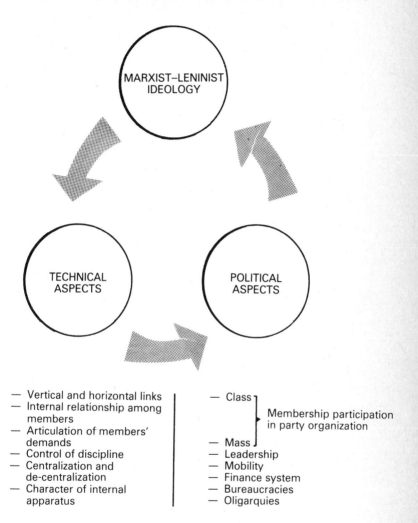

Figure 2.1 PSCh organization: a scheme of interdependence

Thus the self-proclaimed Marxism of the party contributed to the creation (as will be shown later in this work), at least in theory, of a structure which tried to reproduce that of the classic Leninist party. This fact did not prevent the party from adopting practices that were far from being orthodox in general Marxist terms. The result was a mixed, flexible structure in which classic Marxist and/or Leninist principles of organization appeared alongside the practices of liberal democratic parties.

If ideology was a compelling, inescapable issue for the PSCh, reality demanded an even greater attention. The problems of class origin of members and leaders, the ever-present challenge of a cadre (or a mass) model of internal structure, a faulty finance system in a party that theoretically depended heavily on regular payment from its members, and a variety of related issues, all contributed to creating a gap between the needs arising from a compelling ideology and the needs arising from the party as a working unit.

The 'technical aspects' that reflect how the party works on a day-to-day basis appeared separate from the 'political aspects'. The party apparatus, designed to achieve the party's politics in both internal and external relationships, lacked the resources that theoretically were being asked of it. Furthermore, methodology compels the researcher who intends to cover both technical and political aspects to separate them for the sake of accuracy. It would be a difficult and confusing task to try to describe, analyse and eventually establish a set of *a priori* and/or *a posteriori* hypotheses by merely grouping issues which refer to different circumstances and situations. The *isolation* of matters according to these two central criteria appears then as necessary, always taking into account the fact that a particular ideology reflects the character and *working habits* of each political party. Thus, by studying the technicalities of a given political party, the researcher is not explaining it all, because he fails, either consciously or not, to provide the much-needed content insights inherent to any association of human beings. By studying only the social and political content, the researcher fails to provide the much-needed view of the day-to-day functions of a given party. These assertions are not intended to dismiss partial approaches to the study of political parties as irrelevant or incomplete, as long as in each case the author concerned clearly specifies the scope of his research. But the limitations of these methods are clear: they can only explain a limited aspect of a party's organization. It is obvious that a synethesis of certain elements could eventually achieve, in these cases, what the partial studies by themselves cannot achieve. We shall attempt to provide an explanation of the structure and organization of the PSCh up to 1973.

THE PSCh AS A MARXIST PARTY

Introduction

To define a 'Marxist party' comprehensively is an endless task. Many authors, both Marxist and non-Marxist, have, of course, tried to achieve a comprehensive and generally acceptable definition of what in fact constitutes a 'proletarian party'.

Though the subject occupies a very important place in the work of Marx and Engels, it was developed sporadically rather than systematically and on few occasions. 'Moreover, within the broad general framework of their theory of class struggle and of revolution, they evolved their ideas on the forms and functions of proletarian parties as they went along, and related them to their analyses of often very different historical situations'.[4]

It is generally accepted that the term 'Marxist party' can be considered synonymous with the term 'proletarian party', but this does not necessarily mean, of course, that all parties with all or part of its membership belonging to the working class should be automatically considered 'Marxist', nor that a self-defined Marxist party is immediately entitled to be considered a proletarian party.

Marx, Engels and, later, Lenin completely identified both terms. Most other writers have continued using both terms interchangeably, also identifying the terms 'Marxist' and 'proletarian' with the expression 'revolutionary'.[5]

The approaches of various authors after Marx have, of course, related to the historical circumstances of each period. Thus Marx's writings were closely linked with a particular stage in the development of the capitalist system. The great issue for Marx and other revolutionaray theoreticians of his time was not so much the problem of the nature and character of the organization of the party as such (or, in other words, the main characteristics the 'proletarian party' was supposed to exhibit), but rather the problem of the development of the proletariat into a social class, by means of a political party. More specifically, the given political conjunctures with which the working class were confronted did not require, at that time, a complete and systematic definition of the nature and character of the proletarian party.

That being so, the organizational problems analysed by Marx and Engels correspond with the low level of capitalist development. Besides, one should not forget the thesis that the consolidation of the capitalist system in a higher stage was, for Marx, a precondition of the proletarian revolution. The triumph of the 1917 Bolshevik Revolution in Russia actually contradicted that thesis when it was demonstrated that a successful socialist revolution was, after all, possible under pre-capitalist conditions and where the development of productive forces was at an early stage.

Marx, however, saw the proletarian party as the only instrument capable of transforming the proletariat into a class, viewing the party as an organizational element rather than as a vanguard of the working class, as Lenin saw it.

Lenin saw a need for the existence of a sophisticated élite of revolutionaries, whose aims would be the indoctrination of the proletariat with 'scientific socialism'. Lenin, agreeing with Kautsky, stated:

the vehicle of science is not the proletariat, but the bourgeois intelligentsia: it was in the minds of individual members of that stratum that modern socialism originated, and it was they who communicated it to the more intellectually developed proletarians who, in their turn, introduce it into the proletarian class struggle where conditions allow that to be done. Thus, socialist consciousness is something introduced into the proletarian class struggle from without, and not something that arose within it spontaneously.[6]

The synthesis of the Leninist schemata or élite party revolution was expressed very clearly in Lenin's own words: 'Without revolutionary theory there can be no *revolutionary* movement'.[7]

The concept of the 'proletarian vanguard' is the most important Leninist contribution to the Marxist theory of the party. This does not necessarily mean that the 'proletarian vanguard', despite the semantic implication, should be provided by the working-class itself. On the contrary, it can come, and in fact it most frequently does come, from the petite bourgeoisie.

The idea of a highly sophisticated, presumably educated political leadership to head the party of the proletariat was linked to that of the professional revolutionary, entirely dedicated to the party and with no right to claim a 'private' life. Rosa Luxemburg dissociated herself from the classic Leninist party model when she accused Lenin of perverting the real sense of the Marxist party, transforming it into an almost religious sect, united by a military solidarity, distant and different from the real problem and conditions of the working class.[8]

Luxemburg stressed the importance of the spontaneous element in the shaping of the party of the proletarian class, in opposition to the centralized, somewhat élitist leadership that Lenin considered a *sine qua non* condition of it. Her aims were mainly directed at providing a theoretical insight as well as practical political guidance for the party. This insistence on the need for spontaneity tried to rescue in a positive way working-class values which were somehow disregarded by the 'vanguard' approach of Lenin. In opposition to the almost inevitable petit-bourgeois leadership in the party of the working class, Luxemburg tried to stress the need for working-class leadership for the party.

On the other hand, for Lenin, 'the party was an organization of cadres, with great discipline and a high level of consciousness, whose thorough selection, arduous trials, and long apprenticeship consolidated its own vanguard character',[9] while Luxemburg's model was undoubtedly closer to the idea of the mass party.[10]

Notwithstanding the existence of open differences between Lenin and Luxemburg as regards the best organization for the party of the proletariat, there exists what could be called a 'minimum consensus' among Marxist theoreticians before, then and afterwards, on what the 'ideal' party of the working class should be.

Ever since Marx and Engels published *The Communist Manifesto*, the idea of a sort of universal, international working class has always been present. This has meant that in the national struggles of the proletarians of different countries, they point out and bring to the fore the common interests of the entire proletariat, independent of nationality.[11] In other words, the interests of a given working-class party are supposedly the same as those of workers everywhere.

Second, the organization of the party should be one able to guarantee the greatest internal democracy.

Third, within the party a centralized, powerful apparatus is needed to represent the interests of the membership. This apparatus, which in turn exerts leadership, is in charge of articulation and execution of party policies without undue interference from party members, a principle called *democratic centralism*.

Fourth, the total allegiance of the membership to the party is required to the extent that no distinction exists between 'private' and 'public' life.[12]

The ideal Marxist party and the Socialists

The party's interests and the interests of the workers of the world

The first generally accepted defining feature of the 'ideal' Marxist party is that the interests of the party are identified with the interests of the workers of the entire world. Of course, this assertion is sufficiently ambiguous to permit a great deal of flexibility. It has been difficult to establish on objective lines what the supposed 'interests' of workers are in general, and in particular, circumstances.

It is not our concern to discover whether it is possible to empirically identify the existence of a given set of principles which one can firmly consider as representing the interests of workers in general. Nor is it our concern to trace a line dividing circumstances which favour the workers' interests, and those which do not. The fact is, however, that the preoccupation with this aspect of classic socialist ideology has been present in the PSCh's written principles since the organization was inaugurated in the 1930s.

The main founding document, written in October 1933, said that 'the socialist doctrine is of international character and requests a co-ordinated action in solidarity with the workers of the world'.[13]

Ever since, the party has used each and every opportunity to stress this point, leaving no room for doubt about their position. It is important to note that even when the party suffered from one or another of its divisions, the conflicting factions always, at least, agreed in this aspect. The concept of an agreement between 'the interests of workers' everywhere and the interests of the PSCh has been one of the most uncontroversial aspects of the party's ideology throughout its history.[14]

The practice of internal democracy

The need for the existence of *internal democracy* within the party is the second great universally accepted principle among Marxist theoreticians and writers. It should not be confused with the concept of *democratic centralism*, whose characteristics will be dealt with later. At the moment it will suffice to point out that the idea of internal democracy refers to the use of classic democratic norms within the party's procedures (equal opportunities, rights to elect and to be elected to offices, one man one vote, etc.), while democratic centralism refers to the abrogation of those rights in order to enable the leadership to carry out the party's policies without interference. While the idea of internal democracy implies the active exercise of rights, the idea of democratic centralism implies their subordination in favour of the superior interests and party discipline. We found that the concept of internal democracy has been present in the party's literature from the very moment the party was created. There is no problem at all in tracing the relevance of this aspect in PSCh ideology. However, as shall be revealed below, the same cannot be said of the concept of democratic centralism.

The practice of democratic centralism

The PSCh's statutes defines democratic centralism as:

— Democratic election of all leaders,
— Systematic check on the procedures and behaviour of the leadership by those who gave them office,
— Discipline: decisions taken by any authoritative body should be obeyed,
— Subordination of minorities to the majority and mutual respect.[15]

The definition above was written for the PSCh 1967 Chillán Congress and it represents a fairly complete analysis. However, it should be noted that it was only then that the party's preoccupation with the concept became obvious. Although the Chilean Socialists had long defined themselves as Marxist–Leninist,[16] an explicit mention of the principle of democratic centralism in official party literature could not be found until the early 1950s, and even then only in unofficial documents and letters.

Salomón Corbalán, a Socialist MP, stated in 1953 in a letter to the parliamentary chief whip, Oscar Naranjo:

our party cannot go indefinitely without furnishing a complete, comprehensive concept of democratic centralism, as we understand it. The Socialist Party has been proud of its doctrinaire purism [an obvious allusion by Corbalán to party preoccupation and sometimes obsession with ideology], but the same cannot be said of its organization. We should not be afraid of writing out a set of principles to govern our internal behaviour, and democratic centralism should be in the forefront of it.[17]

Without doubt he was referring to the fact that democratic centralism was supposed to be a normal practice in internal procedures from the outset of the party. However, apart from the repeated acceptance of the existence of internal democracy, no specific statement about the existence and practice of the principle had been made up to then.

The clearest declaration on the subject came only in 1967, when the *Estatutos Orgánicos del Partido Socialista*, approved by the Chillán Congress, were issued:[18]

Marxist parties have always been looking for a synthesis between the right and freedom for each man to fight for his own point of view, and the need to centralize and co-ordinate these individual stands so as to make them generally useful. This is the guiding principle of internal relations called democratic centralism. It is a function of the hierarchical centralization of party activities, and it is a form of internal democracy.[19]

The party, however, considered democratic centralism a necessary limitation on internal democracy. It asserted that 'internal democracy is the right of the member to intervene in all affairs of the party, and to fight for his own ideas on the best way to pursue the party's policies'. But once a given policy is adopted, the leadership has the responsibility for its execution. From then on, all members should obey the instructions of the party leadership. No member can overcome the hierarchy, notwithstanding his length of service, the offices he has held, or holds within the party, or any other reason he can assume is important'.[20]

The need to restrict the practice of democratic centralism to enable the exercise of internal democracy was also contemplated in the document:

The practice of democratic centralism requires a high political consciousness by all members of the party. They should be able to disengage themselves from anarchist, personalist and caudillist tendencies which can only distort and weaken a true implementation of the party's policies. On the other hand, an appropriate interpretation of democratic centralism should avoid deformations which could lead to excessive dominance of the party leadership over the members. The development of a despotic bureaucracy can be avoided only through a permanent and broad discussion of problems. However, in the last resort the concrete conditions of each given case will determine whether democratic centralism should prevail over internal democracy or the reverse.[21]

The party provide a statement of the conditions which would direct which course to take: 'For example, under the difficult conditions of underground struggle, it will not be possible to make a full use of all personal rights within the party. On the other hand, under a régime of bourgeois legality which permits the normal work of the organization, there will be no reason to avoid the discussions needed to solve problems'.[22]

It is rather difficult to determine whether the written rules on democratic centralism, as stated in 1967, were normal procedure within the party before then. It is clear that to theoretically define democratic centralism, and to establish how its practice should occur as a day-to-day procedure within the party, has nothing to do with actual practice. In the case of the first of the previous elements analysed as generally accepted prerequisites of the 'ideal' Marxist party—identification of the workers' interests with those of the party—there is only one way of asserting whether the party committed itself to it or not, and that was done, as already stated, through an examination of the more appropriate party literature. It is obvious that the same methodological procedure will prove inadequate in explaining the party's real behaviour on the issue of internal democracy and democratic centralism (as the clear assertion of the party on both items is not sufficient here). Evidence is needed to determine when, and how, one or both were actually being adopted as usual internal procedures within the party.

It has already been said that official recognition of the principle came explicitly only in 1967, but this did not preclude its use in full or in part before. In fact, the practice of internal democracy, for example, at least theoretically, was clearly contemplated in most relevant party literature from the very beginning of the party as a formal political organization. Our main concern here is, therefore, to prove—or disprove—whether internal democracy and democratic centralism existed in reality within the party. Both items seem to be linked, as the existence of one appears to be a prerequisite for the existence of the other.

Three main sources were available to provide evidence on these issues: the opinions of five former Socialist leaders who at one time or another had held important positions within the party bureaucratic structure; a survey of some top- and intermediate-level leaders; and our own experience as party members for almost twenty years. We hasten to recognize the shortcomings of such methods, but given the circumstances affecting Chile at the time of our research, and the character of the subject matter, we could (and even now can) foresee no alternative method of collecting relevant data which would throw some light on this subject. It would have been impossible to carry out a representative survey covering the last thirty or forty years.

However, a questionnaire was used to collect data on this and other issues. It was primarily aimed at producing empirical evidence on the acting leadership's perception of a variety of subjects related to party organization, ideology and the Chilean political situation at that time(1973). Three Regional Committees were allowed by the party leadership to be interviewed. Ten members of the Political Commission of the Central Committee were also given permission to answer. We were authorized to select both the Regional Committees and those Political Commission members at our own discretion (there was one Regional Committee, at least, in each of the twenty-five Chilean provinces, and the Political Commission had a membership of fifteen, including the secretary-general, who was not included in the sample).

We decided to proceed with an intentional sample in the case of the three Regional Committees to be interviewed. The criterion adopted was the following: to choose each one of the Regional Committees in accordance with certain socio-economic features which characterized the different provinces. After carefully studying each province individually, we decided to take one in the northern part of the country (RG1), one in the centre (RG2) and another in the south (RG3).

RG1 was selected because it is predominantly a mining zone (Antofagasta), RG2 because it is primarily industrial (Santiago) and RG3 because it is mainly agricultural. These three features constitute the main basis of Chilean economic life.

Each Regional Committee was composed of twelve members, all of whom were interviewed. Ten out of fifteen members of the Political Commission of the Central Committee (PC) were also interviewed.

Two central hypotheses were drawn:

1. The party could in fact exhibit a good record in achieving internal democracy throughout the years. The full practice of democratic rights was normally respected and there was no evidence to suggest the contrary from our own experience as members of the party.
2. The party could, on the other hand, exhibit a rather dubious record regarding the practice of democratic centralism. This hypothesis was based

mainly upon the fact that it is normal procedure within the party—in contradiction to the written rules—that groups and even recognized leadership levels (i.e. Regional and Sectional Committees) commit themselves publicly to policies which are antagonistic to the official policies of the party. Examples are drawn from the several years of Socialist–Communist alliance (first in FRAP—Frente de Acción Popular—and later on in the Unidad Popular). During this period the party officially sustained a comprehensive policy of alliances with the PCCh at all levels of the Chilean political fabric. This meant, in theory, that in each and every election (whether it was a student, labour or parliamentary election), the two parties should present themselves jointly or, at least with a joint platform, or independently if tactical reasons made that advisable. But it would not fit into the party's policy of Socialist–Communist understanding to allow for Socialist candidates to make alliances with other political forces.

It was a matter of fact, however, that Regional and Sectional Committees of the party officially sanctioned that sort of alliance repeatedly during most of the period from 1960 to 1970.[23] Our hypothesis went on to imply that the trend had been present in normal procedures during most of the party's history.

The data collected from former and existing leaders suggested that there existed a strong agreement on the idea of real internal democracy within the party. On the other hand, they tended to view the practice of democratic centralism as having been rather inconsistent. The interpretation and application of these principles on the part of some intermediate leadership levels was particularly noted for its inconsistency.

The former leaders perception of internal democracy and democratic centralism. The answers were obtained in an informal fashion, mainly through conversations on a variety of issues, not necessarily directly related to the research. The five respondents were all known, knowledgeable members with thirty or more years of membership at that time. All of them had actively participated in the party and had had the opportunity to elect and be elected, to be members of the lower organizational units (*núcleos*) and its leadership, to be members of the intermediate leadership levels (Sectional and Regional Committees) and even, on one occasion, to form part of the Central Committee. In addition to this, on at least three occasions, they all had participated in one or more of the auxiliary bodies of the leadership (mainly Departments).

Obviously, their experience as party members and party leaders had been very rich. Their opinions seemed to be, for that reason, indispensable. Mainly for security reasons we agreed to keep secret the names of the five former leaders interviewed.

Table 2.1 Interview responses of five former leaders of the PSCh

	Period from 1935 on: internal democracy	Period from 1935 on: democratic centralism
Leader 1	Yes	No
Leader 2	Yes	No
Leader 3	Yes	No
Leader 4	Yes	No
Leader 5	Yes	No

Table 2.1 shows, in a summarized version, the answers obtained from interviews with five ex-leaders. It should be noted that there was complete agreement on all answers—unanimously 'Yes' to the question of whether internal democracy was practiced within the party, and unanimously 'No' to the question of whether democratic centralism was normal internal procedure.

We should emphasize that there were no straight questions but a flexible, informal conversation into which we introduced, when considered appropriate, those questions we were most interested in. The respondents would not answer straight questions mainly due to two reasons: First, all of them were 70 years old or more, and it was very difficult to get straight answers to direct questions; and, second, as it has already been explained, the political climate in Chile at that time would not allow for formal research being carried out in an open fashion, as the suspicions it would cause would endanger the development of future work.

To get the opinion of each former leader on the first item, it was explained clearly to them what meaning was attached to the concept 'exercise of internal democracy'. A formal definition was avoided. Instead, we set up examples of 'active', 'practising' democracy within party life; for example, the opportunity to elect and be elected to any office, the right to one vote for every member of the party in every election, the right to be judged by pre-established, regular party tribunals for party offences, and so on. Examples were cited on each specific issue.

The results obtained from all five former leaders shows that the concept of practising internal democracy had been very strongly internalized by them, presumably as a consequence of their roots in actual party procedures. At no stage did any of the five deny that internal democracy was a reality within the party. They were eager to use their experiences in the party to illustrate the existence of internal democracy.

When it came to the second aspect—democratic centralism—the answers were also strikingly homogeneous, as they all considered it non-existent in normal party procedures. The central argument given was: democratic centralism has not usually been respected by the intermediate leadership, which commonly disregarded official party policies in order to implement their own.

The existing leadership's perception of internal democracy and democratic centralism:[24] The following question concerning *internal democracy* was presented to them:

With which of the following assertions would you agree?
(a) the congresses of the party express the internal democracy that prevails, delegates are freely elected and without any kind of undue pressures from either groups or persons. They all have the same opportunities to participate in discussions with limitations imposed only by mutual respect. In reality, any delegate can elect and be elected to any post through the practice of normal electoral procedures.
(b) The party congress expresses different group interests, and delegates represent the views that those groups hold. The group with more power will be the one that eventually will win and its delegates will get most of the important posts.

Table 2.2 shows the answers given by the respondents. These indicate that Regional Committee 1, Regional Committee 2 and the Political Commission of the Central Committee unanimously considered internal democracy, as understood in definition (a), as a practising reality within the party. Only three members of Regional Committee three disagreed, considering definition (b) more appropriate.

The result obtained here clearly indicates that a significant majority of the three intermediate leadership levels interviewed held a perception of internal democracy as an existing reality within the party. This was similar to the views held by the ex-leaders of the party. It is interesting to note that while unanimity is found in both cases of those RCs based in the predominantly

Table 2.2 Choice of definition of 'internal democracy' of three PSCh Regional Committees (RCs) and the PSCh Political Commission (PC)

	Definition (a)	Definition (b)
RC1	12	0
RC2	12	0
RC3	9	3
PC	10	0

mining and industrial zones, respectively, it is not found in the RC located in a predominantly agrarian zone (RC3). However, the three dissenting minority leaders do not effectively reflect the economic-social peculiarities of the zone, as one of them is a physician, the other a secondary-school teacher and the third a primary-school teacher. This view proved to be untypical of the view held by the majority of this particular Regional Committee. In informal discussions with the remaining members, we found that they all supported definition (a). Those Political Commission members interviewed also gave unanimous answers, considering defintion (a) as correct.

From the evidence it can be said that the first hypothesis proved correct—and in fact the party can exhibit a fairly adequate record regarding the practice of internal democracy, both in the past and at present.[25] As the answers were so homogeneous, there were no significative differences along class, education or any other lines of interest. The only exception (three middle-class leaders in a predominantly agricultural zone), cannot be interpreted as indicative of a signficant tendency, as absolutely all other middle-class leaders both in the Regional Committee and the Political Commission agreed upon definition (a) (twenty-five out of twenty-eight). In the case of the working class leadership, the result is completely homogeneous, showing that all of them, without a single exception, (nineteen out of nineteen), agreed upon definition (a).

The following definition of *democratic centralism* was presented to them:

The Socialist party statutes say that democratic centralism means:
— Democratic election of all leaders.
— Systematic checking of procedures and behaviour of the leadership by those who gave them office.
— Discipline: decisions taken by any authoritative body should be obeyed.
— Subordination of minorities to the majority and mutual respect.[26]

Two questions were asked of the respondents:
(a) Do you agree or disagree with that definition (Table 2.3)?

Table 2.3 Responses to question (a) concerning the PSCh definition of 'democratic centralism'

	Agree	Disagree
RC1	12	0
RC2	12	0
RC3	12	0
PC	10	0

Table 2.4 Responses to question (b) concerning the reality of 'democratic centralism' in the case of the PSCh

	Yes	No
RC1	12	0
RC2	12	0
RC3	9	3
PC	0	10

(b) Do you think that this is true in the case of the PSCh (Table 2.4)?

All of the interviewed leaders agreed that the official party definition of 'democratic centralism' was appropriate, as is shown by Table 2.3.

Table 2.4 shows that, again, there is an homogeneous answer in the case of RC1 and RC2, but again disagreement can be found in RC3, where three out of the twelve respondents considered that democratic centralism, as defined officially in the party statutes, was not normal practice in party procedures. It is important to note that although the dissenting members of RC3 are by no means a significant percentage, they are the same respondents who also dissented from the majority in the appreciation of internal democracy as a normal party procedure (see Table 2.2).[27]

The unidimensional perspective of life: the full devotion to the party

The fourth acknowledged component of what could be considered the 'ideal' Marxist party is the unidimensionality of life, to which each and every member of the party should adhere completely. This means, in other words, that a member of the party cannot claim a private life distinct from his public life in the party. The two are incontrovertibly linked together.

The assertion that all persons—and moreover those whose lives are devoted to public affairs—are entitled to this distinction, is widely accepted within the framework of liberal democratic political systems. Parties which call themselves Marxist, on the other hand, claim to reject the assertion, and the origin of this stand can perhaps be found in the classic Leninist assumption that the revolutionary party—especially its leadership—should be integrated by full-time members whose lives are entirely devoted to the party.[28]

The PSCh, however, does not incorporate this view among its written principles. An examination of the most relevant party documents since its foundation, revealed that the subject had been completely left out of party ideology throughout most of its history. Only in the 1960s could some indirect remarks be traced. Furthermore, no social or communal organizations to 'observe' individual members of the party existed, other than the party itself.

It is rather surprising to find that these important aspects of Marxist ideology had been conspicuously absent from the Chilean Socialists' theoretical preoccupations for more than thirty years and that only in the mid-1960s were some written though indirect opinions given on the matter. In the party statutes issued in 1967, the loyalty oath taken by the new members asked them to 'concentrate your lives to the unconditional service of the party, the working class and the socialist revolution, to give your spirits and your blood to the great cause of Chile's liberation from the imperialist oppression and capitalist exploitation'. Further, new members were asked to 'accept the party discipline above all other considerations and to be a thorough and loyal socialist'.[29]

Apart from this general notice of the issue, there exists only one identified written statement specifying the character of the supposed unidimensionality of life attributable to the members of Marxist parties.[30]

This statement establishes that 'there is only the militant [or member] of the party', but fails to clarify the nature of that status. Normally, the meaning that has been given to that statement is that there is no separation between a 'private identity' and a 'public identity'. In other words, there exists no such thing as a 'private' person, being opposed, contradicting, or even different to a 'public' person.[31]

The ambiguity of the member's status has been no obstacle for the existing leadership. It has strongly internalized the unidimensionality principle, as can be inferred from the following data.

The acting leadership's perception of the private/public life dichotomy: The respondents were asked the following question:

The party's declaration of principles says that, 'there is only the member of the party' and there is no separate identity between the militant as a private person and as a public person. Do you agree or disagree with this assertion?

Table 2.5 Responses to question concerning the private/public life dichotomy

	Agree	Disagree
RC1	12	0
RC2	12	0
RC3	12	0
PC	10	0

The answers are shown in Table 2.5. The homogeneity of these answers is absolute. The respondents agree unanimously with the party definition, which, in addition to being rather too general and vague, belonged to an old version of the party's statutes (1954). It had not been included in subsequent documents of that nature or any other sort.

An explanation of this phenomenon can be found in what can be considered the traditional extreme ideologies which have always prevailed within the PSCh's internal life. There are a number of issues profoundly and strongly internalized by both party members and leaders, to such an extent as they appear as true party principles and/or facts, whereas they have never formed part of the party's written ideology or established structure. This is an example of one of these issues and in each and every official initiation ceremony new members are reminded that they are now Socialists and cannot claim any right or privileges attributable to a 'private' person. In fact, however, it is clear that, during the last ten years at least, the party has tolerated the co-existence of both a private and a public life for every member. It has been the exception when the party has not accepted as valid, arguments excusing members from complying with party rules, instructions or specific assignments. These arguments have been of a very personal nature, and in considering them as acceptable the party has implicitly recognized the right of each party member to a private dimension in his life.

It is necessary, nevertheless, to expand on the party's record on this issue. First, it is useful to distinguish the various party units in order to understand the depth of this flexibility within the party.

Núcleos: It has been normal procedure within the *núcleos* to permit its members to dissociate themselves from party responsibilities for a variety of reasons. In practical terms this has meant that if a member can produce any legitimate reason to dissociate himself from a certain party assignment, he will normally be permitted to do so. Acceptable excuses have been, among others, sickness, exhaustion, ideological problems, family problems and economic problems. The most superficial analysis of these problems by the party was sufficient. The nature of the reason did not really matter, as long as it effectively existed, and consequently the nature and scope of the 'private' dimension of the member's life appeared greatly enlarged.

But the degree of flexibility regarding the member's right to claim 'private' reasons to avoid party responsibilities is not enough to ascertain the existence of a clearly accepted (though only in fact, and not in written rule) line between the 'private' and the 'public' life of the party member. The *núcleos* are, in addition, a good example of the same flexibility, when it comes to the matter of what is 'morally right' or 'wrong' for a Socialist member.

There have rarely been punishments for a *núcleo* member whose 'moral' conduct has been a matter of social rejection, unless the nature of his fault has been such that it merited official punishment from a public tribunal.[32] This rather lenient attitude has been in sharp contrast with that exhibited, at least in Chile, by the PCCh, whose scrutiny of its members is famed for its rigour.

This second example of the treatment of members within the *núcleos* aids the argument that in real terms there exists no unidimensionality of life for members of the *núcleos* and that, on the contrary, a procedure is clearly practised which amounts to recognition of the classic dichotomy between private and public life.

Intermediate leadership levels (Sectional and Regional Committees)

Traditionally the higher-leadership bodies experienced a lower level of tolerance than that permitted to rank-and-file party members with regard to the private/public dichotomy. Although the party has never had the 'full-time revolutionary' leader nor has it had the full-time member, entirely devoted to the party, there has nevertheless existed less willingness to condone leaders refusing party assignments or responsibilities.

Whereas in the *núcleos* there has always existed a great deal of flexibility to allow members the possibility of a private life, in the higher echelons of the party bureaucratic structure, reality has been different.

This is perhaps the reason for the homogeneity of the answers of the interviewed leaders. As they were holding leadership positions when the survey was being carried out, it was almost natural that their rationalization corresponded to the realities of that moment. In addition to that, the particular tensions that were affecting the Chilean political life at that time should not be disregarded. They were of such a nature that the parties of the governmental coalition tightened the rules that otherwise were applied with leniency and flexibility. This being so, it was rare that a party leader of intermediate importance could be authorized, during the three years of Popular Unity administration at least, to dissociate from the tasks that had been assigned to him while at the same time retaining his office. The normal procedure in such cases would be the removal from office of the troublesome official rather than granting him leave of absence for a given period of time. This tendency, however, cannot be used to imply that the private/public life dichotomy was effectively suppressed at higher levels of the bureaucratic structure, but that only the extreme political situation in Chile at that moment did not allow the governmental parties to permit themselves such a luxury. Incompetent or inefficient *núcleos* members could be permitted to retire temporarily from party responsibilities, but a party leader could not. In the eventuality of such a case, the leader in question should rather give way to another and lose his post. The situation amounted, though temporarily, to the elimination of a 'private' life in the higher party echelons. Leaders were frequently asked to devote themselves entirely to the party. As the organization did not normally pay them, they were allowed indefinite leaves of absence from their occupations. This was not difficult to achieve in the case of public officials, but it created many problems for those in independent or professional occupations. Lenin's idea of the 'revolutionary leader' thus came to be a reality, at least temporarily in the PSCh.[33]

Higher leadership bodies (Central Committee and Political Commission)

As in the case of the intermediate leadership, the Central Committee and its delegated, centralized smaller body, the Political Commission, normally allowed for a rather rigid interpretation of the private/public life dichotomy during the three years of Popular Unity administration. But, as in the two earlier examples, the facts were quite different during most of the previous forty years of the party. All evidence suggests that a lenient course was normally adopted, permitting even Central Committee and Political Commission members to distinguish between their public and their private lives. Leaves of absence were commonly permitted, violations of generally accepted social and/or moral rules pardoned and even legal indiscretions unproved in public tribunals, condoned. The party recognized, in fact, the right of every member to a private life, even under circumstances where the practice of that right could and perhaps should have been legitimately limited.

The former leaders' perception of the private/public life dichotomy: The generalized view of the five former PSCh leaders interviewed was that during most of its history the party had clearly permitted its members the right to both a private and a public life (see Table 2.6). A private life was always allowed with varying degrees of flexibility according to internal and external political circum-

Table 2.6 Five former PSCh leaders' view of the private/public life dichotomy

	Public and private	One dimension only: the member militant
Leader 1	Yes	No
Leader 2	Yes	No
Leader 3	Yes	No
Leader 4	Yes	No
Leader 5	Yes	No

stances. But at no time could any of them remember the party restricting recognition of a separate private life away from the public. There were, of course, periods when difficult problems would cause the leadership to tighten the rules, but that was the exception and not the rule.

The unanimous opinion of the five experienced former party leaders is in contradiction to the opinion held by the existing leadership, as can be inferred from the comparison between Tables 2.5 and 2.6.

Our explanation is that this is due mainly to one reason: all the existing leaders interviewed were, as has already been said, in office at a delicate point in time. In addition to that, they were doing their jobs under particularly difficult conditions of stress, surrounded by mounting tensions in the political and social atmosphere. Their tendency to ideologism, a natural development in the Socialist leadership, was affected by the situation, causing it to be more extreme. A feeling of unrestricted devotion to the party—and often that was the case for many of them under the circumstances—induced them to regard a transitory situation as a permanent one. The former leaders, on the contrary, had the opportunity to know the party for many years, as rank-and-file members, and as intermediate and higher leaders. They were now observers—their situation at that moment was far more relaxed and, consequently, more objective, than the views of full-time leaders under stress. This being so, the former leaders could in fact see their party with more objectivity than the existing leaders.

CONCLUSIONS

Even though it is a subject for controversy, we had to assume, for methodological reasons, that at least four *sine qua non* conditions were attributable to a Marxist party:

1. Identification of the 'interests' of the workers in general with the 'interests' of the given party.
2. An internal organization which is able to guarantee the practice of internal democracy.
3. An internal organization which is able to guarantee the practice of democratic centralism.
4. The absence of the private/public life dichotomy for party members.

Even though more characteristics could be identified, the four we decided to utilize should be considered as perhaps the more relevant.

It is obvious that while the first and the fourth conditions are of an ideological nature, the second and the third are rather of an organizational or bureaucratic nature. However, the line that separates the simple bureaucratic matter from the ideological matter in a Marxist party is difficult to trace. Each and every rule and principle practised by the party is somehow rooted in the general ideological setting of that party, a *body ideological* from which the party cannot be separated without losing its identity.

The Chilean Socialists provide a good example on this subject. Firmly adhered to the general European Marxist ideology, the party had internalized most of the doctrinaire principles which characterize it.

When an analysis of the party as a Marxist party is made, the main point is to distinguish theory from practice. It is usually in the self-definition of the party as Marxist where presumably actual practices are superseded by theory. In other words, it is one thing for the party to proclaim a theoretical truth in both ideology and organization (assuming for the moment that one can be separated from the other); it is something quite different to assert a compatibility between what the party says and what the party does.

Assuming, then, that the party which can exhibit the four already mentioned items (at least as far as its practice) can be called a Marxist party, we came to the following conclusions in each case:

1. It is clear that the idea of the identification of the worker's 'interests' with the interests of the PSCh has always been present in the party's written principles. As has already been said, it is not possible to empirically establish whose those 'interests' are and whether they are in reality the same as those of the PSCh. It should suffice, however, to say that the principle has been systematically included in the official party literature without exception for almost forty years.

2. It was our hypothesis that the party could in fact show a fair record regarding the practice of internal democracy. The opinions of both former and existing leaders corroborated this hypothesis. The reasons that explain this behaviour can be found, in our opinion, in the peculiarities of the social composition of the party membership, which has always reflected interests, if not antagonistic, at least different from one another. The social heterogeneity of the membership (and, of course, of the leadership) contributed to creating a great deal of flexibility in inter-social class relations within the party, a sort of 'pluralism' which could have been more difficult to achieve had the party been socially homogeneous.

The party has never been an homogenous social body with unilateral class representation. On the contrary, both the middle and working classes have always been represented within the party in different proportions according to the times. This has allowed a kind of internal politics in which different cultures and behaviour patterns had to be represented and defended. Had the party been a homogeneous class entity, internal democracy could perhaps have been an empty principle without effective roots in the party procedures, as the conditions for its interplay would have been non-existent. The existence within the party of people with quite different social, economical and educational backgrounds contributed to the development of a working and accepted 'pluralism'. This may sound strange for those who consider themselves as 'Marxist orthodoxists', but in the case of the Chilean Socialists it amounted to the creation of the very conditions which enabled internal democracy to be fully internalized and practised throughout the party's history. As a consequence, something which remained an unattained objective for so many Marxist parties was a matter of day-to-day activity for the PSCh.

3. However, the same conditions enabling the party to practise internal democracy caused its failure when it came to the practice of democratic centralism. Our hypothesis was that the party's record on this matter was rather poor, primarily as a consequence of continuous and persistent violations of party discipline by the intermediate party leadership bodies. The perception that the former leaders had of the issue rather confirmed our belief, but the opinions (shown in Table 2.4) of the existing leadership are quite different. With the exception of three of the twelve members of RG3, all other existing leaders considered democratic centralism a reality in normal party procedures. Why was this so? Why did there exist so radical a difference between the former leaders' position and that of the existing leaders?

One possible explanation has already been given: is it that the former leaders' perception of this and any other problems appeared weaker due to the passage of time? On the other hand, existing leaders were actively engaged in their rôles and undergoing pressures and stress; this could lead them sometimes to reject reality as a healthy but nevertheless non-political self-defence.

When the case of democratic centralism is analysed, the result shows that those who appear to violate it continuously are not in the higher bureaucratic structure of the party but in the intermediate structure. The results on this matter are further clarified when the answers of the Political Commission are examined. Ten members of this body (100 per cent) agreed that democratic centralism was not being achieved in actual party life. The contradiction existing between the highest leadership and the intermediate levels can be attributed to the different scope of the appreciation of the problem: the highest leadership body (the Political Commission) is the body which suffers because of disobedience by the intermediate levels. These latter bodies are the very structures whose behaviour obstructs the practice of democratic centralism.

4. The fourth and last condition of the 'ideal' Marxist party refers to the absolute commitment to the party by party members.

The main conclusion here is that, though exceptions have existed, the general rule has been that this perspective has never been an ideological principle with real roots in the party's development. It has varied according to times, circumstances and to the type of structure, as has already been explained, but these do not amount to the statement that there has existed in the party an absolute commitment to the party by its members. The private/public dichotomy has been widely accepted in party life for most of its members, and for most of its history.

Is there enough evidence, then, to say that the PSCh could be labelled as a truly 'Marxist' party? If this is to be decided according to what the self-perception of the party through its written principles is, the conclusion would be without doubt in the affirmative. If it is to be decided according to the self-perception of party leaders, either former or exsiting, the conclusion would be, to say the least, ambiguous.

Empirical evidence suggests that at least two of the four selected conditions have not been fully practised within the party in a signficant way throughout its history, and this fact clearly endangers the party's pretensions to be labelled as an 'orthodox' Marxist party. The two conditions in which the party fails—democratic centralism and unidimensionality of life—are of such a nature that they considerably weaken any attempt to regard them as secondary or irrelevant. If the party were a self-proclaimed petit bourgeois, or a self-confessed centrist, multi-class party, the above-mentioned short-comings would be irrelevant or, at least, unimportant. In the case of a self-proclaimed Marxist party, the failure in the implemenation of such important theoretical items constitues a clear indication of both a theoretical and an organizational vacuum.

As will be seen in the following chapter, the failure of the party to implement what it whole-heartedly considered were natural ingredients of its ideology, was due to a number of reasons, and among the most important, were the following:

1. The different class origins of its members.
2. The different class origins of its leaders.
3. The defective articulation of the memberships' demands and the lack of appropriate execution of orders and decisions.
4. The faulty internal model of organization and the erroneous perception by the leadership of the kind of party they were actually in charge of.
5. The lack of appropriate financing.

These factors will be discussed at length in the following chapter.

NOTES

1. Jean Blondel, *An Introduction to Comparative Government* (Weidenfeld & Nicolson, London, 1969), p. 119.
2. By *structure*, we understand a given model of a party's bureaucratic apparatus. By *organization*, we mean the way in which the structure expresses itself in practice.
3. Examples of the purely 'empiricist' approach are: Samuel J. Eldersveld, *Political Parties: Behavioural Analysis*, MacNally, Chicago, 1964. Carl Beck, 'Party Control and Bureaucratization in Czechoslovakia', in *The Journal of Politics*, Vol. 23, 1961, pp. 279–94; Lester C. Seligman, 'Political Recruitment and Party Structures: A Case Study', in *American Political Science Review* (APSR), Vol. 55, 1961, pp. 77–86.

    Examples of the purely 'Marxist' approach are: Rossana Rossanda, 'Class and Party', *The Socialist Register*, 1970, pp. 217–31; Monty Johnstone, 'Marx, Engels and the Concept of the Party', *The Socialist Register*, 1967, pp. 121–58; Lucio Magri, 'What Is a Revolutionary Party?', *New Left Review*, No. 60, March –April, 1970, pp. 97–128; The classic works of W. I. Lenin—*What Is to Be Done?* (Progress Publishers, Moscow, 1968); pertinent passages of *Selected Works* (Progress Publishers, Moscow, 1947), Vol. 1; Rosa Luxemburg, *Leninism or Marxism? The Russian Revolution*, ed. Bertram D. Wolfe (Ann Arbor, University of Michigan Press, 1961)—are also in this line. Good attempts to produce a more balanced approach are in my opinion: Blondel, *op. cit.*; Jean Blondel, *Comparative Government* (reader) (Macmillan, London, 1969); Maurice Duverger, *Political Parties* (Methuen, London, 1972); Robert Michels, *Political Parties* (Dover, New York, 1959). This list is by no means exhaustive. It only includes some of the works that reflect the three approaches.
4. Johnstone, *op. cit.*, p. 33.
5. There is no specific work of Marx and/or Engels on the subject of the Marxist party. Lenin's public debates with Rosa Luxemburg on the issue of party organization (among others) provide rich theoretical material. Afterwards, Magri's 'What is a Revolutionary Party?' (*op. cit.*), Johnstone's 'Marx and Engels' (*op. cit.*), and Rossanda's 'Class and Party' (*op. cit.*), are among the best works which deal with the matter. Always interesting from a theoretical perspective are some classics such as Lenin's *What Is to Be Done?* (*op. cit.*), Luxemburg's *The Russian Revolution* and *Leninism or Marxism?* (*op. cit.*), Antonio Gramsci's 'Soviets in Italy', Pamphlet Series 11 (Institute for Workers Control, London, 1970), Milovan Djilas' *The New Class* (Unwin Books, London, 1966), and George Lukac's *History and Class Consciousness* (Merlin Press, London). The list could go on indefinitely, for there is an abundant literature on the subject. But we do not intend here, nor in other theoretical aspects to be discussed later, to engage in lengthy enumerations and discussions. We shall present in each case a summarized version of the theoretical matters involved, as a methodological need rather than as a specific, *per se* issue.
6. Lenin, *What Is to Be Done?* (*op. cit.*), (quoting K. Kautsky, 'On the draft

programme of the Austrian Social Democratic Party', *Neue Zeit*, 1901–2, No. 3, p. 79).

7. Ibid., p. 81.

8. Rosa Luxemburg, 'Organizational Questions on the Russian Social Democracy', 'The Russian Revolution', both in *Leninism or Marxism?*.

9. Lucio Magri, op. cit., p. 107.

10. The problem of the mass and the cadre party is treated later on in this work. Blondel says that 'the distinction between mass parties and parties of "cadres" or committees appeared to correspond to modern realities [he is referring to Duverger's theory on party models]: on the one hand, some parties are merely organizations of professional politicians, held together in order to fill elective posts. On the other, some parties bring within their fold hundreds of thousands of ordinary people who have no personal political aspirations but simply want to promote a cause and help others to gain political power' (Blondel, *Comparative Government*, op. cit., p. 117).

11. K. Marx and F. Engels (eds), *The Communist Manifesto*, A.S.P. Taylor (Penguin, London, 1967).

12. Johnstone (*op. cit*.); Magri, (*op. cit*.) and Luxemburg's works, notably *The Russian Revolution* (*op. cit*), are very relevant. Contemporary Marxist theoreticians, such as Milovan Djilas, Regis Debray, Roger Garaudy and Palmiro Togliatti have stressed the importance of such elements as *sine qua non* ingredients of the 'party of the proletariat'. Antonio Gramsci's works are also important in both the theoretical and the structural organizational perspectives.

13. *Declaración de Principios*, party document, 1933, p. 2. The concept of *ideology* will be used from now on to refer to the idea of 'political ideology' as described by M. Christensen, Alan S. Engel, Dan N. Jacobs, Mostafa Rejai and Herbert Waltzer, in *Ideologies and modern politics* (Thomas Nelson, London, 1972). They say that 'political ideology is a belief system that explains and justifies a preferred political order for society, either existing or proposed, and offers a strategy (processes, institutional arrangements, programmes) for its attainment'. It is a known fact that the term has been and is a matter for continued scientific controversy. As a consequence, our agreement should be interpreted as an operational necessity rather than as a complete acceptance, with all its implications, of the meaning given to the expression. This definition seemed to me appropriate enough to refer to the concept of 'a reasonably coherent body of ideas concerning practical means of how to change, reform (or maintain) a political order'. (Carl J. Friedrich, *Man and His Government: An Empirical Theory of Politics*, McGraw Hill, New York, 1963, p. 90). Both definitions are complementary to one another and could be further specified by saying with Friedrich that 'ideology is a set of ideas which unites a party or other group for effective participation in political life' (Friedrich, *op. cit*., p. 89). By *ideologism* shall be understood an exaggerated adherence to a given belief system, with general disregard for actual political practices, procedures and/or occurrences.

14. The importance of this aspect of Socialist ideology can be assessed by examining the Official Resolutions of the party's congresses, from its foundation, up to the

1970s. There are few occasions when the issue has not been strongly emphasized. Other documents, such as party periodicals (notably *Arauco, Izquierda* and the daily newspaper *Ultima Hora*) contain abundant references to the subject, as is also the case in speeches made by Socialist MPs in different years.

15. 'Estatutos organicos Partido Socialista', internal document, 1967, p. 12.

16. In fact, the categorization of the party as Marxist–Leninist has gone along with its categorization as a party of the working class, and, prseumably, a party which can and does represent the interests of the workers of the world. There is no attempt on the part of the Chilean Socialist to hide the character of the party's ideology. This has been so since the existence of the party, without a single exception being traced.

17. Salomón Corbalán, letter to Oscar Naranjo, November, 1953.

18. 'Estatutos organicos del Partido Socialista', 1967, op. cit., p. 10.

19. Ibid., pp. 11–12.

20. Ibid., pp. 12–14.

21. Ibid., p. 13.

22. Ibid.

23. In student unions' elections, for example, it was an accepted fact that the PSCh made alliances with the extreme-left Movimento de Izquierda Revolucionaria (MIR), that did not belong to Popular Unity. The same thing happened in a conspicuous way in some important trade union elections.

24. The pertinent data provided by the three RGs and the PC will be used here and elsewhere in this chapter, only as supporting evidence in favour or against a given hypothesis. The inclusion of the relevant answers in each case, is not intended to provide a study of the leadership nor to establish any significant correlations or other empiricial tests which could lead to a more detailed analysis of leadership behaviour. This matter is dealth with in Chapter 4, below.

25. It should be pointed out that the opinions of the intermediate leadership instances and the Political Commission can only be considered as valid regarding the period from 1960 to 1970 as most of the interviewed leaders were not prepared to assess the issue for the previous years. For this, the former leaders considerations were the more relevant evidence that it was possible to get.

26. 'Party Statutes', *op. cit*., p. 12.

27. From the evidence provided by the sample as a whole, it is possible to infer that those three middle-class members of RC3 assumed something of a faction. The nature of their opinions placed them far to the left of the official party line, a fact that in informal party talks qualified them as 'Trotskyites', independently of the real links of the subjects with Trotskyist principles and/ or organizations.

28. Lenin stressed the necessity for members', especially leaders', lives to be completely devoted to the party. Duverger notes that this can lead to the creation of a true 'class of professional revolutionaries' and, consequently, to a process of bureaucratization of the party structures and the self-perpetuation of its leadership in power (see Duverger, *op. cit*). Relevant works of Lenin on the subject are:

Selected Works, Vol. 1 (including ISKRA, No. 1), *op. cit.*, and *What Is to Be Done?* (*op. cit*).

29. 'Party Statutes', *op. cit.*, p. 29.
30. The following documents were examined to assess the party's internalization of the private/public dichotomy:

    1. Resolutions of the Ordinary and Extraordinary Congresses, beginning with the I Ordinary National Congress, Santiago, October 1933, up to the XIII Ordinary National Congress, La Serena, November 1970 (totalling twenty-nine separate documents ranging from 1933 to 1970).
    2. Reserved documents:
        (a) Informe Político del Comité Central del P.S. al Pleno Nacional de Diciembre de 1964.
        (b) Boletín del Comité Ejecutivo del P.S.P., Agosto 1956.
        (c) Informes políticos a los Plenos Nacionales de 1967, 1968, 1969, 1970, 1971, 1972 and 1973.
    3. Party periodicals:
        (a) *Núcleo* (Valparaíso), monthly, 1934–36.
        (b) *Acción* (Santiago), 1933.
        (c) *Acción* Socialista (Santiago), 1934.
        (d) *Jornada* (Santiago), 1934–35.
        (e) *Consigna* (Santiago), weekly, 1934–40.
        (f) *Espartaco* (Santiago), 1947–48.
        (g) *La Calle* (Santiago), weekly 1949–55.
        (h) *Izquierda* (Santiago), weekly, 1958–61.
        (i) *Arauco* (Santiago), monthly, 1959–67.

31. 'Party Statutes' (1954), p. 6.
32. In the 1967 Party Statutes it was specifically stated that any member of the party should be 'personally honest and sober and should conduct his life privately or publicly, in a way compatible with socialist principles' (*op. cit.*, p. 30). Article 11 of the document states that a 'dissipated life and drunkenness' are faults against the party, and the same qualification is given to 'personal illegal activities' without further specifying their character (ibid., p. 32).
33. The character of this 'full-time leadership' was, however, weak and inefficient. During the three years of Popular Unity government the PSCh was unable to mount a national full-time organization which would guarantee a fair degree of political management. In fact, 'full-time' leaders were only possible in the big cities. In addition to that, the lack of a similar structure at the lower levels (i.e. *núcleos*), contributed to weaken the overall structure and political work of the party, as the measures adopted by the most important intermediate and higher leadership bodies would not necessarily be firmly implemented by the lower bodies. Before 1970 a very flexible interpretation of the dichotomy was nevertheless accepted and practised.

3 The Political Aspects of Organization

The *problem of class* is one of the most important aspects to be examined when a party's organization needs to be understood. When the party to be studied is a mass party, as is certainly the case with the PSCh, the need for an analysis of 'class' is even more imperative.

Gramsci, Luxemburg, Johnstone, Magri, Dhilas, Rossanda, and indeed Lenin, stressed the point from a Marxist perspective. The central issue became the inescapability of the class problem as one of the most important factors causing a party to adopt a given pattern of organization.[1]

The issue of the party as a representative of given class interests is certainly related to the issue of the party as true representative of a given social class. In other words, a party can in a variety of cases adopt the character of articulator of a social-class interests and, consequently, of that social-class demands.

Blondel establishes a very close relationship between what he calls 'class-based parties', referring to the socialist parties of Europe and the communists. He adds that the size of industrial groups and the nature of society 'account for variations in the size and importance of class-based parties of the socialist (and indeed communist) types'.[2] He states further that 'class-based groups are somewhat peculiar in that their goals are generally opposed to those of the prevailing groups in society', and that where an 'objective base for large trade unions does not exist, class-based parties are unlikely to develop'. The first issue to be approached will identify the class character of the PSCh. This and the subsequent problems arising from the description will form the first section of this chapter's analysis.

SOCIAL CHARACTERISTICS OF THE PARTY

The question of a party being representative and articulator of a particular social-class interest does not explain in itself that party's structure. It is clear, at least in the case of the PSCh, that the class issue is linked to the party also being a *mass* organization. Blondel rightly says, in this respect:

while one quickly had to recognise the shortcomings in the Duverger theory of party, the distinction between mass parties and parties of 'cadres' appeared to correspond to modern realities. On the one hand, some parties are merely organizations of professional politicians, held together in order to fill elective posts; on the other, some parties bring within their fold hundreds of thousands of ordinary people who have no personal political aspirations but simply want to promote a cause and help others to gain political power.[3]

Although the Leninist idea of a *cadre party* is not the same as Duverger's, both have in common the concept of the development of an élite group concentrating one way or another on party affairs, either paid or not. This is in contrast with Luxemburg's model of the working-class party: an egalitarian and necessarily non-selective group of people with more or less general political aims and without fixed, firmly established *a priori* strategies.[4]

The general idea of a cadre party includes the concept of a few people responsible for manipulating the affairs of other people, while the mass idea is indicative of a rather depersonalized political leadership in which, at any rate, the existence of a mass of supporters linked by cohesive general political aims has to be taken into consideration. This is certainly so whether the cadre party is shaped along the Leninist lines of professional revolutionaries devoted entirely to the party or along the more liberal lines of professional politicians held together in order to gain political power on either ideological or purely practical terms.[5]

Duverger emphasized, however, that the difference between a mass and a cadre (or, as he calls it, *committee*) party should not be seen as merely related to the quantity of people involved: 'The distinction between cadre and mass parties is not based upon their dimensions, upon the number of their members: the difference involved is not one of size but of structure'.[6] It is the factor of class and mass membership and participation in the party's affairs which mainly determines party structures.

Once the character of the class membership and participation of the PSCh has been identified, the nature of its internal organization according to the classical cadre or mass models can be described. Blondel's hypothetical assumptions on the mass party identifies at least six patterns which we shall be examining and analysing *vis-à-vis* the PSCh.

1. A party is a mass party if electors identify themselves with it, a matter certainly referring to the quality of support rather than the quantity of it.
2. Mass parties are characterized by a high reliance on voluntary help, while parties of committees are essentially organized on the basis of a small group of clients, paid or otherwise dependent on the local leader.
3. Mass parties assume the existence of permanent organizations, both at the national and local levels. The bureaucratization of the party structure is a consequence of the stability of the institution which, in turn, is characteristic of mass parties. Party oligarchies may develop in this way and some of the 'democratic' features which appear to be associated with mass parties may diminish as a result.

4. A nationally responsible leadership is also a characteristic of a mass party; leaders of parties of committees (or cadres) are responsible to MPs in Parliament or to small groups of leaders outside it.
5. A reasonable access to the use of mass media is also typical of mass parties.
6. The relationship between party images and those of the leaders are a very important element in mass parties.[7]

Although Blondel clearly established that his concept of mass parties reflects the social and political reality of industrial societies, he did not completely rule out the possibility that 'different' types of societies—such as the Chilean, considered as underdeveloped or on the way to development—could also fit into this framework. This is certainly the hypothesis of our research subject, as shall be demonstrated later in this chapter.

The feasibility of a mass class-based party in a pre-industrial society was foreseen by Blondel when he stated that 'often [these parties are] chosen to be the means by which change is achieved'.[8] However, he considers that the logical development in pre-industrial societies is towards the party of committees, because 'mass parties require popular identification with an abstract notion of party, which is unlikely to come naturally in a pre-industrial society. The local notables are more present, more real, than the party; educational achievement is too limited and the impact of mass media too weak to lead to the natural development of a party identification. The groups and associations from which mass parties tend to emerge in modern industrial societies are non-existent, or limited to rather isolated urban areas with which the bulk of the population has very few connections.'[9]

While fully agreeing with Blondel's argument, we should point out that it does not amount to a rejection of the existence of such a party in the Chilean context. Although Chile was, and indeed is, a developing society, large membership bases for trade unions have in fact existed for the last thirty or forty years. The mining industry has contributed to a long tradition of trade unionism in the country. Also, the existence of what Blondel calls special 'circumstances', helped the working and middle classes to achieve some short-term common aspirations. These 'circumstances' (i.e. the emergence of charismatic leaders, a process of decolonization, etc.) are not necessarily fixed or the same in all social and historical decolonization processes; a *developmental* process may encourage the creation of parties that articulate the interests of the middle classes and the interests of the working class (Socialist and Communist). At other stages, a 'de-Americanization' process has provided what amounts to the legitimization of the party within the Chilean political system, and help to establish the organization as a mass party.

The process of industrialization which took place in Chile over the last thirty or forty years created the conditions for this mass, class-based party. The development of trade unions, peasants co-operatives, professional and intellectual associations helped to pave the way for the party from at least the latter part of the nineteenth century.[10]

The class character of the organization

Is the PSCh a class-based party? What has been the development of the party in this respect since its foundation in the early 1930s up to the 1970s? First, let us analyse the *social character* of the party's membership during its three historical stages (as shown in Fig. I.3).

During the first stage, from the founding of the party in 1933 to the party's participation in the Popular Front (in 1939), the average type of membership was as follows: working class—55 per cent; middle class—45 per cent.[11] The second stage, covering the party's governmental duties (1939-53), shows a distinct improvement in the party's working-class membership, as middle class representation declined. The average type of membership for this stage was: working class—65 per cent; middle-class—35 per cent. The third and final period (1953-70), the party without any responsibilities in government (apart from those arising from its opposition status), shows a further increase in working-class representation and a further decline in middle-class representation: working class—70 per cent; middle class—30 per cent.[12]

The first aspect which is clear from the examination of those periods is that the party emerged in the 1930s as an almost pluralist, multi-class body. The passage of time, however, allowed for a deterioration of middle class representation and a consolidation of working-class hegemony within the ranks of the party's membership. The data available suggests that this was mostly due to an increase of working-class membership, while middle-class affiliation slowed down. These figures can be contrasted with those of the leaders, who show the predominance of the middle class over the working class.

A study of the Central and Regional Committees in all three stages shows the following percentages in each case.

1930s: Working class—25
            Middle class—75
1939-53: Working class—55
            Middle class—45
1953-70: Working class—48
            Middle class—50
            Bourgeoisie—2

Table 3.1 Rate of annual growth of the aggregate gross value of industry in Chile, 1914–64

Sectors	1914–25	1925–39	1939–46	1946–53	1953–9	1959–65	1914–65
Food	2.7	0.8	0.1	3.2	6.8	6.4	3.0
Beverages	5.7	0.2	3.8	4.7	4.1	7.7	4.0
Tobacco	3.8	3.0	6.0	-5.1	4.0	-3.3	1.4
Textiles	4.7	10.5	3.7	6.8	0.3	9.6	6.6
Clothing	6.1	-1.2	7.0	1.6	-1.7	-0.1	1.7
Wood	2.3	4.4	2.3	-3.8	1.0	6.2	2.1
Paper	1.6	5.5	7.5	3.3	2.5	8.2	5.2
Leather	2.7	2.3	4.0	2.4	-0.5	8.4	3.3
Chemicals	3.9	7.2	13.5	5.8	6.9	7.6	7.2
Non-metallic minerals	5.9	5.5	9.8	5.4	6.0	10.0	6.3
Metallurgy	13.0	1.8	9.6	11.6	3.9	11.0	7.6
TOTAL	4.5	2.6	5.5	4.0	2.7	7.8	4.3

Source: Oscar Muñoz, *Crecimiento Industrial de Chile, 1914–1965* (Universidad de Chile, Santiago, Chile, 1967), p. 66.

It is clear that working-class representation in membership began only with a slightly higher percentage than middle-class representation (55 per cent against 45 per cent), a characteristic that marked most of the first ten years of the party's development. During the same period, however, working-class representation in the leadership reached only a 25 per cent against a 75 per cent of middle-class representation. This seems to indicate that the party effectively began as a vehicle for the working class, but that the middle class was significant in the leadership.

Industrial growth in Chile experienced a substantial expansion that meant a continued growth of the working class and its social and political demands. Sectors such as the textile, clothing, wood, paper, chemical, mining and metals industries experienced remarkable rates of growth (See Table 3.1).

Although industry progressed, this was not the case with earnings (see Table 3.2).

During 1914–16, the average net income of the Chilean worker was 30.4 Chilean escudos; this went down to 29.2 escudos for 1922–24 and to 26.9 escudos for 1938–40. Only later did this trend reverse, probably as a result of the Popular Front and subsequent centre-left governments that followed (28.8 escudos for 1944–46 and 32.3 escudos for 1951–53).

Although the development of the PSCh came as a result of a vacuum in working-class representation, the initial pressures for the party's foundation came from other social groups. For most of the 1930s, working-class representation in the leadership was rather low. The reasons for this are not entirely clear, but there are at least two factors that might help us to understand this phenomenon:

1. The level of both formal and political education of working-class leaders was significantly lower than that of middle-class leaders during the 1930s. This fact could only change once the process of rapid expansion in education had taken place during the Radical governments (from 1938 on). These governments, headed by Pedro Aguirre Cerda, Juan Antonio Rice and Gabriel Gonzalez Videla, from 1938 to 1952, enabled low income people to attend both primary and secondary schools, thus increasing the possibilities for social mobility.[14]
2. The level of political knowledge of working-class people was, as a natural consequence of poor education, lower than that of the middle class. This was reflected in the intensity and quality of middle-class participation in cultural associations in Chile during the 1930–40 decade, and the weakness of working-class participation during the same period in the same type of associations.[15]

The tendency then, of working-class people to be involuntarily isolated

Table 3.2 Average income of workers in Chile, 1914–64

Sectors	1914–16	1922–24	1938–40	1944–46	1951–3	1957	1960
Food	32.3	32.0	25.6	27.4	30.7	29.1	36.1
Beverages	28.2	33.3	21.9	22.9	34.9	29.7	36.4
Tobacco	20.1	23.5	22.7	31.7	50.3	39.8	20.3
Textiles	39.4	33.1	34.1	34.5	35.3	28.7	40.7
Clothing and shoes	35.8	31.0	25.8	27.5	22.1	22.9	24.4
Wood	33.5	26.7	34.2	26.7	22.4	13.9	19.1
Paper	26.4	18.5	28.4	35.0	38.0	32.2	50.2
Leather	27.3	26.8	24.7	25.5	26.4	22.8	29.1
Chemicals	12.7	12.1	16.2	24.9	34.6	24.0	42.5
Non-metallic minerals	29.3	17.9	20.6	23.0	26.9	25.2	29.5
Metallurgy	27.5	40.3	26.6	30.6	42.7	28.4	32.8
AVERAGE	30.4	29.2	26.9	28.8	32.3	26.2	34.0

Source: Oscar Muñoz, *Crocimiento Industrial de Chile*, *op. cit.*, p. 194.

from cultural and political developments in the country was naturally more acute in the case of cultural and political developments abroad. Thus, increasing international tensions arising from the success of the Bolshevik Revolution in Russia and the development of the social and economic crises in Europe from the world depression, affected working- and middle-class people in Chile. Leadership for protest movements was, therefore, provided by intellectuals and professionals, although the rank-and-file were recruited mainly from the working class. In other words, conditions in Chile were right for a new working-class party to develop, but were not right for allowing a working-class leadership. One class provided the followers, the other provided the leadership. The examination of the second period reveals that working-class membership increased by 10 per cent (from 55 per cent during 1930–39 to 65 per cent during 1939–53). Leadership figures show that working-class representation went up from 25 per cent to 45 per cent while middle-class representation went down from 75 per cent to 55 per cent in the same period.

Reasons for these developments are of course related to the factors which help to explain the reverse course of events during the first period. As has already been said, in the period that began at the end of the 1930s Chile experienced the effects of a growth in education and industry under the direction of the Ministry of Education and the Corporación de Fomento de la Producción (CORFO), founded by Aguirre Cerda's administration.[16] This opened the door for an increased working-class representation in both the membership and leadership of the PSCh.

The third period revealed a consolidation of working-class representation in the membership (70 per cent) and thus a deterioration of middle-class representation (30 per cent). For the first time leadership representation, on the contrary, showed an increase in middle-class representation (from 45 per cent to 50 per cent) and a decrease in working-class representation (from 55 per cent to 48 per cent). Also the figures indicate the existence of 2 per cent bourgeois leaders (mainly industrialists and merchants), a sector that hitherto had been conspicuously absent.

An explanation for this trend in the social make-up of the leaders during this final period is difficult to establish. One could, however, point to the increasing participation of students in politics, both at secondary and university levels. This phenomenon which has characterized Chilean political life acquired a strong consistency during the second Ibáñez administration. It is not clear whether students participated more actively in politics than before, but a numerical increase was without doubt due to the expansion of university education throughout the country. During the 1950s, no less than four provincial *Sedes* (headquarters) were established by the University of Chile alone. The figure went up to eight for the next decade. Between 1960 and 1970 the National Technical University also developed regional centres in the north and the south of the country, transforming medium-level technical training centres into departments of higher education (notably in engineering, metallurgy, biochemistry and building). The Catholic University also followed the same pattern, establishing no less than six high-level centres between 1950 and 1970.[17]

The distribution of centres of higher education throughout the country was a relatively new phenomenon in Chile, and its beginning can be traced to the early 1950s. This obviously dispersed the students. Thus a purely *santiaguino* phenomenon (referring to people living in the capital city, Santiago), was transformed into a national phenomenon. Political life that in the provinces had been confined, in the case of students, to secondary pupils, came to be shared by university students and lecturers from the new, expanding higher-education centres.

These developments provoked an increase in both the quality and quantity of political activity in the provinces. In the case of the PSCh, Regional and Section Committees were invaded by university students and lecturers, who began to participate in politics from 1950 onwards.

As 90 per cent of university students in Chile between 1950 and 1970 were of middle-class origin, their importance in the internal political life of Chilean parties should be noted.[18] In addition to this, 70 per cent of the student unions in the provinces during this period were controlled by the left (Communists, Socialists and MIR, either separately or together).

The appearance of a new social strata, the bourgeoisie, representing 2 per cent of the leadership during this period is also a rather surprising phenomenon. This strata had never had any representation in party life. An explanation for their presence at this stage can only be speculative. These might have been a need for the party to include the very small number of rich people who for one reason or another had come to join the organization. Perhaps the special personal qualities of these leaders might also have been a factor.

From the point of view of its social composition, the party had clearly been a working-class party. From the point of view of its policies, it had also articulated in a reasonable way the demands reflecting working-class interests. The same trend could be observed in the analysis of the party's main ideological stances.

Their representation in the party's leadership does not, however, prevent the party from being considered a class-based party, representing the interests of a particular class. Furthermore, the party satisfied Blondel's two main preconditions for class-based parties: (1) the antagonistic nature of the party's goals with respect to society's goals, and (2) the existence of an 'objective' base for trade-union development.[19]

Blondel's hypothetical preconditions for the class party: the case of the PSCh

Antagonism between party's and society's goals

To determine the extent of antagonism between what could be considered 'society's goals' and 'party goals', we isolated ten fundamental issues included in the Chilean Constitution of 1925. These issues provided the base for the country's social, political and economic system until the government of President Salvador Allende was overthrown in 1973. They reflected the main characteristics of a liberal democratic, Western type of system. The ten selected issues shown in Figure 3.1 were then correlated with ten fundamental issues included in official party documents from 1933 to 1970. The analysis indicated a clear, direct antagonism in every case considered.

SOCIETY'S GOALS	PARTY'S GOALS
A. *General Political*	A. *General Political*
1. *Division of formal powers (presidency, legislative, judiciary).*	1. *Centralized power (People's Assembly).*
Statement: 'No authority, person or reunion of persons can, under any circumstances, exercise powers other than those which have been given to them by the law.'[21]	*Statement*: 'All the power should go to the People's Assembly and the artificial and hypocritical "division of powers" should be brought to an end immediately.'[22]
2. *Periodical elections.*	2. *Country's leaders chosen by Assembly (indirect elections).*
Statement'The president will be chosen by direct suffrage by the citizens who can legally exercise that right.'[23]	*Statement*: 'A People's Assembly should be entitled to reform the actual presidential, extreme autocratic system, and replace it by one in which all responsible leadership is exercised collectively.'[24]
3. *Freedoms (or rights): full exercise along liberal model.*	3. *Freedoms (or rights): clearly limited.*
Statement: 'All inhabitants of the Republic are assured of . . . freedom of education.'[25]	*Statement*: 'All so-called "individual rights" should be limited in accordance to collective needs. The so-called "freedom of education" is a pretext for a education for the rich and an education for the poor.'[26]

B. *Social*
1. *Equalities before the law, justice and general guarantees to employees.*
Statement: 'All inhabitants of the Republic are assured equality before the law . . . in Chile there are no class privileges.'[27]

B. *Social*
1. *Equalities understood in a collectivist perspective.*

Statement: 'In Chile there are two classes: one exploits the other. One works and produces and the other just exploits the other and gets the surplus value. The only system that can guarantee equality is the socialist system, as there is no possible equality in the present system.'[28]

C. *Economic*
1. *Public requisitions strongly controlled.*
Statement: 'All inhabitants of the Republic are assured of . . . the inviolability of all properties, without any discrimination . . . nobody's property can be expropriated without specific law or a decision of the Judiciary.'[29]

C. *Economic*
1. *Public requisitions normal.*

Statement: 'Private property should always be limited by social interest. There should be easy available ways to acquire, by public interest, all private properties belonging to individuals or corporation.'[30]

2. *Public ownership strongly limited.*
Statement: 'The conditions to make any private property public are: [there] should exist clear reasons of public interest, this public interest should be declared by law, compensation should be adjudicated to the owner and paid in advance and in complete agreement.'[31]

2. *Public ownership desirable.*

Statement: 'An extended area of public ownership is the only guarantee that a just redistribution of income is going to be undertaken . . . the legal means to enable this are inadequate and reactionary and tend to perpetuate an intolerable situation.'[32]

3. *Compensation guaranteed.*
Statement: See the statement immediately above.

3. *Reluctance on compensations.*
Statement: 'No compensation should be given for those expropriated properties that already receive excessive benefits . . . this is certainly the case for the copper companies.'[33]

4. *Freedom of industry and commerce.*
Statement: 'No industry can be prohibited unless it is contrary to the security of the country, health of the public or normal accepted social uses.'[34]

4. *Limitations to private industry and commerce.*
Statement: 'The development of private industry and commerce should be limited very clearly by the public interested.'[35]

Figure 3.1 Prototype statements on the society's and the PSCh's goals[20]

The ten selected issues from the 1925 Constitution were selected according to three central criteria:

1. *General political*, referring to the basic philosophical foundations of the system as a whole.
2. *Social*, referring to class aspects of the legislation.
3. *Economic*, referring to the economic aspects of legislation.

The same method was used to select the corresponding issues out of official party literature.

An examination of Figure 3.1 shows that there has been almost complete antagonism between what has been considered as 'society's goals' and those considered 'party goals'. This satisfies Blondel's preconditions for *class-based* parties. However, some of the issues we compared require further explanation.

It is clear that issues 1 and 2 of *Part A (General Political)* Figure 3.1 are absolutely opposed to each other, but, results in the case of issues 3, *Part A* and 1 to 3 *Part B (Social)*, need further explanation. Issues 1 to 4 *Part C (Economic)* also prove conclusive and need no further explanation.

In the case of issue 3, the examination of the documents indicates that although the PSCh has stressed the need to increase 'freedoms' in a wide sense, this stand should be understood from a Marxist perspective. This is no doubt different, if not in opposition to the stand taken in the liberal perspective of the Constitution. Only in the case of education have the Socialists consistently opposed, at least theoretically, private education. They have always supported state education. With respect to other 'freedoms' mentioned in the 1925 Chilean Constitution, the party has never had a clear position, but its overall behaviour suggests that they have understood them to be within the general framework of a Socialist, centralized, society. The same is also true of the three issues of *Part B* in Figure 3.1. The concept of 'equality' from the Marxist-

Table 3.3 Growth of union membership in Chile, 1932–69[6]

Year	Plant	Craft	Rural	Total
1932	29,400	25,400	—	54,800
1942	122,400	71,600	—	193,000
1952	155,000	128,300	1,000	284,300
1964	143,000	125,900	1,700	270,600
1969	196,100	233,000	104,700	533,800

Leninist perspective is of course different from the liberal orientation. It does not mention the full exercise of individual rights, considered independently or in opposition to the state, as is the case in liberal orientated positions.

Our firm impression in this respect is that the party's goals have been consistently opposed to society's goals. The opinions of both former and active leaders confirmed this belief.

Trade union development

The second of Blondel's preconditions for the development of class-based parties refers to the existence of 'objective' bases for trade union development.

An examination of Table 3.1 indicates that the industrial infrastructure of Chile allowed for the development of trade unions. Trade union (officially registered) membership from 1932 to 1969 supports this hypothesis.

Table 3.3 includes only 'legal' trade unions, which for most of the period did not cover unions with less than twenty-five members (in the case of the *sindicatos industriales*, or industrial trade unions), so development was really far greater than indicated by these figures. The table also excludes the majority of *sindicatos agrícolas* (rural trade unions), which had to include at least twenty members to be declared legal. (Only a sixth of all farms could fulfil that requirement when the 1947 law on rural trade unions was enacted. Before, provisions were even worse, but they improved with new legislation enacted in 1967.)

Our concern here, however, is not so much to analyse the quality and extent of the Chilean trade union movement, but to stress the fact that the ecomomy was sufficiently developed to allow the fast and efficient development of unions.[37]

Blondel's hypothetical preconditions for the mass party: the case of the PSCh

The fact that the party is class-based is related to it being also a *mass type*. 'It remains [therefore] to see whether mass parties are likely to develop in non-industrial societies', says Blondel, after identifying the existence of this type of party in industrial societies. He considers that these parties naturally develop in industrial societies, and in fact prove 'functional' for a variety of reasons (size and quality of industry and trade unions, sophistication and extension of education, highly specialized propaganda machines, etc.).[38]

The characterization of a party as a mass organization, on the other hand, means from the structural point of view that its character would undoubtedly influence the bureaucratic apparatus and the entire organizational structure.[39]

The six main features of the mass party which Blondel accurately developed, can reasonably be identified in the PSCh. Furthermore, Blondel's assertions that 'certain conditions are more likely than others to permit a successful imposition of a mass party in a pre-industrial society' seemed to be appropriate to the case of the Chilean Socialists. 'Mass parties are also helped by the emergence of "charismatic" leaders; and the struggle for decolonization, particularly where it was difficult, established more firmly the position of these leaders', he adds. 'But these mass parties remain somewhat different from the mass parties of modern industrial societies because they are imposed on a social system which is not really suited for them. Identification with the party has constantly to be fostered—and one of the ways by which it is fostered is by relying either on the nationalistic past or on the identity between leader and party'.[40] All these patterns, as will be seen below, could also be observed to some extent in the PSCh.[41]

Blondel goes on to say that, 'admittedly, with the gradual industrialization which may be taking place, groups such as trade unions will come to have a greater impact on the population; political life in the large cities will come to have some of the characteristics of mass party politics, but this comes rather slowly and, in the large cities, modified parties of committees are likely to develop'.[42]

On the whole, this is what has happened with the PSCh: a mass class-based party, consistently acquired and developed habits normally associated with the committee-party. Although a final analysis should regard the party as having a 'mass-type character', some distinct and without doubt deviant patterns should not be overlooked. There are three aspects of the party which shall be examined by the application of Blondel's preconditions:

1. The actual character of the party: is it a cadre (committee) or a mass-type party?
2. The deficiencies in organization arising from the differences between the ideology adopted by the party and its daily operations as a practical political unit.
3. The widespread aspiration in the party leadership to overcome the problems of party bureaucracy. Their efforts can be seen in the attempt to create a cadre party along Leninist lines.

Each of these questions shall be examined in greater detail later.

ELECTIONS (years)	37	41	45	49	53	57	61	65	69	
PERCENTAGES	11.2	16.7	12.8	9.3	14.1	10.7	10.7	10.3	13.3	
DEPUTIES	17	15	5	11	24	11	12	15	15	
TARAPACA	1				1	1	1			
ANTOFAGASTA	1	1		1	2	1		1	1	1
ATACAMA					1					
COQUIMBO	1	1	1	1	2		1			
ACONCAGUA							1			
VALPARAISO	3	2		1	2	1	1	1	1	
SANTIAGO 1	3	3	2	2	2		1		1	
2	1	1	1		1	1		1	1	
3	1	1		1	1	1		1	1	2
4		1		1	1			1	1	
O'HIGGINS	1	1		1				1	1	
COLCHAGUA		1						1	1	
CURICO										
TALCA										
MAULE										
LINARES							1			
ÑUBLE 1				1	1	1				
2										
CONCEPCION	2			1	2	1	1	1	1	3
ARAUCO							1	1	1	
BIO-BIO					1	1				
MALLECO					1	1				
CAUTIN	1	1			1	1	1			
VALDIVIA	1	1					1	1	1	4
OSORNO							1	1	1	
LLANQUIHUE					1					
CHILOE					1					
MAGALLANES	1	1	1	1	1	1				5

Figure 3.2 The continuity of electoral support

THE MASS AND CADRE MODELS OF PARTY

It is difficult to attempt a thorough-going definition of mass and cadre party, and we do not intend to make it here. Nor do we wish to discuss the feasibility of both terms.[43] Their present usage seemed quite appropriate in this case to the extent that they provided the means to lead our research into a more detailed analysis of the party organization.

It is clear that the typology regards a consideration of the *membership* as one of the most important, if not the most important, element. From there on, the whole party apparatus could be broken down into component parts and analysed: the extent and quality of its bureaucracy, the way in which it works, how resolutions are adopted, the degree of participation in decision-making, the forming of oligarchies, and so on.

On the whole, it can be said that a mass party is a political structure whose membership is characterized by its impersonality, while the cadre party stresses the importance of the individual *per se*. Mass parties count on massive support of people, either on a direct (as individuals) or on an indirect (as members of trade unions or other associations) basis. Cadre parties rely exclusively on individual support, and elements as prestige, fortune and other factors play an important role. Mass parties theoretically rely on a constant and systematic cash flow from party members, while cadre parties depend on money collected from rich contributors who are either members or in sympathy with the aims of the party.[44]

The list of differences could go on indefinitely, creating a dichotomy that does not always correspond to reality, as some parties have features of both mass and cadre party together. As this has been certainly the case of the PSCh, we preferred to tackle the problem of the mass or cadre organization using Blondel's six hypothetical preconditions for the mass party. This revealed the extent to which the party structure satisfied these requirements:

1. *A Party is a mass party if electors identify with it*. This assumption refers to 'the stability of electoral support'. In the case of mass parties, the electors 'will continue to vote for their party, whether their current MP chooses to be loyal or disloyal', whilst generally in the case of parties of committees, 'the elector tends to follow the man if the man changed party'.[45]

The PSCh exhibits a definite tendency as regards this factor, as can be seen from Figures 3.2 and 3.3. In fact, there have been five electoral zones in which the party has always been strong: the north, including Tarapacá, Antofagasta and Coquimbo provinces; the centre, mainly Santiago and Valparaíso; Arauco and Concepción; and Magallanes. The lake zones (mainly Cautin and

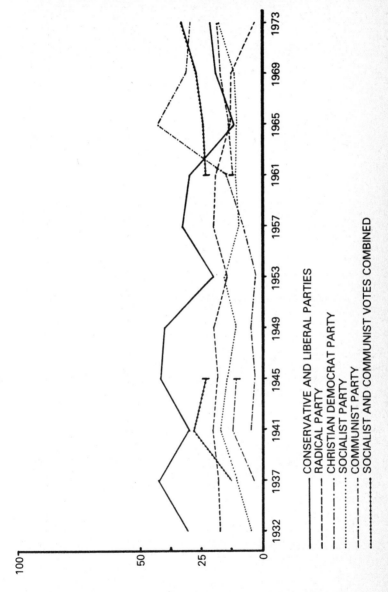

CONSERVATIVE AND LIBERAL PARTIES
RADICAL PARTY
CHRISTIAN DEMOCRAT PARTY
SOCIALIST PARTY
COMMUNIST PARTY
SOCIALIST AND COMMUNIST VOTES COMBINED

Figure 3.3 Chile congressional elections, 1932–73

Valdivia provinces) have also shown a relatively high degree of electoral support for the Socialists, although here the trend has always been weaker.

Figure 3.2 shows the continuity of electoral support for the PSCh in which we have called *zones*, from 1 to 5. Each of these zones reflect certain social and economic characteristics that certainly explain to an important extent the character of that support.[46] Nationally, there has also been a certain consistency in the support obtained by the Socialists from 1937 to the present (see Fig. 3.3). Their percentage of the vote has never been lower than around 10 per cent and never higher than around 14 per cent before 1970. The lowest vote came in 1949, when the three factions into which the party was then divided received a total of 9.3 per cent. The highest percentage polled was 14.1 per cent in 1953 (counting the vote of both the Partido Socialista de Chile and the Partido Socialista Popular), a fact that can be attributed to the popularity of the Ibáñez administration in which the Partido Socialista Popular played an important role.

Thus the 'stability of electoral support' has clearly been important in most of the PSCh's lifetime.

2. *The second characteristic of mass parties in Blondel's typology refers to the type of members' work and financial help which the party gets.* While 'parties of committees are essentially organized on the basis of small nuclei of clients paid or otherwise dependant on the local leader', mass parties 'are characterized by a high reliance on voluntary help, both in kind and cash'.[47]

The PSCh has certainly been dependent almost entirely on voluntary work by its members and paid functionaries have been absent for most of the party's history. Furthermore, the finance system has been, at least in theory, one based upon fixed contributions from members.[48]

The absence of paid officials is related to the voluntary help in kind and in cash on which the party could rely. The 'class of professional revolutionaries' which Duverger envisaged in extremely centralized mass parties could, therefore, not develop in the PSCh. It was also true in this case that the Leninist ideas of full-time revolutionaries whose lives should be entirely dedicated to the party could not exist because the internal mode of organization and the existing finance system would prevent it. It would be interesting to discover if the nature of the party in these respects had any influence on the development of party oligarchies. This question is examined in some detail next.[49]

The evidence only allowed for a general tendency to be observed. This suggested that in the case of the party's Central Committees, the greater percentage of posts were almost always occupied by people with no more than three terms of office, a fact that is hardly indicative in itself of either an 'oligarchy in leadership' or devoted full-time revolutionaries. However, as it has

NUMBER OF TIMES IN OFFICE

YEARS	1	2	3	4	5	6	7	8	9	10	11	12	13	14	15	NUMBER OF MEMBERS	MONTHS
APRIL 1933 OCT. 1933	21															21	5
OCT. 1933 DEC. 1934	1	11														12	14
DEC. 1934 JAN. 1936	4	2	5													11	25
JAN. 1936 MAY 1937	4	2	—	5												11	16
MAY 1937 DEC. 1938	3	2	1	1	4											11	19
DEC. 1938 DEC. 1939	3	1	2	1	2	3										12	12
TOTAL														TOTAL X̄		78 13	91 15.13

Figure 3.4 Number of times in office of Central Committe members and duration of terms 1933–9

YEARS	NUMBER OF TIMES IN OFFICE															NUMBER OF MEMBERS	MONTHS
	1	2	3	4	5	6	7	8	9	10	11	12	13	14	15		
JUNE 1941 MARCH 1942	6	—	1	1	2	—	1	1								12	9
MARCH 1942 JAN. 1943	9	4	1	1	—	1	—	1	1							18	10
JAN. 1943 JULY 1944	8	2	1	—	1	—	1									13	18
JULY 1944 OCT. 1946	12	7	—	1	1	1	2	1								25	27
OCT. 1946 JUNE 1948	6	2	2	—	1	1										11	20
JUNE 1948 JUNE 1950	2	5	1	3	—	—	1	1								13	24
JUNE 1950 MAY 1952	4	4	1	2	2											13	23
MAY 1952 OCT. 1953	4	1	5	1	1											12	17
TOTAL															$\bar{X}$	117 14.30	148 18.50

Figure 3.5 Number of times in office of Central Committee members and duration of terms 1941–53

NUMBER OF TIMES IN OFFICE

YEARS	1	2	3	4	5	6	7	8	9	10	11	12	13	14	15	NUMBER OF MEMBERS	MONTHS
OCT. 1953 OCT. 1955	7	1	—	4	—	1										13	24
OCT. 1955 JULY 1957	5	3	1	—	3	—	1									13	21
JULY 1957 OCT. 1959	7	4	2	1	1	1	1	1								18	27
OCT. 1959 DEC. 1961	3	2	2	1	—	3	1	1	1							14	26
DEC. 1961 FEB. 1964	6	1	1	1	1	—	2	—	1	1						14	26
FEB. 1964 JUNE 1965	5	2	3	2	2	—	—	2	—	1	1					18	16
JUNE 1965 NOV. 1967	8	2	2	3	—	1	1	—	—	—	1					18	29
NOV. 1967 JAN. 1971	17	5	2	1	—	—	—	1	—	—	—	1				27	38
TOTAL																TOTAL 135 X̄ 16.86	207 25

Figure 3.6 Number of times in office of Central Committee members and duration of terms 1953–71

TIMES IN OFFICE	MEMBERS
1	36
2	7
3	2
4	1
5	1
9	1

NON-OLIGARCHICAL

OLIGARCHICAL

(1) This Central Committee was still in office when the overthrow of President Allende's Government occurred on 11, September 1973. A Congress to replace it was supposed to be held sometime during 1974.

Figure 3.7 Last recorded Central Committee January, 1971

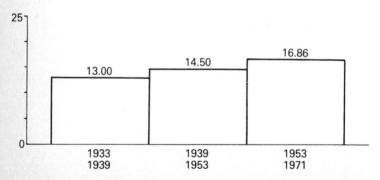

Figure 3.8 Average Number of Central Committee members 1933–71

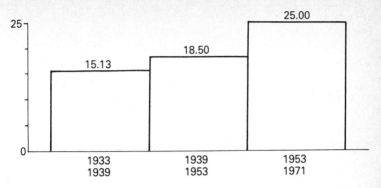

Figure 3.9 Average duration of Central Committee terms (in months) 1933–71

already been said, the analysis should not go further than simply illustrating the general frequency of Central Committee membership. Figures 3.4 to 3.9 clearly suggest the fact that oligarchic tendencies could hardly be detected within the leadership with the available information. On the contrary, the totality of these figures indicate a quite clear mobility trend.

3. *The third characteristic of mass parties according to Blondel is related to the nature of the bureaucratic-political structure which pervades the party at all levels*.[50] Mass parties rely on permanent organizations, both at national and local levels. 'The bureaucratization of the party structure is a consequence of the stability of the institution which, in turn, is characteristic of mass parties. Party oligarchies may develop in this way and some of the "democratic" features which appear to be associated with mass parties may diminish as a result'. Furthermore, 'the contest is to take over the machine, to be in a position to act on behalf of the local organization and thus to be recognized by the electors and party identifiers as "representatives" of the party'.[51]

4. *The fourth characteristic of mass parties, according to Blondel, is a 'national responsible leadership'*.[52] This is a condition undoubtedly related to the permanent character of the organization and also to the last of Blondel's six hypothetical preconditions; namely, the existence of 'widespread party images'.

The PSCh relied on a national responsible leadership, as opposed to leaders 'responsible to MPs in Parliament or to small groups of chiefs outside it'.[53] As with most mass parties the PSCh leadership needed to identify themselves and respond to the mass of electors and supporters (members) whom the leaders would like to attract to the party, or to retain in it. As Blondel puts it, 'as long as party identification exists, the leader, however, popular, has to remain responsible'.

The highest bureuacratic party structure, the Central Committee, and also its delegated body, the Political Commission, were both national organs responsible to the party as represented by the congresses. These, in turn, were composed of delegates representing all internal bodies, from the bottom of the party organization (*núcleos*) up to the ones at the top, including both the acting Central Committee and Political Commission, whose members had considerable influence in the congresses (see the PSCh structure shown in Fig. 3.10, and national structure shown in Fig. 1.1 to 1.4).

The PSCh has certainly always had the structure of a permanent organization. The bureaucratic structure at both the national and the local levels were designed to work on a day-to-day basis, although most of the leaders operated as part-time officials and without any financial reward. The financing system has not in fact been the same throughout the party's history, and, there are various problems involved in financing a permanent political organization.

First, financing was based upon *equal fees* paid by the members. This method originated in the party's first years and continued until the mid-1950s, when a system of *proportional fees* was instituted. The proportional system was maintained up to 1970, when a *progressive* system was drawn up and implemented by the leadership.

None of the three systems actually worked well, thus confirming Christian Anglade's contention that financing by membership contributions is unsatisfactory in almost all the cases studied by him in Latin America. He says in fact that 'it does not seem that financing by membership contribution is satisfactory anywhere', and he gives the example of Acción Democrática of Venezuela, a party that tried hard to 'impose compulsory levies on public servants who are party members, but has met the same difficulties as have traditional parties like the Colombian Liberal Party'.[54]

Anglade's assertion also covers the case of the PSCh, notwithstanding the tremendous efforts of successive leaderships to overcome the problem.

A voluntary financing system was first established in 1934, but it did not last long. It was based on the assumption that every member had a superior sense of duty that would compel him to voluntarily pay fees according to his income. Compulsion was then not contemplated. In fact, a Memorandum dated 13 December 1934 reminded the members that fees were voluntary and that 'each member would pay according to his personal financial situation'.[55]

Apparently the system did not serve the party adequately, and a compulsory finance system was established. This was enacted in 1935 and was based on the principle of 'equal fees', independent of the member's income. The

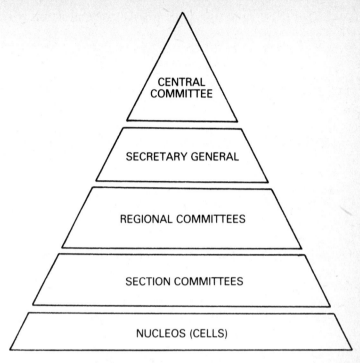

Figure 3.10 PSCh formal structure

fees were to be paid monthly to the nearest local party treasurer and fines were also instituted for those who inexplicably failed to pay for more than three months.[56] The proportional system was based on the principle of fees proportional to incomes, on a fixed scale. Everyone in the party would pay the *same proportion* but not the same amount.[57]

In 1970 the party drew up a system that was never actually put into extensive practice. It was based on the principle of higher incomes paying higher proportions, and lower incomes, lower proportions. These went from as low as 0.5 per cent to as high as 20 per cent.[58]

The money raised by all three systems never satisfied even the most modest of party needs. This caused anguish in the leaders and officials and the reluctance of members to accept the posts of treasurer at the different party levels.[59] Reliable party figures establish that an average of no more than 10 per cent of all the money raised came from the three systems of members' subscription.

Table 3.4 Parties and the sources of their funds

Parties with some degree of financial autonomy	Parties without financial autonomy

1. Membership parties: two-thirds of their normal non-election-year expenses come from membership dues.*
 2. Official parties whose expenditure is covered by:
   (a) membership dues.
   (b) More or less enforced contributions from some socio-professional milieux (industrialists, civil servants)†
   (c) More or less institutionalized official financing by the government.
 3. Parties whose expenditure is covered by (a) and (b) or (c) of category 2, plus some percentage of external financing. The actual influence of 'external' financing depends on its percentage within the financing of the party as a whole and on the strength of the party (whether it is a dominant or a competitive party); such influence may also depend on the occasional or permanent character of 'external' financing.
	4. Parties whose financing, covered by membership dues and/or enforced contributions, represent only a small percentage of their non-election-year expenditure.‡
	 5. Parties for which dues and/or enforced contributions constitute a negligible percentage of the overall financing; the parties must then rely on 'external' resources whose nature and sources vary.§

* No Latin American party falls into this category.

† Most donations made to this type of party seem to be different from those made to non-official parties, and should perhaps be classified as more or less enforced contribution.

‡ This is the case of most Western parties, whose dues cover on average 20 per cent of their normal expenses.

§ Under this category may be included parties whose financing is carried out by the candidates personally.

Source: From Anglade, 'Party Finance and the Classification of Latin American parties', in *Comparative Political Finance: The Financing of Party Organizations and Election Campaigns*, ed. A. S. Heidenheimer (Heath, Lexington, Mass, 1970), p. 171.

How did the party manage to survive? There was the problem of the bureaucratic apparatus that, although very small and essentially part-time, had a permanent status. There was also the problem of elections (municipal, parliamentary and presidential) which put the party in very difficult financial situations every two years (without taking into consideration by-elections).[60]

This phenomenon is, however, in no way exclusive to the PSCh. Anglade reports that no Latin American party is in fact financed by its membership and that, on the contrary, in most of the cases, their expenses covered by the membership subscription 'represent only a small percentage of their non election-year expenditure', as is also the case of most Western parties, whose income from membership fees covers an average of 20 per cent of their normal expenses.[61]

The PSCh correspond to what Anglade calls 'parties without financial autonomy' (Table 3.4).[62] The only exception is perhaps the three years in which the party shared governmental responsibilities with the Communist and the Radical parties from 1970 to 1973. Then, it may be assumed, the party began to acquire the character of those parties Anglade calls 'parties with some degree of financial autonomy', but no evidence on this could be gathered.

If the party was, for most of its history, an organization without financial autonomy, how was it able to survive? This would not be a problem for a party whose only need for finance was immediately prior to elections, although at election times spending would increase significantly. However, besides elections, the PSCh had to add the financial burden arising from the following aspects:

(a) *Party bureaucratic machinery*. Even though the party bureaucratic apparatus was part-time, it is also true that it worked on both *permanent* and *national levels*. Clerical officers were needed in each of the provincial regional bodies. These officials were non-political and consequently had nothing to do with party political work, but they were mostly paid. The rest of the bureaucratic apparatus, namely officials with political responsibilities, were unsalaried, as has already been said.

(b) *Party buildings*. To operate on a permanent and national basis the party needed buildings to set up its headquarters.

(c) *Political education*. The party attributed great importance to the political education of the membership and maintained a chain of 'schools' throughout the country, at least during the last decade. This required teachers, materials and an education structure.

(d) *Public Relations*. The party used to maintain a permanent, nationally organized public relations campaign through the massive diffusion of periodicals, bulletins, advertisements, and so on.

(e) *Mass Communications*. The party maintained various instruments of mass media that, on the information in hand, were mostly unprofitable.

(f) *Election expenditure*. The spending in elections ranged from costs of printing pamphlets and general advertising to the more sophisticated campaigns involving mass media techniques which proved extremely costly.

The question arising from the fact that no more than 10 per cent of the party's spending was financed by members' dues (in contravention of written regulations) is clear: how did the party manage to survive as a national, permanent organization for almost forty years? How did it manage to maintain national and regional headquarters; clerical officers; propaganda before, during and after election periods; a media which was essentially non-profit making; and, at least during the period from 1960 to 1970, permanent, well-staffed schools for political education?

There are no official records which can provide absolutely reliable data on this matter. There was unanimity, however, among both former and present leaders interviewed as to the manner in which the party filled the gap: donations from well-to-do sympathizers and members.[63]

The fact that 90 per cent of the party's expenses were covered by donations from wealthy sympathizers and/or members, raises the question of the extent of the influence of these people on the party's policies. It is almost impossible to exactly determine the extent of this influence, if any. However, the recollections of reliable old party members allowed us to at least establish certain personal characteristics of those members and sympathizers who supported the party's finances:

(a) During the first ten or fifteen years of its development, the party relied heavily on voluntary donations from sympathetic industrialists and big merchants. The proportion of party funds coming from this sector amounted to almost 80 per cent, while the rest came mainly from donations given on a month-to-month basis by medium and small merchants, resident mainly in the provinces.

(b) During the next twenty or thirty years, the party's finances began slowly to diversify, moving towards a different source: the international bureaucracy. Santiago was the regional headquarters of a number of United Nations' technical bodies. A host of international conferences as well as a proliferation of highly placed, well-paid officials followed. It is reported that from the mid-1950s the PSCh received important contributions from a significant number of sympathizers in international organizations. These sympathizers, both Chilean and non-Chilean, were even able to donate in foreign currency (most US dollars). The high exchange rate on the Chilean black market would allow considerable increases to be made on the initial contribution. It is not known how many officials contributed nor the amounts given, but it is certain that their contributions amounted to an estimated 50 per cent of total party funds which were received from wealthy members and sympathizers, during the period from 1952 to 1960.

(c) The last ten years of the party's history (1960–70) registered an increase in contributions from the international bureaucracy, up to 60 per cent of the total income coming from wealthy sympathizers and members.[64]

The existence, then, of a permanent organization was only possible because of the existence of a network of wealthy contributors that were or were not members of the party. The rank-and-file contributions amounted to no more than an average 10 per cent and the party could well do without them.

5. *According to Blondel, 'access to and utilization of the mass media' is also a characteristic of mass parties, 'because the mass media are the means through which the "image" of the party is presented to citizens'*.[65] It is clear that 'mass parties, based on popular support, cannot, except in the very peculiar cases of a narrowly circumscribed geographical minority, develop and be maintained without press, radio and television. Both the requirements of identification and that of responsible leadership are dependent on mass-media utilization'.[66]

There is evidence to suggest that this has been the case for the PSCh, mainly in the last twenty years. Television only developed in Chile in the 1960s, but the PSCh did manage to make a comprehensive use of the available mass-media before, during and after TV appeared on a national scale. During the period beginning in 1960, the party was able to create a national broadcasting network, distributed throughout all twenty-five Chilean provinces. There are no official records, but reliable party officials revealed that the party itself owned the following means for media coverage for at least the 1960–70 period:

1. *Broadcasting*. Forty-two radio stations distributed throughout the country and covering all twenty-five provinces. This network included four stations able to reach the entire country with medium and short waves, and thirty-eight regional stations covering certain geographical zones and also able to link themselves, when needed, to the four most powerful broadcasting networks.

2. *Newspapers and periodicals*. The party itself owned eight regional daily newspapers, covering 70 per cent of the country. In addition to this, the party

had a strong influence on the Santiago evening daily newspaper *Ultima Hora* , whose publication began in the mid-1940s and continued with interruptions up to the overthrow of President Allende's government in September 1973.[67] *Ultima Hora* was sold in three major Chilean cities (Santiago, Valparaíso and Concepción) and also the surrounding towns and villages. In the mid-1960s its daily circulation of 80,000 was very good by Chilean standards. Although it was not nationally distributed, it was widely considered as an important 'influence newspaper' whose opinions were valued either by people holding power to those generally considered as holding 'influential' positions in society (politicians, trade union officials, education leaders, civil servants, businessmen, church leaders, etc.). The PSCh opinions on national and international issues were normally officially printed in *Ultima Hora* , and its editorial comments reflected the party's position on many issues.

The party also owned no less than two nationally distributed weeklies, with a collective circulation that oscillated between 3,000 and 30,000.

3. *Television* . There were no private TV networks in Chile, but it is generally acknowledged that the Left and, more specifically, the PSCh and PCCh were always able to create, maintain and expand their influence on television from its origin under state- and university-controlled networks in the late 1950s and early 1960s.

During the latter half of the 1960s, unofficial records estimate approximately 70 per cent of journalists working on both the National TV Channel (No. 7) and the University of Chile Channel (No. 9) either belonged or were openly sympathetic to the PSCh. The example of the third Chilean TV Channel (No. 13, run by the Catholic University) was different. There the influence of the Christian Democratic Party was always very strong and the voice of the Left went unnoticed for most of the time.[68]

The party's comprehensive access to the mass media was greatly facilitated by the existence of a significant number of Socialist journalists working on non-Socialist newspapers and broadcasting networks. Official party records established that about 20 per cent of all registered journalists in the country in 1970 were either members or sympathetic with the aims of the PSCh. Of those journalists specializing in political, economic, labour and international and social problems in 1970, approximately 35 per cent were PSCh members or sympathizers.[69]

6. *The existence of 'widespread party images' is the sixth and final characteristic that Blondel attributes to mass parties* .[70] This refers to the degree of association, by the membership or sympathizers, between their image of the leaders and of the party. In other words, leaders of mass parties tend to associate themselves with the party's general image, held by supporters and/or members. Blondel

says that 'these images play the part of flags and of myths. They lead to certain reactions. They also reinforce party identification and party allegiance against outside attack' to the extent that 'the success of party leaders among the electors often depends on the capacity of these leaders to fit the images which followers have of the political party'.[71]

The generally accepted popular image of the PSCh as an extreme leftist party standing to the left of the PSCh certainly played a part in sustaining the influence of extreme leftist tendencies within the top and intermediate levels of bureaucratic power structure within the party. Internal voting records on a variety of issues, from 1933 up to 1970, also confirmed this trend. Moderate or mildly rightist positions were consistently defeated in all congresses, as were moderate and mildly rightist candidates for bureaucratic offices. There was always a consistency, then, between the public image of the PSCh as an extreme leftist political organization and the behaviour patterns of the leadership. Candidates for internal offices with positions which did not respond to this widespread party image were sometimes successful, but they were never able to form a majority. Political views considered moderate were also consistently defeated, as again they did not respond to the members' image of the party as an extremist, uncompromising political organization.

A congruence between the party's public image and the images cultivated by the leadership clearly existed. As we have said, departures to the right by leaders normally either led to defeat or they found themselves in the minority.[72]

The party was rather loosely structured along the lines of the mass model. Features which are normally associated with cadre (committee) parties (i.e. disproportionate influence of notables, factionalism, 'democratic' excesses, 'electoralism', etc.) also appear, however, present in day-to-day practices, at least over the last twenty years. The examination of documents and periodicals covering previous periods, and the opinions of the old leaders interviewed, substantiated this conclusion.[73] As the evidence that came out of the available data clearly confirmed, the party continuously stressed the need for rank-and-file members not to yield to 'alien' influences (i.e. local notables), to avoid unnecessary discussions which might lead to the degeneration of democratic practices and disrupt the party as an organization working on a permanent basis and not merely for electoral purposes. All the old leaders interviewed were of the same impression, showing strong criticism of these shortcomings.

Perhaps the best summary of this situation can be provided by the following paragraph of an internal letter sent by the Central Committee to all Regional and Section Committees on 23 July 1961:

We should remind all comrades that this is a Leninist party, deeply committed to the transformation of the capitalist society ... how this can be achieved through sporadic, part-time work during election periods only, using the goodwill of some comrades who happen to hold important positions in our society, it is something that has to be seen. Furthermore, this vicious tendency to question everything, to discuss irrelevant matters up to the point of exhaustion, is a practice worthy of bourgeois parties, but not of our own.[74]

This tendency has in fact constantly recurred throughout the party's life since the 1930s.

The influence of important party figures and the role of party factions in shaping the mass party will be analysed below.

FACTIONS AND NOTABLES IN THE PSCh

The role of internal groups within the party is a rather challenging and difficult matter, for there are no scientific studies on Chilean pressure groups which could provide an appropriate framework for analysis. Some attempts, however, have been made to identify active factions and pressure groups within political parties. One of them is particularly interesting, because it is centred on the Italian Socialist Party, which, we think, shares many ideological and even structural similarities with the PSCh.[75]

This work, by Raphael Zariski, reveals how the Italian Socialists had within the party, sharing the same structural, formal organization, many groups with somewhat different values and political attitudes (extreme-left Trotskyites, intellectual Marxists, social democrats, trade-union-minded sectors).

Zariski uses, to summarize as much as possible, the following method to identify groups within the party:

1. Examination of voting of leaders on important issues.
2. Examination of social, educational, economic, geographical and religious origins or leaders.
3. Deduction, by association of results thus obtained, of possible active groups and their motives and goals. Common interests are then detected, together with possible shared values, links to more prominent leaders, opportunist temporal coalitions for mere administrative-bureaucratic motives, and so on.

He discovered in one specific period at least three more or less differentiated groups, and mini-factions within each of them (the 'left-wingers', for example, included the *carristi*, open supporters of an alliance with the Communists, as well as veteran Maximalists of the pre-fascist era, intellectuals with Leninist ideals but with strongly anti-Stalinist attitudes, and bureaucrats linked to the control appratus of the party; the so-called 'Autonomist' faction exhibited an even broader spectrum of internal factionalism). The model was interesting enough to encourage its use, if possible, for the purposes of our research. However, only a partial test was possible in measuring the extent of active factions within the party. This was an examination of the voting record within the party's Central Committee from 1949 to 1970.[76]

The issues examined ranged from apparently purely internal administrative matters to major political decisions regarding voting on laws in Parliament. The material on voting appeared in several different documents, but these were kept in the safe for *reserved documents*, in a special archive, in the party's headquarters in Santiago. It had been put together by party officials in 1970 as part of a programme to create a party library.[77]

A total of eighty-seven decisions qualified as 'important' (meaningless votes on such matters as the site for the party's summer political school each year, or the appointment of secretaries, were not taken into consideration) were examined, and they can be classified in the following manner:

1. Political decisions regarding voting arrangements in Parliament (nationalization of private concerns, increases in taxation for higher-income groups, agrarian reform, workers' participation in the administration of private industries, limitations on private education and reinforcement of state education, increases of social benefits for the poor, limitations on the amount of foreign currency for those travelling abroad, creation of workers' powers at different levels, strengthening and financing for the Chilean TUC, and so on).
2. Political decisions regarding internal matters (reorganization of internal bodies, representatives for congresses, election of candidates to municipal, parliamentary and presidential elections, calling of extraordinary congresses, nomination of internal commissions, and so on).

The results can be summarized as follows. Factions appeared and disappeared over a period of between three and six years. There was always a strong *extreme leftist faction* dominant in more than 90 per cent of the decisions. The main factions detected were:

1. An extreme leftist faction, in favour of radical measures in the direction of the needs of a socialist society.
2. A 'practical' faction without clear ideological standing, always worried about the public image. This faction would adopt 'moderate' stands, if only because they did not like the party being labelled as 'over-heated'.
3. A Trotskyite faction espousing purely 'doctrinaire' arguments (world

revolution, non-participation in liberal democracy, party's isolationism for the sake of 'purity', etc.).

4. A social democratic faction trying to stress the need for accommodating the party's ideology and aspirations with those of the PCCh. This faction had Allende as its leader.

Although these factions maintained their identity through the years, the leaders associated with them were continually in flux. This is to be expected from a party which we have already shown was free from any tendencies to oligarchy.

An overall control of the party by the extreme leftist faction appears throughout the period examined (determining the results of approximately 90 per cent of the available resolutions). The remaining 10 per cent is fairly equally divided between the other factions. We might conclude, therefore, that they have had virtually no say on the party policy.

The result of this part of our research raises an important question: how, with such a small social democratic influence, did Salvador Allende manage to get nominated four times as the party's presidential candidate? This point is related to the wider context of the influence of charismatic leaders in the shaping of mass parties.[78] The PSCh has been led by many leaders, some of whom have dominated the party's activities beyond question: in the 1930s and 1940s, Marmaduke Grove and Oscar Schnake, and in the 1950s and 1960s, Raúl Ampuero and Salvador Allende. These four leaders, gifted with undoubted charismatic virtues, provided the unifying element to an organization always divided by eternal discussions and disagreements. The personalities of these men superseded the division within the party's ranks, although their individual stands might not agree with present party policy. Of the four, only Ampuero was never a presidential candidate. All of them had been secretary-general of the party at some time, and MPs and senators.

On several occasions they were all left in the minority within the party, but this did not cause loss of influence or prestige. The only reason for this phenomenon can be found in the charismatic nature of their personalities. Only the personality of a charismatic leader could rise above internal party problems, could provide the much-needed impetus which would allow such a party to develop, gain influence and ultimately, power.

The charismatic nature of these leaders coupled with the anti-Americanism of the PSCh gave the party an opportunity to develop a strong mass-base which would help to construct a party along European lines.

CONCLUSIONS

It must be said that from the evidence collected there appears to be little foundation for the argument that oligarchies existed within the PSCh. The absence of full-time, paid functionaries wihin the party's bureaucratic structure is an important, perhaps determinant, factor on this matter. A course of events that is only natural in other mass parties' organizations (i.e. some communist parties in Western Europe, some African and Asian one-party systems, and even some Western European socialist parties) would hardly develop in this case. The existence of paid, full-time leaders would at any rate encourage the development of oligarchies. The existence of voluntary, unpaid, part-time leaders would, on the other hand, encourage the development of some democratic patterns in a party's internal practices.

A permanent organization based upon voluntary work could protect the party from oligarchical developments but also created the conditions for clear weaknesses and shortcomings in the party.

It is obvious that a full-time party, based on both middle- and working-class support could not rely on a part-time unpaid leadership. The existence at all stages of the party's history, however, of a number of MPs could have prevented these organizational/operational problems. Had the party distributed the MPs among the most important formal bureaucratic bodies, it would perhaps have been able to avoid the most common problem deriving from its faulty internal model of organization: deficiencies in the articulation of the members' demands, lack of correct execution of orders coming from higher political bodies, and a disregard of ideology in practical situations, mainly by the intermediate leadership.

The allocation of posts to 'civilians', as opposed to parliamentarians, has been a tradition in internal party procedure and behaviour. The pretext has been that the parliamentarians should concentrate on 'mass politics', meaning that they should work with the people at large rather than completely involve themselves in party politics. This fact is reflected in the low proportion of MPs within both higher (Central Committee and Political Commission) and intermediate (Regional Committees) leadership offices. Between 1933 and 1939, only 18 per cent of members of Central Committees, 16 per cent of the Political Commissions and 40 per cent of the Regional Committees were MPs. The averages decreased further in the next period (1939–53) to 17, 15 and 3 per cent, respectively, and even further in the last twenty years (1953–1973) (15, 13 and 2 per cent, respectively) (Fig. 3.11).[79] The low proportion of MPs holding leadership positions also reflected the PSCh's desire to put the organization firmly under what in party lexicon was

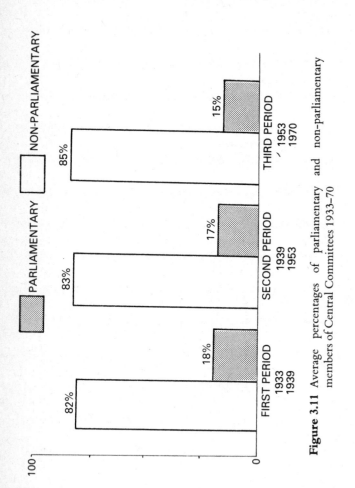

Figure 3.11 Average percentages of parliamentary and non-parliamentary members of Central Committees 1933–70

known as 'civilian rule'. This trend was also seen in the fact that no member of the party holding reasonably important government posts was ever allowed to hold party bureaucratic positions at the same time.[80]

All these elements, together with the voluntary character of the organization, provided the basis for the development of a system of internal mobility which can be better illustrated with regard to the following information. Of all leaders occupying Central Committee posts between 1946 and 1973, 80 per cent had made their way up to the highest party echelons after beginning at either the local or the intermediate levels. Further, of all leaders occupying Regional Committee posts during the same time, 90 per cent had come from either Sections or *núcleos*. Of all leaders occupying Section posts, almost 100 per cent had come from the *núcleos* (Fig. 3.12).[81] These percentages show a distinct mobility trend within the party bureaucratic structures and refutes any suggestion of oligarchical tendencies. This supports previous arguments outlined above.

The permanent character of PSCh organization did not avoid, however, the development of organizational/operational problems as outlined above.

Surprisingly, the existence of mobility within the bureaucratic structure did not help the party. On the contrary, we would suggest that the very existence of this democratic feature in such a class-based and mass-type party contributed to weaken it and had a significant share in accounting for the party's weaknesses.

As the party did not have full-time, completely devoted paid officials, mobility caused organizational vacuums at times when strict discipline and concentration were required. With parliamentarians operating at either the level of Parliament or 'the masses', and part-time party officials continuously changing positions, there remained no permanent organization that could really work continually and effectively. Thus, in the case of the members' demands on a variety of issues (social pressures such as increases in wages, student aspirations for participation in the administration of the educational system, peasants petitions for agrarian reform of various categories, miners' continuous demands for wage increases, etc.), the party would fail to do anything until the last moment, when it would support the stand taken by other parties (mainly the PCCh).[82]

In the case of the execution of orders, whatever their nature, the intermediate and lower leadership offices would in many cases make their own interpretations and 'adjustments'. The tendency to mobility, then, was related to a pattern of bureaucratic instability which, in turn, reflected the practice of democratic elements within the leadership apparatus. However, the changing positions within the bureaucratic structure required from the leaders certain patterns of behaviour which were characterized as follows:

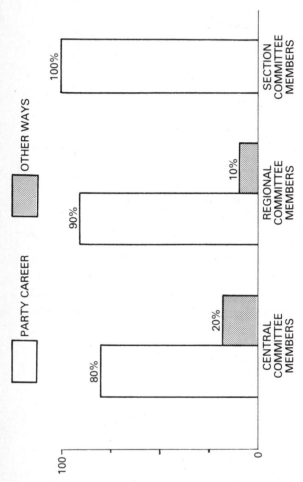

Figure 3.12 Mobility trends in leadership 1946–73

1. Eagerness to present themselves well 'to the left' on most general ideological and concrete political matters.[83]
2. The need to maintain a 'be alert' attitude towards future internal elections, which caused widespread disorganization. Officials devoting an important part of their party time (already not very significant) to self-preservation and promotion activities could hardly cope with pressing internal and external political issues to which the party had to direct its attention.[84]
3. Disregard for petitions from rank-and-file members and an excessive care for pressures and/or demands coming from other leadership levels. This fact helped to isolate the leadership from the membership and to distort the effectiveness of real democratic practices. The satisfactory treatment of other leaders' demands was normal, whilst in the case of the rank-and-file members' demands, little appears to have been done.

Points (1), (2) and (3) above will be expanded below where a detailed analysis of disorganization within the party will be undertaken:

1. The need to adopt extreme leftist positions seems to be strongly correlated to the needs arising from self-preservation and promotion within the party's bureaucratic structure. An examination of important issues upon which the party had to decide a course of action showed that in nearly all cases the successful positions were those standing to the extreme left while those suffering defeat had put themselves in moderate positions. This, in turn, was only the consequence of the results of most internal party elections for Regional and Central Committee members, in which left-wing positions constantly overcame moderate positions. Those who offered the delegates resolutions considered mild and not revolutionary were continually risking defeat.

There is, in fact, no single party congress where the moderates gained a majority, although sometimes they managed to win up to 40 per cent of the available seats.[85]

As well as this ideological trend, the need to be ready to face internal elections and to gain promotion within the party's bureaucratic structure created tensions and vacuums the party was unable to overcome. Already it was an important weakness that no party official devoted his full-time attention to the party, and the attitude towards elections only aggravated matters. Overlaps of internal party electoral works and important political problems were not uncommon, causing delays on decisions and ultimately the party, in the absence of its own stand, came to support that of other organizations on certain issues. This was the case, for example, of an important number of laws enacted between 1941 and 1964, according to the opinion of reliable

Socialist MPs at the time. It was also certainly true of many of the most important issues affecting the Frei period (1964–70).[86]

2. The disregard of demands made by the rank-and-file members has been, in the opinion of three secretary-generals holding the post for more than three periods each, one of the most pressing problems throughout the party's existence. This has also been related, in our opinion, to the inability of the party to provide itself with an efficient bureaucratic machinery. It could also be related to the absence of paid officials, especially internal relations men, who should have provided a much needed permanent, stable link between higher leadership, intermediate leadership levels and the rank-and-file membership. Instead, what prevailed was a complete lack of consistent interrelationships between leaders and members, bureaucratic insecurity by people holding voluntary posts, which led to irresponsibility and a lack of enthusiasms, and perhaps the gravest of all consequences, the inability to satisfy both internal and external demands. All this together led to the verbosity which has always characterized the PSCh leadership. The exact reasons could hardly be isolated, but they certainly lie in the complex interrelationships existing between leaders and members. Whether members' and followers' demands determined extreme leftist stances and language by the leaders, or whether extreme leftist stances and languages appealed to a certain type of person is, however, a matter that this work cannot answer.

3. Disregarding general ideological positions have been a fault which has mainly affected intermediate leadership levels. The area of Socialist-Communist relationships has been where this pattern has been more widely observed, but other related areas, such as the relationships with centre-left parties (Radicals and Christian Democrats, principally), socialist countries and education, have also been affected.

In the case of Socialist–Communist relationships, the strong anti-Movimiento de Izquierda Revolucionaria (MIR) attitudes of the PCCh caused repeated embarrassments to the Socialist leadership, especially when some important trade union and student elections were at stake. The official party line of a continuing alliance with the Communists was challenged several times by Regional and Section Committees wishing rather to ally themselves with the MIR.[87] The urgent Communist plea for political cooperation with 'moderate leftist' parties and, consequently, recognizing as 'progressive forces' the social strata which those parties allegedly represented (namely, the middle class), always encountered strong resistance from Socialist quarters. Despite this, most of the important pleas ended in Socialist acceptance. Again and again, intermediate leadership officials failed in the implementation of these policies and defied orders.[88]

On the whole, the evidence gathered suggests a loose mass party with committee-party practices. The next chapters will hopefully show how this reality was never understood by Socialist leaders, who repeatedly wanted to see their party as a revolutionary vanguard, structured along the lines of the Leninist *cadre model*. The internal realities of the party did have decisive consequences over a variety of important issues, ranging from internal party relationships to external political stands.

Up to now we have shown, we hope, the main factors in the party's history and structure. The next chapters will try to clarify the party's organization, and the views held by the 1973 leadership on their own party.

NOTES

1. Antonio Gramsci, *Maquiavelo y Lenin*, (Biblioteca Popular Nascimento, Santiago, 1968). *Soviets in Italy*, Pamphlets Series No. 11. Rosa Luxemburg, *Leninism or Marxism? The Russian Revolutions*, ed. Bertram D. Wolfe (Ann Arbor, University of Michigan Press, 1961); Monty Johnstone, 'Marx, Engels and the Concept of the Party', in *The Socialist Register*, 1967, pp. 121–58. Lucio Magri, 'What Is a Revolutionary Party?' *New Left Review*, No. 60, March–April, 1970, pp. 97–128; Milovan Djilas, *The New Class*, (Unwin Books, London, 1966); Rossana Rossanda, 'Class and Party' *The Socialist Register*, 1970, pp. 217–31; Lenin, *Selected Works* (Progress Publishers, Moscow, 1947) and *What Is to Be Done?*, (Progress Publishers, Moscow, 1968). To assess the importance Marxist researchers and theoreticians give to the class element in the shaping of the party apparatus, see Duncan Nallas, Tony Cliff, Chris Harman and Leon Trotsky's *Party and Class* (Pluto Press, London, 1970).
2. Jean Blondel, *An Introduction to Comparative Government* (Weidenfeld & Nicholson, London, 1969), p. 108.
3. Jean Blondel, *Comparative Government* (a reader) (Macmillan, London, 1969), p. 117.
4. Detailed description of both models can be examined in: Rosa Luxemburg, *op. cit.*, and Maurice Duverger's *Political Parties*; Lucio Magri's discussion about the party in 'What Is a Revolutionary Party? (*op. cit.*). Lenin's *What Is to Be Done?* and *Selected Works* (*op. cit.*).
5. See Duverger, *Political Parties* (Methuen, London, 1972), pp. 133–201.
6. Duverger, ibid., p. 63.
7. Blondel, 'Mass parties in Industrialized Societies', in *Comparative Government* (*op. cit.*), pp. 117–26.
8. Blondel, 'Types of Parties and Types of Societies', in *Comparative Government* (*op. cit.*), p. 135.
9. Ibid., p. 134.
10. See Historical Introduction and Chapters 1 and 2 for further details. Blondel's *Comparative Government* (*op. cit.*) (mainly his two articles, 'Mass Parties in Indus-

trialized Societies', and 'Mass Parties and types of modern societies' include a detailed description of the mass model of party. His *Introduction to Comparative Government* (*op. cit.*), pp. 108–10, provides useful explanations on the character of class-based parties.

11. It refers to *present* class position.

12. Unofficial statistics provided by internal sources. They show average percentages for each period. Official statistics were not available.

13. The percentages represent the average, taking into consideration all Central Committees from 1933 up to 1970 and a representative sample of Region Committees during the same period. (Official party records, 1940, 1950–60 and 1970). Robert Michels ever-relevant observations on the German Social Democratic Party's leadership social characteristics can be more or less observed here, although middle-class preponderance in leadership appears to be less important in the PSCh (see Michels, *Political Parties*, Dover, New York, 1959).

14. For further details on education achievements during the 1938–50 period in Chile, see the 'Official Statistics on Educational Development', Ministry of Education, Santiago, Chile, 1952. For details on industrial growth in Chile, see Oscar Muñoz, *Crecimiento industrial de Chile 1914-1965* (Universidad de Chile, Santiago, 1967).

15. The examination of ten associations of writers, journalists, readers' clubs, newspapers' supporters and political associations of various categories in the 1930–40 period revealed a 95 per cent membership of middle-class origin against 5 per cent of working-class origin. Most of the people included in this 5 per cent were at the same time leaders of leftist groups who had managed to educate themselves guided by intellectual, middle-class friends. The autodidact phenomenon was by no means representative of a tendency or a trend in the working class at that moment.

16. There were 54,800 legal union members in 1932. The figure went up to 284,300 in 1952. It does not include 'illegal' unions (some peasants co-operatives and associations, small unions, etc.) during the same period. The figures are indicative of the extent of working-class participation in their own affairs and suggests the development of social consciousness which was certainly related to the progress made in education and industrialization (figures from Alan Angell, *Politics and the Labour Movement in Chile*, Oxford University Press, London, 1972, p. 54; Source E. Morgado, *Libertad Sindical*, 1967, p. 120). Angell's book includes an acute analysis of the development of labour forces in Chile *vis-à-vis* the development of political and social consciousness of Chilean workers.

17. Figures were provided by the respective offices for the universities concerned in 1972.

18. During the first years of this final period, the figures were even more categoric: 98 per cent of students were of middle-class origin, against 2 per cent of working-class origin. Figures provided by the Direccion Nacional de Estadisticas y Censos, Santiago, Chile, 1971.

19. Blondel, *An Introduction to Comparative Government* (*op. cit.*), p. 118.

20. The society's goals statements were selected from the Chilean Constitution of 1925. The party's goals were selected from primary sources, in order to reflect official party ideology and not individual or factional opinions. However, the examination of speeches of leaders and parliamentarians, official or unofficial party periodicals and other documents confirms the clear antagonism existing between the PSCh goals and those of Chilean society as reflected in the Constitution of 1925.

21. Article 4, Chilean Constitution of 1925. The paragraph is reflecting Locke's and Montesquieu's theories of the separation of powers. In fact, the Chilean Constitution of 1925 does not state the principle explicitly, but rather establishes it throughout the different sections of it, under the titles which specify each power's responsibilities.

22. Internal Resolutions of the PLENO of 1972, p. 3.

23. Article 63, ibid. The same principle is established to elect Members of Parliament.

24. Internal Resolutions of the PLENO of 1963, p. 5.

25. No. 7 of Article 10, *Constitution*. Other guaranteed freedoms are: association, reunion, religion, press, opinion, petition.

26. 'The State of the Country', special document on education, internal party document, issued by the XIII General Ordinary Congress, Santiago, 1950, p. 6.

27. No. 1 of Article 10, *Constitution*.

28. Report to the XX General Ordinary Congress, 'On Equality Before the Law', internal party document approved by majority, Concepción, Chile, 1964, p. 7.

29. No. 10 of Article 10, *Constitution*.

30. 'Economical Report to the XXIII General Ordinary Congress of the PSCh', Valparaiso, 1959, p. 11 (internal document).

31. Part 2, No. 10 of Article 10, *Constitution*.

32. *Party Bulletin*, mimeographed document, Santiago, 1953, p. 6.

33. Internal Special Report to the Central Committee on the 'Chilenization' measures of President Frei, memo, 1968, p. 5.

34. No. 14 of Article 10, *Constitution*.

35. Approved party standing on private industry, internal party records, 1949. This stand was greatly clarified in successive documents. Also important, the comments of Mario Bernarschina, *Constitución Política y leyes complementarias* (segunda edición), Manuales Juridícos No. 57 (Editorial Jurídica de Chile, Santiago, Chile, 1958).

The party's goals are suggested by the following documents: Eugenio Gonzáles Rojas, *Fundamentación Teórica del Programa del Partido Socialista, in Pensamiento Teórico y Político del Partido Socialista* (reader), ed. Alejandro Chelén y Julio César Jobet (Editorial Quimantú, Santiago, Chile, 1972), pp. 67–93; Eugenio González Rojas, 'El Socialismo frente al Liberalismo', ibid., pp. 93–118; Raúl Ampuero, 'Reflexiones sobre la Revolución ye el Socialismo', ibid., pp. 145–67; Salomón Corbalán, 'El Partido Socialista de Chile', ibid., pp. 181–209; Luis Zuñiga, 'El Partido Socialista, Partido del Pueblo', ibid., pp. –21. Oscar Schnake, 'El Partido Socialista no es un partido más', ibid., pp. 13–17. Adonis Sepúlveda,

'El Partido Socialists en la Revolución Chilena', ibid., pp. 227–59. Aniceto Rodríguez, 'El Partido Socialista plantea la nacionalización del hierro', ibid., pp. 259–307. Carlos Altamirano, 'El Parlamento, "Tigre de Papel"', ibid., pp. 307–29. Carlos Altamirano, 'El Partido Socialista y la Revolución Chilena', ibid., pp. 329–42; Julio César Jobet, 'Teoría, Programa y Política del Partido Socialista de Chile', ibid., pp. 426–66.

The following party's official documents were also taken into consideration: ordinary Congresses resolutions from the first one, on the 28, 29, 30 and 31 October, 1933, to the XXIII Ordinary Congress that met in La Serena, Chile, on 28, 29, 30 and 31 January, 1970 (official party documents).

The Chilean Constitution of 1925 which was only cancelled after the overthrow of President Salvador Allende in 1973, has been widely regarded by constitutionalists as a prototype liberal democratic constitution. See Mario Bernarschina, *Constitución Política y Leyes Complementarias* (*op. cit.*); Carlos Andrade, *Elementos de Derecho Constitucional Chileno* (Editorial Jurídia de Chile, Santiago, 1971); Julio Heisse, *Historia Constitucional de Chile* (Editorial Jurídica de Chile, Santiago, 1950); Carlos Estévez, *Reformas que la Constitución de 1925 introdujo a la de 1833* (Universidad de Chile, Cuadernos Jurídicos y Sociales, XXIII, Santiago, 1942); Gabriel Amunátegui, *Manual de Derecho Constitucional* (Editorial Jurídica de Chile, Santiago, 1950). Against this acknowledged liberal background, the Chilean Constitution of 1925 stands clearly in antagonism to the collectivist, centralized principles of the PSCh.

36. Angell (*op. cit.*), p. 54.
37. Angell, ibid., gives a detailed description of trade unionism in Chile and its relationship to the development of the Left in the country.
38. Blondel, *Comparative Government* (*op. cit.*), pp. 127–41.
39. For a detailed discussion of the *mass* and the *cadre* types of parties, see Duverger (*op. cit.*), pp. 62–132.
40. Blondel, *Comparative Government* (*op. cit.*), pp. 134–6.
41. Leaders such as Marmaduke Grove, Oscar Schnake, Salvador Allende, Raúl Ampuero and others played a protagonic role in shaping the party's ideology and reinforcing its firm anti-American stand. If not a *decolonization process*, a *de-Americanization* process served the same purposes of *anti-colonialism* in the case of the PSCh, always under the firm guidance of a charismatic leader. Their specific role, however, in shaping concrete models of structure and organization and policies, is difficult to determine, but it was certainly important.
42. Blondel, *Comparative Government*, (*op. cit.*), p. 134.
43. See Duverger, (*op. cit.*), pp. 61–132, for a description and discussion on the problem. Jean Blondel, *Comparing Political Systems* (Weidenfeld and Nicolson, London, 1973), also provides a concise view on the subject.
44. Duverger (*op. cit.*), pp., 62–132, treats the subject exhaustively.
45. In Blondel, 'Mass Parties and Industrialized Societies', in *Comparative Government* (*op. cit.*), p. 122.
46. *Zone 1* is predominantly mining and contains 60 per cent of the country's mining population. *Zone 2* is predominantly industrial, and contains 70 per cent

of industrial workers in the country; *Zone 3* is both mining and industrial. *Zone 4* is mainly agricultural but also industrial. *Zone 5* is both agricultural and industrial. There is no place where industry is important and the Socialists do not have strong, continued and persistent electoral support. There is no place where mining is important and where the same phenomenon does not occur. Industrial workers and miners seem to have been the main source of electoral support for the party throughout its history, but middle-class support should not be entirely ruled out, mainly in Zone 2, where a big bureaucratic apparatus exists. The agriculture-orientated provinces (mainly Colchagua, Curicó, Talca, Maule, Linares and Nuble) reveal that electoral support for the PSCh there has been inconsistent.

Figure 3.2 considers all elections for the Chamber of Deputies from 1937 up to 1969. The party was founded in 1923 and in 1937 it confronted the first elections. After 1970, the only election held was that of 1973, in which the PSCh obtained 22.5 per cent of the national electorate, a phenomenon very much related to the fact that the president was the socialist Salvador Allende.

47. Blondel, *Comparative Government* (*op. cit.*), p. 122.
48. There exists no official or known unofficial documents establishing the existence of paid party workers. In addition to this, nearly all party statutes from 1933 on have stressed the voluntary character of party work. Financial help has come traditionally from rank-and-file members, though in a rather insufficient and faulty way, thus creating the need for sporadic financial help from wealthy party supporters, but always on a voluntary basis.
49. In addition to what has already been said on the theoretical problems of defining and determining the existence of oligarchical tendencies in the leadership, the case of the PSCh provides problems of its own. First the top-level decisions have been traditionally adopted by the Political Commissions, smaller bodies emerging from the Central Committees and whose compositions in most cases are unknown. Second, the number of members of both Political Commissions and Central Committees have varied significantly throughout time, thus changing the patterns of power-holding: it is not the same thing being in a nine-members Central Committee as it is to be in a 25-member Committee. Third, the period of duration of both Central Committee and Political Commissions have also been different at different stages of the party's development, and again, it is not the same to integrate a Central Committee of five months as one lasting three years (see Figs. 3.8, 3.9). It would certainly be interesting to attempt to isolate these variables and perhaps through regression and other analyses to draw conclusions on 'real' power-holding and oligarchical tendencies among leaders. The matter would require a number of theoretical and practical assumptions whose scope would be, to say the least, very controversial. But the issue remains open for future research.
50. Duverger, (*op. cit.*), pp. 133–201, 151–7, treats the subject thoroughly. See Lenin, *What Is to Be Done?* (*op. cit.*), and *Selected Works* (*op. cit.*) to assess the Leninist concept of the full-time party official, which is supposed to be the basic operational element of the bureaucratically centralized, power-concentrating Leninist

party model. Durverger (*op. cit.*), pp. 151–68, refers to the problem of 'oligarchy in leadership' in political parties of all sorts. The concept is along the lines of Robert Michels' idea of oligarchy being inherent in any kind of organization, although Duverger is not as categoric (Michels, (*op. cit.*). Michels' observations were primarily drawn from his study of German social democracy, but his book did not provide any empirical tests to assess the existence and extent of oligarchies in political parties.

   To begin with, how do we define a party oligarchy? It is not enough to establish that a representative percentage of leaders have been holding power positions for an unreasonable period of time. It would also be necessary to know their ages; how they came to support or reject given positions throughout their terms in office; how and when were they replaced by new leaders and how these new leaders behaved over a reasonable period of time; where the old and the new leaders came from and how they got into their power positions; how they reacted to significant membership demands—whether they tended to satisfy them or rather to neglect them—and a variety of other important issues as well. As Michels suggests it, other issues to be analysed should be, among others, the problem of financial power of the leaders, the relationships and 'cultural superiority' of leaders. The list could go on indefinitely. The available data on the PSCh leadership, however, did not amount to examining the issues mentioned, making it almost impossible for a comprehensive empirically tested analysis of the existence, if any, of an 'oligarchy in leadership'. On the same subject, see Robert McKenzie, *British Political Parties* (Heinemann, London, 1955). He considers that Michels' 'technical' and 'psychological' factors causing the development of oligarchies within political parties were certainly a fact in the case of his observations in Britain, but he clearly dissociates himself from Michels' absolutely deterministic, somehow fatalistic approach, which presupposes the phenomenon to be almost inevitable. But Blondel, *Comparative Government* (*op. cit.*), p. 123, develops the central points relevant to our study.

51. Blondel, ibid., pp. 123–4.
52. Blondel, *Comparative Government* (*op. cit.*), p. 124.
53. Ibid., p. 124.
54. Christian Anglade, 'Party Finance Models and the Classification of Latin American Parties', in *Comparative Political Finance*, ed Arnold J. Heidenheimer (Heath, Lexington, Mass., 1970), p. 177.
55. *Memorandum* to leaders and members, mimoegraphed document, internal use only, 1934, p. 2. The memorandum was referring to the fact that no official policy on financing had been established yet and appealed to the 'comrades to show themselves generous' to the party (p. 3).
56. There is no written evidence that the date on which the new system was instituted is correct. However, old party members remember that the previous system had a very short life, certainly not more than six months. There is no written evidence either on how the system actually worked, as there are no documents on the issue available. Our information here comes primarily from conversations with old and reliable party members and leaders.

57. 0.5 per cent of the member's personal income was the proportion considered most of the time. At some stages (elections), this was raised to 1 per cent.

58. 0.5 per cent was normally requested from unskilled workers, only; 20 per cent was normally requested from members occupying international posts paid in foreign currency.

59. There is an interesting collection of internal *memos* at different times, urging the intermediate leadership officials and members to pay their fees. It was in the private collection of an old Socialist leader who was himself treasurer at various levels, and who managed to get cash from wealthy party sympathizers, when needed. His memory of the task of getting money for the party is both appealing and appalling, because it shows the striking contradiction of a mass, class-based party, with a strong following in trade unions, unable however to set up a reasonable system of finance.

60. Christian Anglade distinguishes four categories of party expenditure in elections: (1) general expenditure on election propaganda; (2) 'operational' expenses (printing electoral lists, campaign tours, meetings, banquets, payment of electoral agents); (3) buying of votes; (4) election-day expenses. (Anglade, *op. cit.*, p. 178). All but category (3) undoubtedly were ordinary financial needs of the PSCh.

61. Anglade, *op. cit.*

62. Ibid., pp. 163–89. Table 3.4 in this chapter appears in Anglade also. Anglade compares his approach based on party finance with the models devised by A. Heidenheimer, in order to describe the relation between political finance and the stages of socio-political development. Anglade's approach to the study of parties in Latin America, based mainly on finance, 'bears in mind the incomplete data available'. This is certainly one of the most difficult problems that the researcher will encounter, and this was so in the case of the PSCh, whose official records on the matter were unavailable. See also Arnold J. Heidenheimer, 'Comparative Party Finance: Notes on Practices and Towards a Theory', *Journal of Politics*, Vol. 25, No. 4 (1963), pp. 790–811 and John D. Martz, 'Dilemmas in the Study of Latin American Political Parties', *Journal of Politics*, Vol. 26, No. 4 (1964), pp. 590, 531.

63. The opinions of all five old former leaders and all present leaders interviewed were unanimous in considering that this was how the party met approximately 90 per cent of its permanent costs.

64. Sources of information: A party leader who had been Treasurer at different levels, including the Central Committee, for more than twenty years, and five former leaders. The matter of the party's finances remained one in which the strictest secrecy was requested. No clear written rules exist, and the persons nationally responsible for finances have normally enjoyed considerable autonomy.

65. Blondel, *Comparative Government*, (*op. cit.*), p. 125.

66. Ibid., p. 125.

67. The party bought the majority of shares in *Ultima Hora* in 1971.

68. Sources: Information provided by two party officials in charge of mass communications, August 1972. For a detailed account of mass media ownership in

Chile, see Elmo Catalán, *La Propaganda instrumento de presión política* (PLA, Santiago, Chile, 1970).

69. *Internal official records*, 1970 (restricted and confidential use, only). The records registered data on the 1960–70 period. Information on previous periods was unavailable.

70. Blondel, *Comparative Government* (*op. cit*.), p. 125.

71. Ibid., pp. 125–6.

72. A number of the eighty-two editorials on PSCh political behaviour, written between 1950 and 1968, were examined. Twenty-seven of them appeared in the centre-right daily newspaper *La Tencera de la Hora*, thirty-two in the Conservative *El Mercurio* and the rest evenly distributed in the Communist *El Siglo* (seven) the Christan Democratic *La Patria* (sixteen) and the Socialist *Ultima Hora* (eleven). All of them coincided at least in one point: the PSCh stood consistently to the left of the PCCh. As the examination made covers sixteen years, the findings are of relevance at least for the 1950–70 period. A survey made by the party's own Technical Department in 1969 confirmed the existence of this popular belief: 81 per cent of those interviewed (a sample of 1,500 nationally distributed, men and women with voting ages) thought the party *far* to the left of the Communists (S.P. Technical Department, 1970, internal and confidential document).

73. Periodicals examined covered the 1933–73 period, and included the following official party organs: *Núcleo*, Valparaíso, 1933–36; *Acción*, Santiago, 1933; *Acción Socialista*, Santiago, 1934; *Jornada*, Santiago, 1934–35; *Consigna*, Santiago, 1934–40; *Espartaco*, Santiago, 1947–48; *La Calle*, Santiago, 1949–55; *Izquierda*, Santiago, 1958–61; *Arauco*, Santiago, 1959–67; *Ultima Hora*, Santiago, 1950–73. All are weekly periodicals, with the exception of *Arauco* (monthly), *Núcleo* (monthly) and *Ultima Hora* (daily). Also examined: internal correspondence between different leadership bodies, during the 1933–70 period (Central Committee, *reserved documents*, Santiago, 1971).

74. *Circular interna* of 23 July 1961 (Central Committee, to all Regional and Section Committees), p. 3.

75. Raphael Zariski, 'The Italian Socialist Party: A Case in Factional Conflict', *APSR*, June 1962, pp. 372–90; John Martz, 'Dilemmas in the Study of Latin-American Political Parties', *The Journal of Politics*, August 1964, pp. 509–31, suggests a similar approach.

76. Due to the reasons explained in the Preface, further data on this subject was unavailable. Furthermore, the data that it was possible to gather, i.e. voting records in the Central Committee, was rather incomplete. The results of this test should not, therefore, be treated as conclusive.

77. Most of this data is presumed lost by now, as the party's headquarters were virtually 'invaded' by the military the very day of Allende's overthrow on 11 September 1973. The headquarters were set on fire by the invading units. The fate of thousands of party documents and private libraries is also uncertain, but there is widespread fear that most of them were destroyed.

78. For discussion, see Blondel, *Comparative Government* (*op. cit*.).

79. Statistics were given to the author by reliable party officials, but there are no official records on the matter.
80. For example, posts at ministerial or under-secretary levels, directors of government enterprises, and so on.
81. Unofficial party statistics. Percentages for previous years were not available.
82. The character of demands reflects the most common social and political interests which the party was called to represent.
83. See the following internal party documents: *Bulletin*, August 1939, mimeographed; *Bulletin*, August 1941, mimeographed; *The Situation of the Country*, report to the PLENO of 1944; *Bulletins* from 1945 to 1963 (half-yearly, three-monthly and monthly). See also party periodicals, notably *Consigna* (1939–40), *La Calle* (1949–55), *Izquierda* (1958–61) and *Arauco* (1959–67).
84. This was also true to an important extent in the case of members of Parliament. At least two known reports exist criticizing parliamentarians for having an 'electorally-orientated mind' ('On Behalf of a Mass Politics', report to the Central Committee, Santiago, 1964; and 'Towards the People's Assembly', report to the Political Commission of the Central Committee, 1971). Self-incriminating documents on the part of the leadership were less common, but nevertheless there is evidence which suggests that they used their meetings to strongly criticize fellow leaders and themselves for 'arrogant scornful' attitudes and for falling into 'bourgeois, electoralist tendencies'. Strong evidence of this was given to us by reliable party leaders and our own experience during the 1960–70 period confirm it.
85. This was the case of the Nineteenth Ordinary Congress, December 1961, Los Andes (38) and the Twentieth Ordinary Congress, June 1965, Linares (40). At different stages, the 'moderates' got between 15 per cent and 35 per cent. On the other hand, the 'extreme leftists' were never an homogeneous group, but a mixture of Trotskyites, pro-Cubans, pro-Chinese and others who managed to present a united front against what have been always labelled as 'social democratic deformations' of the moderates.
86. Lengthy discussions on the agrarian reform, the 'Chileanization' of the copper, the educational system reform, the tax reform and others, which took place during this period, ended with the socialists' adhering to the PCChs' generally well-documented stances, although sometimes reluctantly. The party's propositions appeared to be too mild in the eyes of the Socialist party.
87. As it has already bee said, elections in a variety of student bodies mainly between 1960 and 1970 provided important data on this. The same can be said of an important number of trade union elections. Oddly enough, somewhat anti-communist attitudes sustained by previous highest echelons leaders before 1960 found rejection in some intermediate instances that tried then to achieve alliances with the Communist party.
88. Voting with these parties in Parliament has been a common practice for the Socialists. The Unidad Popular coalition in 1970, which included the Radicals, was also accepted reluctantly by the PSCh.

4 The Technical Aspects of Organization

The practical operation of the PSCh does not necessarily reflect the written rules on organization established in successive Ordinary Congresses and special *ad hoc* meetings. Duverger says rightly that 'we must therefore not allow ourselves to be misled by the letter of the constitution, but must analyse its application in practice before coming to a conclusion'.[1]

The case of the PSCh provides an excellent example of the problem insofar as the party had tried very hard to overcome the many defects of its internal structure, which in turn had posed many problems to both leaders and members (Figs. 4.1 and 4.2).[2] In fact, the party was often able to introduce modified schemes for organization but was unable to implement them. Between 1933 and 1970 at least eight plans for reorganization were made. These do not include several minor adjustments made at different levels and at different historical stages, which are difficult to describe with reasonable accuracy. However, in only four out of these eight could real differences be distinguished and analysed, all of which can be seen in Figures 1.1 to 1.4 (pp. 17, 21, 31). These are the following:

1. The original scheme for organization adopted when the party was founded in 1933.
2. The major reform project adopted by the Special National Conference on Organization in November 1939, later sanctioned by the Sixth Ordinary Congress (1940).
3. The major reform project adopted by the Special National Conference on organization in December 1953.
4. The reforms adopted by the National Conference on Organization in 1966, later sanctioned by the Twenty-Second Ordinary Congress of Chillán (1967).[3]

In all the schemes there were some common elements that prevailed:

1. *Centralization*: Efforts were made to try to eliminate or at least reduce the continued and persistent tendency towards a diffusion of power from top to bottom. It was considered that this resulted in indiscipline and anarchy.
2. *Democratic efforts* which tried to avoid, on the other hand, the development of *autocratic* features as a result of centralization.

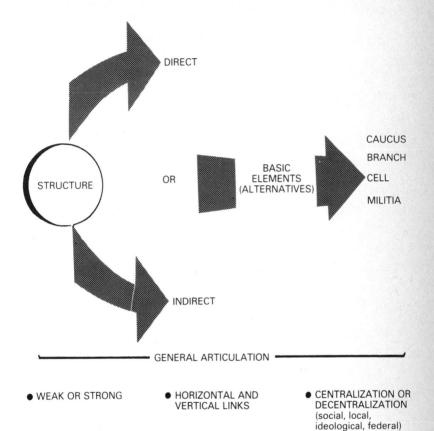

DIRECT

STRUCTURE

OR

BASIC
ELEMENTS
(ALTERNATIVES)

CAUCUS

BRANCH

CELL

MILITIA

INDIRECT

GENERAL ARTICULATION

● WEAK OR STRONG   ● HORIZONTAL AND   ● CENTRALIZATION OR
                           VERTICAL LINKS   DECENTRALIZATION
                                                      (social, local,
                                                      ideological, federal)

(1) Interpreted from Maurice Duverger's *'Political
    Parties'*, op. cit. A complete explanation of this
    typology can be there examined (pp. 4–61).

Figure 4.1 General typology of party structure (Technical aspects)

PERIOD	GENERAL ARTICULATION		CENTRALIZATION		HORIZONTAL LINKS		VERTICAL LINKS	
	WEAK	STRONG	WEAK	STRONG	WEAK	STRONG	WEAK	STRONG
1933–9		↘		↘	↘			↘
1940–53	↘		↘		↘		↘	
1953–67	↘			↘	↘			↘

Figure 4.2 PSCh real working structure

3. *Organization efforts* which tried to produce a balance between individual freedoms and the collective responsibility of members. These were expected to harmonize centralization, the practice of democratic centralism, a workable system of both vertical and horizontal links and, as a consequence, a reasonably acceptable system of general articulation of demands and decisions.

The intended results of an improved system of organization would be:

(a) *Efficiency*: This was understood as a system in which decisions adopted by the different bodies were correspondingly implemented by subordinate bodies without undue change and deletions.
(b) *Discipline*: This was understood as a system in which decisions were accepted and implemented by subordinate bodies without public complaints or disagreements.
(c) *Continuity*: This was understood as a system in which consistency was requested of decisions at various levels. This would help avoid as much as possible, contradictions between both ideology and bureaucratic rules.[4]

PSCh STRUCTURE, 1933-9

The first period of the party's development registered what apparently could have been the most consistent scheme of party organization *vis-à-vis* party management (see Fig. 1.1).

In fact, the first organizational scheme adopted by the party in 1933, proved inadequate for the party's needs during the 1930s. It had the following characteristics:

1. A hierarchical, centralized bureaucratic structure in which important decisions were only to be made by the Central Committee, and only a very limited amount of power-sharing was permitted to the intermediate and lower bodies (Regional Committees, Section Committees and *núcleos*). A system of strong centralization existed.
2. A system of both vertical and horizontal links was instituted. This allowed the passage of information in all directions of the structure, the co-ordination of policies and the correct implementation of decisions. The secretary-general had diffused powers, as a direct system of links of Central Committee members with lower levels existed. Concentration of power in the hands of one man only was thus believed to be avoided.
3. As a consequence of 1 and 2, general articulation was intended to be practised on a strong and permanent basis in order to enable the full

exercise of both the member's individual rights and collective responsibilities.

The first model can be examined in Figure 1.1. As it proved rather inefficient, the end of the 1930s saw a special Conference on Organization in 1939 to introduce what were considered necessary changes to improve the party's working conditions. Later, in 1953, new measures were recommended, when the measures adopted in 1939 again proved to be unsatisfactory (see Figs. 1.2 and 1.4).

The first six years of the party's history were, as stated above, adapting to the prevailing circumstances and were devoted to establishing an internal model of organization.

At the top of the bureaucratic structure, a Central Committee was established. This, in turn, delegated the most important decisions to a smaller body, the Political Commission, which worked on a more permanent basis. The average number of sessions of the Central Committee from 1933 to 1939 was once every fortnight, whilst the Political Commission met weekly.

Only the National Congress was placed above the Central Committee, but this body, which had representatives from all intermediate and lower bodies, met only once a year. At the intermediate level, two types of bodies were established: *Regional* and *Section Committees*. Regional Committees were established in each provincial capital and Section Committees in each city or town. At the bottom, the *núcleos*, organized as cells, formed the basic party units.

The ideology behind the organization was to create 'a Leninist structure which could successfully articulate the working class's fight for socialism. This means an organization of revolutionary cadres whose superior formation will lead and educate the masses'.[5]

As the first period was one of enthusiasm and growth, the extremely centralized system worked fairly well for at least two years. During this period there were in fact no more than eight Regional Committees and twenty-one Section Committees throughout the country. Furthermore, five out of the eight Regional Committees were placed in the Centre (Santiago, Valparaíso and Concepción), and so too were fourteen of the twenty-one Section Committees. This factor allowed strict overall control by the top bureaucratic bodies, notwithstanding the fact that then, as afterwards, the party could not count on full-time paid officials.

Consequently, the system of both vertical and horizontal links worked well at least during 1933, 1934 and 1935. The vertical links were intended primarily to pass on decisions and information, while the horizontal links were only supposed to provide information.

As we have said, at the bottom of the party structure, the *núcleos* provided the basic working units. More than merely deliberative bodies, the *núcleos* were supposed to be structured in a way similar to the *cell*. Implementation of decisions and not ideological discussions were therefore their *raison d'être*. The congresses at the various levels were the natural organs for deliberation. However, from the very beginning of the party's organization, the *núcleos* showed a clear tendency towards deliberation, adopting a working model that was very near to the *caucus* or the *branch*.[6]

As the numbers of *núcleos* were obviously larger than those of other bodies (a recorded total of seventy-three for the first six years, according to unofficial party records), their deliberative character necessarily influenced party policies to a considerable extent. This feature helped to create both democratic features and also defects in the implementation of some of the party's policies.

The consistent behaviour of the *núcleos* towards discussion caused at least two strong reactions from the Central Committee in 1937 and 1938. In one report to the Political Commission, Central Committee member A. Pezoa stated that 'the *núcleos* are increasingly overlapping the congresses powers, through the discussion of a variety of ideological and political matters. Some *núcleos* have even gone as far as to discuss and reject Central Committee official policies, though not publicly'.[7]

The preoccupation with the *núcleos* by the Central Committee came to a peak in 1938, when former secretary-general and then Central Committee member Marmaduke Grove reported that 'again and again the party is being destroyed by bourgeois tendencies at the very bottom of its structure. A number of *núcleos* insist on placing themselves as purely deliberative organs, while there is no implementation of the party's policies. Congresses are therefore useless organs to provide an appropriate environment for social life'.[8]

At the end of 1938 the party exhibited the distinct signs of a weak organization whose main characteristics can be summarized as follows:

1. Technically, the system of general articulation was working reasonably well but was being increasingly weakened. This was due basically to both the limited geographic extension of the internal party organization and the geographical centralization of most of the party's intermediate and lower bodies. These facts enabled the rapid growth of an efficient system of internal coordination, communications and mutual information, but one which deteriorated when the party began to grow after two or three years.
2. The system of both vertical and horizontal links began to fail at the level of the *núcleos*, especially in their relationships with both intermediate and higher bodies.

The centralized system, therefore, in 1937 was already failing to achieve permanent, stable channels of communications from the top to the bottom. Decisions taken by responsible bodies at the various levels were being discussed and in some cases rejected by the *núcleos*, at the same time as the *núcleos* were gradually usurping the role of the congresses as deliberative organs.

The negative effects of such practices were, among others, the following:

1. Failure in achieving consistent policies on any issues as decisions adopted by the higher bodies were not being implemented by the basic units. The party exhibited ideologically clear commitments but they remained only as written declarations of intention.
2. Disenchantment among the intermediate leaders, who were being blamed by the Central Committee as responsible for the lack of liaison between the top bodies and the basic units. This stimulated a massive process of resignations at Regional and Section Committee levels which reached a peak of thirty-seven individual resignations between 1936 and 1939.
3. Development of *caciquista* tendencies among both *núcleos* and Central Committee members, who tried to build for themselves power positions which would eventually elevate them to higher positions.[9]

The existence of what party leaders considered as the 'negative effects' of the *núcleos*' behaviour did not preclude the development of some positive features as well.

First, the party acquired some prestige because of its democratic practices at the lowest levels. This was recognized by Grove in his report, when he wrote:

even though we are being consumed by a rampant disorganization process, one would be careful not to fall into authoritarian practices for which the Socialist Party has no place. Our internal democracy should be rather limited, discipline respected and individual members' rights clearly implemented. The tendency to deliberation and indiscipline in our *núcleos* should be corrected by the way of persuasion, because our main strength is in our system of practising internal democracy. Let us not go from one extreme to the other. Other parties' examples of authoritarianism and disrespect for individual freedoms should guide our behaviour ... our prestige as a working-class party is at stake.[10]

Second, an increasing number of intellectuals and educated people were seeking membership status as a result of the generally observed internal flexibility within the party. This in turn helped to shape a party whose public image was one of 'respectability' to the middle class. Other working-class parties were generally considered consistently classist and violent, and they made only a very limited appeal to the middle class and, more specifically, to the intellectuals. This feature can be better illustrated by the following statement made to us by former party secretary-general, Central Committee member for several times, MP and senator, Salomón Corbalán:

During the first six years or so of our development, we strongly appealed to intellectuals and professionals because the disenchantment with Communist policies was very strong indeed. People 'in the middle' were afraid of the 'extremism' of the Communist Party, its commitment to Soviet policies, its class warfare. On the other hand, we in fact had potential for a far more extremist stand that the Communists, as we were not committed to the contingencies of any foreign country. This meant in practice that if, as it was later proved, Soviet needs requested restraint on the part of communist parties in Chile and elsewhere, we would not follow that pattern at all. The Molotov Von Ribbentrop pact, for example, temporarily took the Communists in Chile out of the national anti-nazi struggle. We did not accept that, and continued as firmly opposed to totalitarianism as before. The same happened with the Popular Front policies, which legitimized class collaborationism as a means of achieving power . . . we never accepted it, but however had to yield in order to keep our understanding with the Communists going.[11]

Corbalán went further, adding:

besides, our party consistently developed democratic practices in its internal behaviour that greatly appealed to the Chilean educated middle class, which was always committed to democracy in the liberal sense. A socialist party that, on the one hand, proclaimed its interest in socialism and, on the other, was allowing permanent fraternal discussions at the basic levels was an interesting, attracting new fact to them, accustomed as they were to hear terrible things about internal Communist Party practices.[12]

PSCh STRUCTURE, 1940–53

The existence of problems in the party's internal organization at the end of the 1930s affected morale in the leadership, both at the top and the intermediate levels. Whilst leaders' resignations were already frequent (37 between 1936 and 1939, as already stated), the *núcleos* continued to be disobedient, refusing to carry out orders and policies. Furthermore, vicious *caciquista* practices were driving the party into several factions, in which areas of influence were being developed by Central Committee members, through the Regional and Section Committees, right down to the lowest levels, the *núcleos*. However, the most characteristic trend was that of a direct horizontal link between Central Committee and *núcleos'* members, simply bypassing the intermediate levels' powers and, even worse, the authority of the secretary-general.

It is true that the secretary-general did not have, according to the party's written rules, a direct command over Regional and Section Committees and *núcleos*. This task was handled by the executive Central Committee. This fact, nevertheless, could not and should not preclude the top party authority from having an overall control over the party apparatus. What happened instead was that the established authority of the Central Committee over all other leadership levels enabled the building of various power blocs, and the secretary-general could do nothing to prevent it.[13]

The state of internal affairs was so grave in the middle of 1939 as to induce the secretary-general to call for an extraordinary Conference on Organization, to be held in Santiago in November 1939. Only a few days later, the hectic Sixth Ordinary National Congress, held in Santiago for December 20 to 23, precipitated one of the major crises in the party's history, when five deputies left the party to set up another organization.

Although the major causes were, according to Chelén,[14] of an ideological nature (namely, the 'collaboration with the Popular Front'), the Conference on Organization suggested that bureaucratic problems had a part in the crisis. The Conference heard the complaints of disenchanted intermediate leaders, whose authority had been continuously ignored by the Central Committee and *núcleos* members. The prevailing sentiment can be seen from the words of the delegate from the Valparaíso Regional Committee, Néstor Maturana, who declared that 'our existence is no longer necessary within a party that has shown every disrespect for our authority and our work. We propose, therefore, that Regional and Section Committees be dismantled and command over the *núcleos* be from now on directly exercised at its discretion by the Central Committee'.[15]

No doubt the dismantling of the intermediate party machinery was absolutely out the question for everyone. The words of the Valparaíso delegate, as those of other delegates, reflected the resentment of the intermediate leadership of the party and declared their intention to regain their lost powers. The First Conference on Organization considered and approved the following changes in relation to the previous model (compare Figs. 1.1 and 1.2).

1. As in the previous scheme, a hierarchical, centralized bureaucratic structure was adopted. As before, the main decisions were to be in the hands of the Central Committee, placed at the top of the structure, which in turn could delegate powers to the Political Commission. The conference, however, considered it was now appropriate to delegate some of its power to the

intermediate leadership levels, namely Regional and Section Committees, thus establishing for the first time a certain degree of decentralization at the local level, a factor mentioned by Duverger.[16]

2. The existing system of both vertical and horizontal links were reinforced. The rules for permanent co-ordinating policies between the various bureaucratic levels were established in detail. The main goals were to maintain a lively, dynamic internal information policy and to avoid the misunderstandings that had caused the degeneration of previous bodies.

In order to avoid the development of areas of influence and at the same time the concentration of excessive power in the hands of one man, a compromise system of hierarchical subordinate relationships was adopted. This allocated direct responsibility for handling Regional and Section Committees to an *ad hoc* body to be called the Departmento de Organización y Control (Control and Organization Department). This, in turn, would keep in permanent contact with, and should inform the secretary-general.

3. As a result of points 1 and 2, above, it was hoped that general articulation would be as strong as during the first two or three years of the party's existence.[17]

All other aspects of organization remained untouched, notably in relation to the congresses at the various levels and the *núcleos* as cell-type bodies. But in order to compel the *núcleos* to perform their duties as the party expected, a superior body for discussions and deliberation was set up in the form of a congress. These were to be held twice a year and would include delegates from all *núcleos* belonging to each Section Committee. In this way the party hoped to satisfy the need of members to permanently discuss political and ideological matters and not limit themselves to obeying orders. The caucus-type deviations exhibited by the *núcleos* from around 1936 on would now be avoided.

An analysis of the actual working habits of the party during this period shows, however, rather disappointing features in relation to the leadership expectations, as can be inferred from the examination of the following aspects:

1. The attempt to reinforce the system of general articulation through local decentralization and a detailed ruling on internal relations failed for most of the period. According to repeated internal party statements after 1943, Regional and Section Committees grossly misinterpreted their new power-sharing responsibilities. This in fact created a very strong sub-system of general articulation among them exclusively, which included strong vertical and horizontal links as well. This meant in practice the isolation of the basic political-bureaucratic bodies, the *núcleos*, which now were prevented

from any sort of meaningful and permanent relationship with higher bodies. Furthermore, these developments also isolated the top bureaucratic body, the Central Committee, and its delegated smaller body, the Political Commission, from any sort of meaningful and permanent relationship with the lower bodies.

2. The party as a whole, therefore, fell apart, divided in practically three sections: at the top, the Central Committee and the Political Commission stood as élite entities whose policies did not take into account the opinions of the other bodies; in the middle, Regional and Section Committees established a powerful structured general articulation sub-system of their own, including a system of both vertical and horizontal links; and at the bottom, the *núcleos* developed into useless bodies whose only hope lay with the twice-yearly congresses, where they would present their grievances.[18]

3. As an overall consequence of the above, the party was, in 1950, affected by a mounting internal crisis which it could not avoid. The *núcleos* by then had reached a numerical peak of 179, distributed throughout the country. Regional Committees already existed in all twenty-five provinces and the Section Committees amounted to seventy-two. This success, however, was challenged by the failure of the party bureaucratic apparatus to cope with an enlarged party structure. It was only natural that if the party had proved incapable of providing a rational infrastructure to administer the far simpler organization of the 1930s, it would almost certainly prove incapable of providing an infrastructure to cope with the problems created in the 1940s.

The fact that the party would again be affected by a division in 1952 (see Chapter 2) came as no surprise, therefore. Together with the publicly acknowledged reasons traditionally considered as the most important ones in causing the new schism, undoubtedly the old bureaucratic problems of a faulty party model had a signficant effect. As Senator Salvador Allende, the leader of the rebellion put it:

This party is now no *one* political party, but *several* political parties. Worst of all, no ideology seems to sustain different groupings, but small, irrelevant interests arising from bureaucratic posts. People work to perpetuate themselves in power positions without caring for the disintegrating party structure. The Central Committee stands aloof as a chosen superior body without commitments to organization as a whole. The Regional Committees and the Section Committees misuse the power which was granted to them to make the party more democratic. The *núcleos* only want to discuss, to reject or just sit and see, and no obligations or a sense of discipline exists.[19]

Salvador Allende recognized the problems of a bureaucratic nature which lay behind the new crisis together with other reasons of a political and an ideological nature when he added:

now we have to tolerate the new bosses—the Department of Control and Organization, which has come to replace the *caciquista* practices of Central Committee members in the past. Each comrade there considers his right to build a power structure of its own, misusing in a very old-fashioned and, let me say, absolutely anti-Leninist way, the responsibilities handed over to them by the party. We can no longer tolerate this, which constitutes blatant disregard for our most precious virtue as a working-class party: our democratic practices in each and every of our acts.[20]

Instead of Central Committee members building areas of influence, the party now had the members of the Department of Control and Organization reproducing the old *caciquista* practices that had affected the party during the past and which they had originally intended to curb.

PSCh STRUCTURE, 1953–67

The Fifteenth National Ordinary Congress held in San Antonio in October 1953 discussed at length the new management crisis that was affecting the party. It was considered so grave that it was decided to instruct the new secretary-general, Senator Aniceto Rodríguez, to call a Special National Conference to discuss exclusively that problem.

The conference was held in Santiago the following December and had delegates representing all bureaucratic offices throughout the country.

The main changes adopted there were the following (see Fig. 1.4). The secretary-general was given strong powers, and for the first time since the party was founded in 1933 he was given direct responsibility for all bureaucratic and political offices and other matters related to internal organization. In this way the party hoped to restrain the development of *caciquista* policies by individual members of the Central Committee, the Department of Control and Organization or any other bureaucratic body. The new model envisaged a secretary-general with broad powers and responsibilities, namely:

1. He would be responsible to the Central Committee for discipline in relation to the Central Committee, the Regional and Section Committees and the *núcleos*.
2. His powers would only have the limitation of triennial sessions by the Central Committee, and, naturally, the Regular Ordinary National Congresses of the party organization.

The new powers granted to the secretary-general meant in practice that he had been legally established as a virtual dictator. This reveals the extent of party dissatisfaction with a situation that was described as an 'anarchist, uncontrollable situation' by Central Committee member Mario Garay.[21]

The rest of the party apparatus remained the same as before. It is clear, however, that the only major change approved actually reversed, at least theoretically, the operationalization of the old principles of democratic centralism and internal democracy of which the party had been so proud throughout its history. The process of decentralization that had granted a certain degree of local autonomy to several leadership offices at levels other than the Central Committee, was also brought to an abrupt end by these new reforms.

An analysis of the new party structure reveals that the most probable goals desired by the party were:

1. *Extreme centralization*, even at the risk of exaggerating the already extreme centralized Weberian concept of bureaucratic structure, which recognizes the need for absolute leadership and command at the top of the party structure. At the same time, lower bodies remained as merely administrative organizations (see Fig. 3.10). The main purpose of this was probably to enforce discipline.

2. *The suppression of all systems and sub-systems of horizontal links*, in order to avoid the creation or the reinforcement of existing areas of influence at different levels. Furthermore, the central system of vertical links was improved and clarified. This came in the form of new stronger powers for superior offices over their subordinates. This went down to the lowest bodies, the *núcleos*, which were restricted to simple administrative tasks. Again, the most probable purpose here was discipline.

3. *As a consequence of points 1 and 2 above, the system of general articulation was supposed to be more expedient, quicker and certainly, stronger than the previous ones*. Further to these powers, the secretary-general was given powers to summarily expel rebel members. An appeal against expulsion could only be made at the next National Ordinary Congress. This would readmit the expelled member as long as his excuses proved valid.[22]

The most obvious underlying purpose of the new system was the reinforcement of discipline among the members. The majority of delegates to the Third Conference and party leaders at different levels approved the reform with enthusiasm. Delegate and Central Committee member A. Zuñiga recalled:

The fact that we would have from then on to restrain our verbose behaviour, our traditional indiscipline, our disrespect for hierarchy did not deter us from eagerly agreeing to the reform. We knew that we were risking the very fabric of our party, which could be converted into an autocratic, even despotic apparatus which would crush dissent arbitrarily. But we also knew that the risk was a worthy one, because the party could not continue in that way.[23]

In fact, the fears of some party members regarding the risk of despotism mentioned by A. Zuñiga proved to be unjustified. Future developments showed that no party secretary-general misused the strong powers granted to him and created a ruthless, or even a mildly autocratic, party structure. On the other hand, future developments consistently re-emphasized the old party weaknesses in organizational matters: party members continued to be indisciplined, party officers at different levels continued implementing policies of their own, and political language acquired a distinctly violent, markedly verbose style which came to characterize the party for much of its remaining twenty years.

An examination of the party's bureaucratic practices during this period can be summarized as follows:

1. At the top of the structure, the secretary-general could not or did not want to use the strong powers that he was able to exercise. Successive secretary-generals (Raúl Ampuero, Salomón Corbalán and Aniceto Rodrí-guez) tried to pursue a persuasive policy towards indisciplined party members. Despite this, some cases culminated in expulsion and others with the 'suspension' of the member's rights (a milder punishment than expulsion). This did not deter the rebel members from offending party discipline again and again.

2. Central Committee members practically bypassed the powers of the secretary-general, creating a completely illegal, even if informal, system of vertical links with Regional and Section Committees. This enabled the emergence of a new power, shared by Central, Regional and Section Committee members that sometimes acquired the appearance of factions. The real power of the secretary-general, therefore, was greatly diminished, and he frequently decided to adopt a policy of appeasement in order to avoid a new division within the party.

3. At the bottom of the structure, the *núcleos* came to be almost completely isolated bodies. They practised policies of their own, their vertical links were ineffective, and their horizontal links inefficient in an already overextended party with as many as 435 *núcleos* distributed throughout the country in 1965.

4. The system of general articulation was as a result very weak, showing marked features of typical caucus-type behaviour at all levels of the party apparatus.

5. As a result, by 1966 the party displayed three identifiable bureaucratic levels:

(a) The first, at the top of the party apparatus was the·secretary-general, isolated in fact from the rest of the party machinery.

(b) The second, in the middle of the party apparatus, represented the bulk of the intermediate leadership officers, namely the Regional and Section Committees.

(c) At the bottom of the party apparatus were the *núcleos*, also isolated from other levels.

These three levels worked almost independently from one another after 1956, despite a three year period in which party discipline functioned in a fairly efficient way. However, major political matters were always decided by the secretary-general, and the other bodies normally respected and implemented his decisions. Successive party congresses (held in 1955, 1957, 1959, 1961, 1964 and 1965) ignored existing problems and thereby sanctioned a weak structure to deal with internal affairs. They preferred to concentrate on more attractive national and international political issues. In 1967, the party reached a new major crisis which culminated in the expulsion of former Secretary-General Raúl Ampuero and a small number of Central, Regional and Section Committee members.[24]

The expulsion of Ampuero, who was not at that time a Central Committee member, was explained as necessary to eradicate from the party 'factionalism', 'misuse of power', 'anti-democratic behaviour' and 'gross violations of the party's most precious principles on internal organization'.[25] The majority of the Central Committee believed that he had in fact been trying to build a party machinery to suit his own purposes, in opposition to the existing party apparatus. 'The ultimate goal', it was said, 'would be the division of the party'.[26]

Although Ampuero did in fact establish a new organization called the Unión Socialista Popular, there exists no evidence to support the majority claim against him, and he was presumably the scapegoat of the new party internal crisis. It was obviously easier to blame a person who had held important bureaucratic positions in the past for many years for the permanent defects of the party machinery than to admit any collective responsibility. An acceptance of the latter might have caused the fall of many leaders from their positions of power.

The important fact remains that from 1953 to 1967 Raúl Ampuero occupied the position of secretary-general in this period for a total of five years. His attempts to build a disciplined, efficient party apparatus were never recognized by the party and, later he even came to be blamed for the very faults that he had earnestly tried to overcome.

The repeated acts of indiscipline at different levels caused him to adopt often draconian measures, which undoubtedly engendered resentment against him inside the party's ranks. No less than 125 members were expelled, including Central, Regional and Section Committee leaders, during his five years in office. In addition, no less than 234 suspensions were also registered, ranking from a mild two months to an extremely harsh two-year suspension.[27]

Future events proved that many of the suspended and expelled members continued to participate in party activities under the protection of some Central, Regional and Section Committee members. This eventually deterred other secretary-generals (notably Aniceto Rodríguez and Salomón Corbalán) from adopting similar strong tactics. A firm, determined effort to strengthen discipline within the party came to an end.

In August 1966 a new National Conference on Organization again decided to undertake a major structural reform project. This was later confirmed by the Chillán National Ordinary Congress held in November 1967. (The new scheme adopted can be examined in Fig. 1.5, p. 34).

The party was entering the 1970s with the same faulty organization that had allowed discipline, verbosity and the fragmentation and diffusion of power. But now the problem had been compounded by other developments. The simple, small party apparatus of the 1930s, which had had to cope with eight Regional Committees and twenty-one Section Committees, had now became a mass, class-based party with strong ideological and political commitments. It covered the whole of Chile with thirty-two Regional Committees, 184 Section Committees and an estimated 854 *núcleos* in which 80,000 members were involved.[28]

PSCh STRUCTURE, 1967–70

Figure 1.5 shows the structure given to the party by the Twenty-Second General Ordinary Congress, held in Chillán in 1967. It involved a detailed distribution of power (including a system of both vertical and horizontal links and the description of the degree of centralization and/or decentralization).

The very detailed character of the charter approved in Chillán in 1967 tried in fact, for the first time 'to leave nothing to the leader's or the member's imagination: all was there, in writing, in order to avoid repetition of the faults of the pasts. We sincerely hoped to overcome indiscipline and irresponsibility, because now anyone in doubt would have only to go to what had been previously stated to cover the specific situation'.[29]

The new established party's internal apparatus created in fact a very strong system of general articulation, an extremely centralized power structure and a reinforced system of vertical links. All this helped to affirm both the desire for centralization and the need for a strong general articulation system. It can certainly be said that the general ideology behind the new bureaucratic apparatus was the same as that behind the old and already faulty system which it was supposed to replace. Like the scheme approved in December 1953 in Santiago, the new one envisaged strong centralization, reinforcement of the system of vertical links while at the same time weakening the system of horizontal links and, consequently, a system of strong articulation. The great difference was in the extent to which each scheme had stipulated the actual methods of working. While the old system had been full of ambiguities which had permitted all kinds of interpretations, the new system established a detailed code of practice.[30]

At the top, a Central Committee of forty-five members and a smaller Political Commission of nine members whose power was derived from the Central Committee were established.

The character of the vertical organization remained unchanged: Regional and Section Committees and *núcleos* formed the skeleton of the party bureaucratic machinery. In order to facilitate the 'technical' aspects of the increasingly complicated Chilean political life, departments with clear-cut powers and functions were created: 'No longer would people go around asking who has to do this or that, just to find that nobody is doing it, or, worse, is going to do it'.[31] The departments were those of defence, labour, housing, peasants, propaganda, political education, municipalities, solidarity, elections, organizations and finance, the entire structure resembling in fact a ministerial cabinet. All departments would depend on the Political Commission and the Central Committee jointly.

These *ad hoc* organizations with autonomous bureaucratic structures, were created to deal with women's, youth and parliamentary matters, respectively. These bodies were supposed to have organizations of their own, but were still absolutely responsible towards the Central Committee and their actions guided by the rules and ideology of the party.

To assist the Central Committee and the secretary-general in administering the vertical system, a Department of Organization and Control was created and given very strong powers. They were to see to the discipline of all members and leaders and that violations be punished.[32]

At the bottom, the *núcleos* were clearly established, for the first time, as both deliberative and administrative bodies.

As *deliberative bodies*, the *núcleos* were supposed to have a very flexible internal system of debate and discussion, but with the sole aim of 'invigorating' the party:

'Invigoration' was understood as the process by which the party maintains a system of permanent discussion of ideological and practical, concrete political matters at all levels of its bureaucratic structure. This, on the other hand, shall be done internally, without putting in danger the party's official stance on any matter. Proper representations can be done to immediately superior bodies, and not to other bodies. It is for the Central Committee, at the top, to interpret the party's stance, to determine policies, etc. Resolutions cannot be adopted by anybody, other than the Central Committee, but petitions can and should be presented, whenever it is judged appropriate, to the proper bodies.[33]

As *administrative bodies*, the *núcleos* should comply with the party's resolutions and implement them when necessary. Policies of a broad nature were to be implemented by Regional and Section Committees.

During the three years from 1967 to 1970, the party apparently began to correct some of is 'normal' defects in organization. According to a report submitted in May 1970 to the Central Committee, 'our party can say now that it functions as a Leninist organization'.[34]

The findings of the report were confirmed by the opinions of five Central Committee members that at the time of the Chillán Congress were very active in the party's organization. Three of them were members of the Commission which wrote the report, and all five had been engaged in part-time organizational tasks, especially commissioned by the party, from 1967 to 1970.[35] These findings can be summarized as follows:

1. The enactment of the Chillán scheme was considered as the most important achievement in the party's organizational history. For the first time it clearly established roles concerning the obligations and powers of particular bodies. Overlapping was still possible, but proved more difficult than before. For the first time the scheme also established in detail the system of internal relationships and centralization, which resulted in a general system of strong articulation that was working reasonably well in 1970.

2. The level of disobedience observed in the *núcleos* before 1967 was greatly reduced. The establishment of the deliberative executive role for the *núcleos* enabled the members to discuss ideology and policies without having to violate discipline but at the same time allowing the possibility for them to be administrators of the party's policies. Superior bodies, notably Regional and Section Committees, apparently learned from experience and began to provide good and expedite channels of communication, with the Central Committee and the Political Commission.

3. The 'sectorization' of the party observed earlier quickly disappeared, apparently as a result of the clarification of their power and duties within the Chillán scheme and the new areas open for participation.

4. Consequently, vertical links worked well (horizontal links were practically eliminated) and centralization was strong and efficient. The general system of articulation was stronger than ever, a fact that was reflected in the reduction of punishments to members during this three-year period. There were only three suspensions and no expulsions. Given the impressive growth of the party, the new sense of discipline and control appeared as a truly impressive and valuable achievement after more than thirty years of disorganization at all levels.[36]

CONCLUSIONS

1. The party fought hard to establish a rational system of internal management, enjoying in the last ten years of its development a strong system of vertical links. This was aimed at reinforcing discipline and at preventing the disobedience so common within the party's previous structure.[37]
2. Consequently, the system of horizontal links deteriorated considerably, to the detriment of internal democracy, as inter-body relationships came to be severely restricted.
3. Although the above-mentioned phenomena were related to the trend towards extreme centralization, general articulation processes continued to be as weak as those betwen 1940 and 1967. Only during the first six years of the party's development in the 1930s was general articulation strong, probably because such factors as the relatively smallness and the initial enthusiasm of the party prevented it from undesirable organizational developments.

The failure to achieve a strong general articulation system was, indeed, the major internal problem the party had to face throughout the years—a matter for grave concern in a self-declared Marxist party.

NOTES

1. Maurice Duverger, *Political Parties* (Methuen, London, 1972), p. 56.
2. Duverger's typology of internal party structure will be used (see Figs. 4.1 and 4.2). According to this typology, the PSCh has always worked with what Duverger calls *direct structure* (as different from *indirect structure*), the first based on direct affiliation of members to a party, and the second to affiliation through

other bodies (trade unions, associations, etc.) which become affiliated as such, thus associating individual people indirectly to a given party. As for the other features of Duverger's typology (namely, the problems of *general articulation* and related matters, such as *centralization* and *decentralization*, *vertical* and *horizontal links* and the overall problem of a *weak* vs. a *strong* articulation), the party exhibited different schemes that are analysed throughout this chapter (see Duverger, *op. cit.*, pp. 4–61). Figures 4.1 and 4.2 explain this with greater clarity.

3. Other adjustments were made in 1937, 1944, 1947, 1949, 1957 and 1965, but they were minor ones.

4. These elements are included as basic requirements for a workable internal party structure, in the following documents: *Party Organization*, internal documents, mimeographed, Santiago, 1933, 1939 and 1953; *A Discussion on Our Faulty Organization*, confidential and restricted internal document, mimeographed, Santiago, August 1956. 'Towards a Leninist Party', report to the Central Committee, restricted document, Santiago, 1966.

5. *Why We Are for Centralization*, report to the Central Committee, internal document, mimeographed, Santiago, 1934, p. 3. This scheme, according to reliable old party leaders, was along the Leninist conception of the proletarian party, as opposed to the Luxemburgist conception which stressed the need for spontaneity in the party of the working class.

6. See Duverger, (*op. cit.*), pp. 4–61. A detailed description and discussion of these concepts is included there.

7. A. Pezoa, 'Report on the Indisciplinary Behaviour of Some Núcleos', internal and confidential party document, Santiago, December 1937, p. 7.

8. Marmarduke Grove, 'The Crisis of the Núcleos', special confidential report to the Central Committee, Santiago, 1938, p. 4.

9. This was greatly facilitated by the fact that Central Committee members were able to establish direct links with the *núcleos*, bypassing the secretary-general, as can be seen in Figure 1.1.

10. Grove (*op. cit.*), p. 9.

11. Salomón Corbalán, in a personal interview with the authors, August 1965.

12. Ibid.

13. Party Secretary General Marmaduke Grove stated in an internal Bulletin issued on August 1939 that 'our organization should be remodelled as soon as possible among more disciplined lines, in order to avoid *caciquismo*, put the *núcleos* into full work and build a bureaucratic machinery able to respond to the increasing requirements of the moment and those ahead' (Marmaduke Grove, *Special Bulletin to Members*, internal document, mimeographed, August 1939, p. 5).

14. Alejandro Chelén, *Los problemas del frente-populismo*, pamphlet, Santiago, Chile, 1941.

15. Néstor Maturana, speech delivered to the First Conference on Organization, Santiago, November 1939. The proceedings of the Conference were not available, but a fairly accurate unofficial record was kept in his private library by a party member that was himself a delegate to the conference. Most of the data used for the analysis of the conference was provided by him.

16. Duverger (*op. cit.*), pp. 52–60, developed the issue of party centralization and decentralization, according to the distribution of power among the various levels of the party's decision-making structures. The notion should not be confused with the concept of vertical and horizontal links, which refers to the co-ordination, exclusively technical, methods of internal party relationships. Decentralization, for Duverger, can be of a local, ideological, social and a federal nature. Local decentralization is commonly associated with a weak system of articulation, as was the case with the French Radical Socialist Party, and indeed with the PSCh during the 1939–53 period. For further details on this typology, see Duverger (*op. cit.*), pp. 4–60. A graphic view of the model, as it worked during the different stages of the PSCh's development, is provided in Figure 4.2.

17. 'Now that we have corrected our faulty internal structure', stated the Central Committee in 1941, 'we hope that internal co-ordination, communications and the overall system of a hierarchical Leninist structure will work well': Central Committee, *Our New Party*, letter to party members, mimeographed, 1941, p. 6. The document also denounced those 'hypocritical, bad Socialists who dared to divide our working-class organization', (p. 2), a reference to the small faction that left the party in 1940 over an ideological and bureaucratic dispute referred to above.

18. Important sources on this matter were: *Bulletins*, issued by the Central Committee on May 1943; August 1944; April and September 1945; July, September and December 1946; February, April, June and November 1946; January, March, May, November and December 1947. (*Bulletins*, internal and confidential party documents, mimeographed. These were distributed to all members through the various party bodies.)

19. Salvador Allende, *Why We Left the Party*, letter, mimeographed, to the members, issued on January 1952, p. 3. Discrepancies over the support for Carlos Ibáñez' candidature in 1952 remain, however, as the known major reasons for Allende's departure. He rejected such a standard and was himself a candidate with the support of the PSCh and the PCCh. Allende and his group considered Ibáñez a populist, a somewhat fascist-orientated politician, fundamentally opposed to Marxism.

20. Allende, ibid., p. 6.

21. Central Committee member for several times, Mario Garay performed duties as under-secretary-general for many periods. He was considered one of the most important party theoreticians and undoubtedly played a significant role in shaping the new party organization which emerged out of the Third National Conference on Organization.

22. The data on this period was mainly gathered from the following documents: (a) 'Unofficial Proceedings from the Third National Conference on Organization', manuscript, private library, Santiago, Chile; (b) internal party *Bulletins* of 1933, 1954, 1956, 1957, 1958, 1961, 1962, 1963, 1964, 1966 and 1967, mimeographed, Santiago, Chile (for use of members, only); (c) conversations with party leaders of the period, mainly Central Committee members Mario Garay, Federico Godoy and A. Zúñiga.

23. A. Zúñiga, Central Committee member and delegate to the Third Conference on Organization (*op. cit.*) in conversation with the authors.

24. In August 1966 the National Conference on Organization recommended that the secretary-general should be elected by the Central Committee from among its members, instead of from the National Congresses of the party, as before. The recommendation was later rejected by the XXII National Ordinary Congress held in Chillán in November 1967. The recommended measure is believed to have been planned to cut down the support enjoyed by Raúl Ampuero among the lower party bodies and to avoid his election in successive periods.

25. Central Committee, *Bulletin*, internal party document, mimeographed, Santiago, November, 1967, p. 3.

26. Ibid., p. 4.

27. Unofficial party records, manuscript document, private collection, Santiago, Chile.

28. Official party records, Santiago, Chile, 1967 (reserved and confidential).

29. Central Committee member Eduardo Paredes, in conversation with the authors, May 1971. The detailed character of the new charter would be an important factor in protecting the full practice of democratic discussion within the party, as we had the opportunity to observe between 1967 and 1973.

30. See *Principios Orgánicos y Estatutos del Partido Socialista de Chile*, Ediciones 'Pasos', Juventud Socialista, Documento Téorico No. 1, (Prensa Latinoamericana, Santiago, 1969). The document is an acute testimony of accuracy. The previous organizational schemes were normally printed by the mimeograph system, its diffusion was very restrictive and the content vague and full of lags.

31. Central Committee member Edmundo Serani, in conversation with the authors, July 1973.

32. Previous schemes also contemplated a Department of Organization and Control, but it normally appeared inserted among other departments, with very diffuse powers, with the exceptions already mentioned in this chapter, and, furthermore, the notable exception of the 1967 Chillán Charter.

33. Central Committee member Victor Barberis, in conversation with the authors, July 1973.

34. *Special Report on the Results of the Chillán Organization System*, reserved and confidential document, Central Committee, mimeographed, Santiago, August, 1970.

35. Edmundo Serani, Erick Schnake, Juan Valenzuela, Arsenio Poupin and Ariel Ulloa confirmed to the authors that the findings of the report were 90 per cent right, and some over-enthusiasm on what the report called 'Leninist practices' of the party (democratic centralism, internal democracy and level of political education) were dismissed by them as 'irrelevant', in view of the major achievements on the main subjects: discipline and organization. (Conversations carried out from January to August, 1973.)

36. In 1970 the party had already established 40 Regional Committees, 210 Section Committees and 970 *núcleos*, with an estimated 95,000 members. The membership went up to 120,000 in 1971, a few months after the triumph of the Popular

Unity coalition in September 1970. Some of the Regional Committees, though, had not been officially recognized by the Central Committee.

37. The assumed existence of factions within the party's different leadership structures no doubt played an important role in the repeated efforts by several Central Committees to consolidate strong vertical links and strong general articulation and centralization systems. However, as it has already been said, the political climate existing at the time of our field research, prevented us from gathering appropriate data on this subject. From the beginning it was made clear to us that information on this matter would not be made available, and we were in no condition to challenge that decision. To do otherwise we would have put in jeopardy other aspects of the research, for which we received reluctant collaboration.

5 The Image of the Party as Held by the Leadership

INTRODUCTION

The description and analysis of the PSCh's internal organization does not wholly explain the real nature of the party. Shortcomings in organization revealed by the examination of the model can be further explained by the image of the party held by the leadership.

The answers to a questionnaire designed to assess the political and organizational perceptions of the leaders (both at the top and intermediate levels) revealed a number of incongruities between the image of the party held by the leaders and actual ways in which the party was structured and organized.[1] In several cases a significant proportion of the leadership held opinions which contradicted reality as far as ideological and structural matters were concerned. On the whole it is clear that an erroneous perception of the party by its leaders led sometimes to controversial management of daily party affairs and the implementation of inappropriate policies.

To begin with, the question of the party either being a mass or a cadre organization is essential in answering the dilemma posed by the ways and means in which all party affairs are to be conducted. Not only the whole system of internal demands' articulation is here at stake, but also other issues as important as the type of organization, bureaucratic models and behaviour, and the execution of certain policies depend on the view of party organization.

Second, do leaders necessarily follow the 'official' ideology, as established in written documents, or do they on occasions represent views of their own or those of certain factions within the party?

Third, the view of class within the party held by the leadership is also relevant to the way in which the party is managed.

Apart from these factors, there are a number of opinions held by leaders on a variety of issues which in some way or another determined their approach to structural and organizational matters. In the pages that follow we shall try to summarize them.[2]

Figure 5.6 describes the social origin, the level of education and the times in office of the interviewed leaders.

THE IDEOLOGY OF THE LEADERSHIP

The internalization of the 'official' ideology

Internalization of what can be called 'official' ideology of the party appears to be fairly good. In fact, 60.9 per cent of the interviewed leaders adhered to

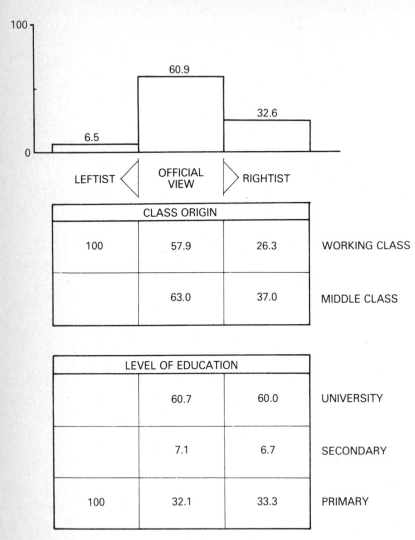

Figure 5.1 Internalization of the 'official' ideology in the PSCh leadership

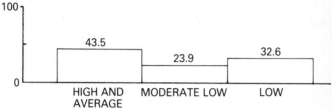

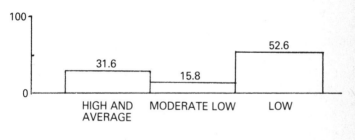

Figure 5.2 Political culture and leadership

party ideology according to certain documents that were presented to them.[3] Views to the left of official ideology were, however, found, in 6.5 per cent of the respondents, and 32.6 per cent exhibited views to the right of this official ideology (Fig. 5.1).

Adherence to the official ideology appears evenly distributed between the working-class and the middle-class leaders: 57.9 per cent of the working class and 63.0 per cent of the middle class agreed with official party ideology. It should be pointed out that, although all leaders of working-class origins showed 'leftist' deviations, 26.3 per cent of them had, at the same time, 'rightist' deviations.

Agreement with official party ideology also appears to be related to education (the more educated, the more 'officialist') and the number of times holding leadership positions (the more years in office, the more 'officialist'). Furthermore, adherence to 'rightist' deviations seemed to be linked to a higher education as well.

Figures here were as follows. Of those assuming 'official' views, 60.7 per cent had had a university education, and all the leaders who had occupied posts on more than three occasions shared the same views. This trend towards conformity among higher-educated leaders is further reinforced by the fact that of those deviating to the 'right', 60.0 per cent had had a university education.

Political Culture[4]

Political culture appears to be rather poor, as 56.5 per cent of the interviewed leaders fitted into either the 'moderately low' (23.9 per cent) or the 'low' (32.6 per cent) categories (Fig. 5.2).

Perhaps naturally enough in the Chilean context, working-class leaders appeared less politically educated than middle-class leaders (68.4 per cent of working-class leaders were grouped in the 'moderately low' and 'low' categories, 15.8 per cent and 52.6 per cent, respectively), but 51.8 per cent of middle-class leaders were grouped in the 'high' and 'average' categories.

The education factor offers a rather surprising result as 50 per cent of those leaders with a university education fit into the 'moderately low' and 'low' categories (30.8 per cent and 19.2 per cent, respectively). However, the other 50 per cent of university-educated leaders appear in the 'high' and 'average' categories (29.9 per cent and 23.1 per cent, respectively). The more politically educated groups appeared to be those with secondary education—66.7 per cent fell into the 'high' category—and the group with only primary education seemed to be the least politically educated —70.5 per cent fit into either the 'moderately low' (17.6 per cent) or 'low' (52.9 per cent) categories (Fig. 5.3).

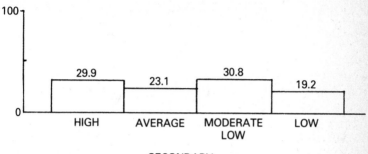

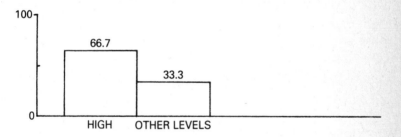

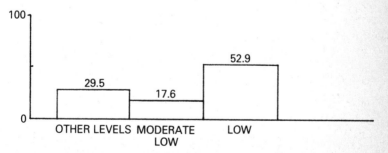

Figure 5.3 Political culture according to the level of education

Of the leaders who had occupied office *twice* or more 77.7 per cent appeared to be scoring either 'high' (33.3 per cent) or 'average' (44.4 per cent) in political culture while 63.6 per cent of those leaders occupying office *once* fell into either the 'moderately low' (33.3 per cent) or 'low' (30.3 per cent) categories. As leaders with one term of office constitute the majority of the sample (71.7 per cent), the results clearly indicate that a significant section of the leadership has a rather low political culture.

The model: the new socialist society

All the interviewed leaders agreed with the view that the ultimate model to be implemented in Chile should be a 'decentralized' socialist system (as opposed to a 'centralized-totalitarian', 'social-democratic/liberal', and 'Christian democratic'). This result indicates a significant degree of cohesion within the leadership regarding long-term ideological goals.

Tactics: concrete orientations in the process of building the socialist society[5]

A clear general tendency towards extreme leftism was showed here by the leadership. This trend was stronger in middle-class than in working-class leaders, and in better-educated than in less-educated leaders. This result suggests that the higher representation that the middle class has traditionally had within the party's leadership could help to explain the persistent extreme leftist policies pursued by successive leaderships.

PSCh ORGANIZATION AS PERCEIVED BY THE LEADERSHIP

The practice of democratic centralism

A clear majority (71.7 per cent) of the leaders thought that the principle of democratic centralism was normally practised within the party, as shown in Figure 5.4.

Working-class leaders tended to see the party as effectively practising democratic centralism, more so than the middle-class leaders (78.9 per cent against 66.7 per cent).

Of leaders with only primary education, 82.4 per cent thought that democratic centralism was a usual, day-to-day practice in internal party

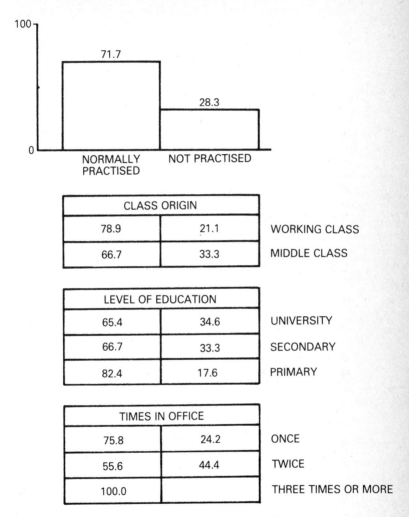

Figure 5.4 View of the leadership on the practice of democratic centralism

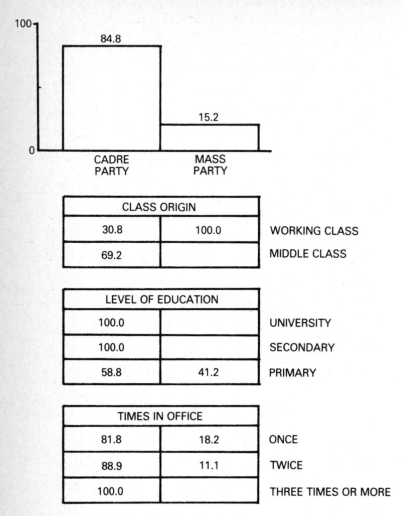

Figure 5.5 The leadership perception of the party's structure

procedures, but only 66.7 per cent of those with secondary education and 65.4 per cent of those with a university education shared the same view.

All leaders with three or more occasions in office were also of the same opinion, whilst a significant 75.8 per cent of those with only one term of office, and 55.6 per cent of those twice occupying leadership posts, shared the view that democratic centralism was a normal party practice.

Mass or cadre model?

Some 84.8 per cent of leaders thought that the party was structured as a Leninist cadre-type organization (Fig. 5.5). It is most significant that only 15.2 per cent believed the party to be a mass organization. It is also revealing that all the leaders viewing the party as a mass organization were of working-class origin, while of those maintaining the erroneous perception of the party as a Leninist cadre organization, 69.2 per cent were of middle-class origin, as against only 30.8 per cent of working-class origin. Furthermore, all the leaders with a university education had an erroneous perception of the party's internal model, all of them thinking it to be a Leninist cadre party.

The number of terms in office did not result in many diversified opinions. Significant percentages in every case viewed the party as a Leninist organization. If anything, seniority seemed to be related to an even more erroneous perception of the party's model.

The representation of social classes within the party

Class and membership

Some 52.2 per cent of leaders thought that the party not only included working-class members but petty bourgeoisie as well; 47.8 per cent thought that the party even included middle bourgeoisie.[6] As to the interests represented by the party in the political system, 84.2 per cent of working-class leaders believed it represented manual workers, peasants and segments of the petty bourgeoisie. The same opinion was held by 70.4 per cent of middle-class leaders.

Less-educated leaders held a far more accurate perception of the 'real' party than the more educated leaders, as shown by the fact that while 82.4 per cent of leaders with primary education appreciated the multi-classist membership of the party, only 30.8 per cent of leaders with a university education did. However, this multi-classism is in fact perceived erroneously if a more elaborate answer is asked for: only 17.6 per cent of leaders with primary education saw it as comprising both working class and medium bourgeoisie, whilst 69.2 per cent of leaders with a university education held the same view.

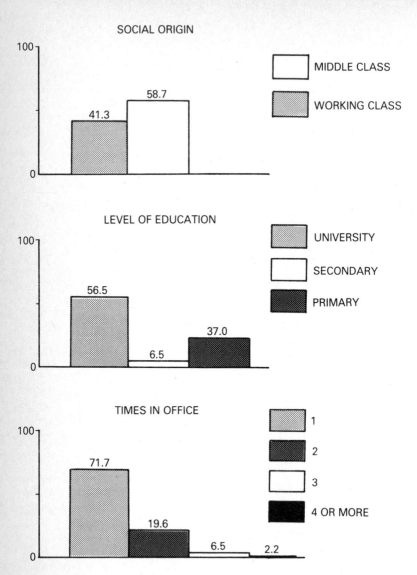

Figure 5.6 Social origin, level of education and times in office of interviewed leaders

Senior leaders seemed to hold more accurate perceptions on this matter, as indicated by the fact that *all* of those with three or more termns of office perceived the party as both a working-class and a middle-class organization.

Class and leadership

Some 58.7 per cent of leaders realized that the party leadership did not in fact exactly reflect class membership. Middle-class leaders seemed to be more conscious about this than working-class leaders (66.7 per cent against 33.3 per cent, respectively). Furthermore, more-educated leaders held a far more accurate perception than less educated-ones, as 65.4 per cent of leaders with secondary education and 66.7 per cent of leaders with a university education shared this view, against 47 per cent of leaders with only a primary education.

ANTI-COMMUNISM IN THE PSCh

The feelings of the leaders towards the PCCh was an important focus for inquiry, given more than twenty years of Socialist-Communist alliance in Chile.

The past and present character of the alliance

Exactly half of the leaders showed 'moderate antipathy' towards the PCCh, while only 6.5 per cent expressed 'open sympathy'. This result suggested that the pattern of Socialist-Communist relationships, both in the past and at present, had been rather unsatisfactory. Furthermore, this view is widely shared by both working- and middle-class leaders, as indicated by the 68.4 per cent and 66.6 per cent, respectively, that fitted into either the categories of 'open' or 'moderate' antipathy towards the PCCh. The same similarity could be observed in the case of both more- and less-educated leaders.

Socialist-Communist relationships in the future

The above-mentioned findings contrast with the results of the survey regarding the system of relationships in the future. In fact, 71.7 per cent of the leaders showed a 'moderate trustful' attitude towards the PCCh in any necessary future co-operation between the two parties, whilst 28.3 per cent went further, their views fitting into the 'strongly trustful' category. No leaders revealed 'distrustful' attitudes.

Sino-Soviet dispute

The Sino–Soviet dispute provided some insight into the nature of the party's anti-communism. The strong pro-Moscow line of the PCCh obviously caused some opposition by members of the PSCh. Only 13 per cent of the interviewed PSCh leaders considered the Soviet Union as the 'correct' party in the dispute. Furthermore, the 45.7 per cent who did not want to commit themselves, and expressed no allegiance to any party in the dispute, can be viewed as presenting the 'diplomatic' answer aimed at avoiding criticisms of the 'brother' party. The 19.6 per cent that named China as the 'correct' party in the dispute was indeed the group aligned to the more extreme leftist positions in the party.

The dilemma of international socialist solidarity

The extent of the criticism of communism was emphasized by the position of the leaders on the question of international socialist solidarity. Some 65.2 per cent of the leaders showed categoric dissatisfaction with the aid given by Eastern European countries to the Popular Unity government. Both poor political support and the lack of financial help were considered as the main shortcomings in this relationship.

Criticism in this respect was stronger among the middle-class than the working–class leaders (63.3 per cent and 36.7 per cent, respectively), and no more than 15.2 per cent considered this solidarity to be 'appropriate' or 'satisfactory'. It was also clear that of the less critical leaders, 71.4 per cent were of working–class origin and only 28.6 per cent of middle-class origin. Furthermore, educated leaders were more openly critical, as indicated by the fact that of those considering the aid as 'unsatisfactory', 60 per cent had had a university education.

CONCLUSIONS

1. Although the internalization of the 'official' ideology appears to be reasonably acceptable, leaders of working-class origin tend to show deviations to the left more than middle-class leaders. This is a rather surprising result, as a generally accepted theoretical assumption suggests that middle-class leaders would show stronger left-wing tendencies than working-class leaders.[7]

A tentative explanation for this result could be the existence, within the leadership, of 2 per cent of leaders of a distinct bourgeois origin. This pheno-menon, in our opinion, created suspicions and contributed to building a class barrier between leaders of different class backgrounds. Working-class leaders presumably reacted in the described way as a reaction to an assumed danger of the party moving to the right as a consequence of too many middle- and lately, 'high'-class leaders in the highest bureaucratic structures of the party.

2. Political culture appears to be definitely poor as a whole (see Figs. 5.2 and 5.3). Not surprisingly, working-class leaders, who are at the same time less educated, tend to know less of a standard political culture than middle-class leaders.

Leaders with a university education, however, appear to know less than leaders with only a secondary education. This could be due to the fact that leaders with secondary education tended, generally, to take more, internal political education courses than leaders with a university education, who wrongly assumed they already knew all that was needed.

The low level of political education is of the utmost relevance to the organization and behaviour of the party. Furthermore, it should not be forgotten that this survey shows trends in the 1973 leadership, when mass communications were at their peak in Chile (national TV and radio, gener-ous editorial policies, broad newspaper coverages, etc.). We assumed the level of communication to be even lower in the past. The consequences of this need hardly be emphasized. They can provide explanations for a wide variety of issues, ranging from the organizational vacuums and insufficiencies, to the contradictions in the handling of policies and the expression of a common ideology.

3. Generally, a variety of issues exhibited radical leftist trends (the socialist 'model' to be created in Chile, revolutionary tactics, concept of justice, anti-communism 'from the left') in the leadership. All these were issues with a strong overall ideological content on which the party always tended to exhibit extreme-leftist leanings. The results came only to confirm the image of the party as left of the PCCh.

This result explains the continued, persistent extreme-leftist behaviour of the party as a whole. It also confirms what Charles A. Micaud called 'the intellectualism of party leaders and militants, which leads to a structural incapacity to present realistic, concrete programs that might be the basis for responsible action in Parliament'.[8]

4. Most of the party leaders believed the party was structured and worked along cadre (Leninist) lines. This is a gross misconception of the real struc-ture and organization of the party, which was clearly organized and worked along mass-type lines. The main consequences of this mistaken perception were:

(a) Mismanagement of internal party affairs as the top leaders presumed an organization that in fact did not exist.

(b) Misinterpretation of the membership's goals, as the lack of communication channels worked against a normal process of internal articulation.

(c) Non-implementation of party decisions at various levels.

Briefly, the rather loose, flexible organization of mass parties required a certain pattern of behaviour on the part of the leaders. The fact was that their real behaviour reflected their erroneous perception of the party as a cadre party, along Leninist lines.

5. Another important organizational fault was revealed by the fact that most of the leaders viewed the practice of democratic centralism as a grass-root reality within the party. In fact, as it has already been explained in this work, this was not so, at least in the case of the intermediate leadership bodies, which tended to disregard orders from top-level officers (Central Committee and Political Commission).

6. Within the party leadership the middle classes were over-represented, a fact that no doubt determined the character of certain procedures and policies. Furthermore, a substantial sector of the leadership was aware of this over-representation. This did not provoke, however, a conscious, concerted effort aimed at correcting this deficiency, but rather the matter was always treated with the utmost indifference.

7. The nature and extent of the anti-communist feeling revealed by the survey only confirmed previous assumptions on the subject. This feeling was naturally exacerbated by the poor showing of Eastern European countries during the Allende administration. The fact that Allende himself was a member of the party is also important; indeed, he made available confidential information to PSCh leaders which reaffirmed the already widespread belief that there was insufficient solidarity with Chile.

Anti-Soviet views undoubtedly held by a significant proportion of Socialist leaders in 1973, did not preclude them, nevertheless, from considering the Socialist–Communist alliance as a *sine qua non* condition for the successful pursuit of the attempt to establish Socialism in Chile. This is, in our opinion, not a contradiction but rather demonstrative of the fierce independence that has characterized the party throughout its history.[9]

NOTES

1. Forty-six leaders were interviewed, (thirty-six distributed through three Regional Committees, and ten members of the Political Commission of the Central Com-

mittee). The survey was carried out in Chile, in 1973. So, all the data shown in this chapter refer to the year 1973, unless otherwise stated.

2. The central purpose of the survey is to provide data on the extent of 'accurate' or 'inaccurate' perceptions of the leaders on the more relevant issues regarding structure and organization. The data available is certainly insufficient to support more ambitious conclusions covering other subjects, such as general patterns of behaviour.

3. Official statements and statutes representing different periods were used.

4. *Political culture* is not used here in the generally accepted manner but is used to refer to the level of *political knowledge*. The authors realize that the term 'political culture' refers to a wide range of subjects, but it was felt that within the context of this research, a term such as 'culture' would be more acceptable than the term 'knowledge', which would be too restrictive.

5. *Tactics* are understood as short- and medium-term measures aimed at the building of a given *strategy*, understood as a long-term ideological and political model.

6. *Middle bourgeoisie* was defined by the interviewees as a group whose activities are generally of an 'exploitative' nature (businessmen employing salaried labour in a limited form, but with productive units heavily dependent on the owner's own work). *Petty bourgeoisie* was considered as part of the higher-paid professional strata, at the private, state and international organization's levels.

7. Robert Michel's *Political Parties* (Dover, New York, 1959) contains this view. Also in the same vein: Hugo Frühling, 'Capas Medias en Chile', unpublished social sciences thesis. University of Chile, Santiago, 1973. This phenomenon is contradictory to the behaviour of the middle class in society at large, which tends to be conservative (see John Raynor, *The Middle Classes* (Penguin, London, 1969), and Herman Lebovics, *Social Conservatism and the Middle Classes in Germany (1914–1933)*, (Princeton University Press, Princeton, NJ, 1969).

8. Quoted by Joseph La Palombara, 'Political Party Systems and Crisis Governments', *Midwest Journal of Political Science*, Vol. II, No. 2, May 1958, p. 119. He refers to Micaud's observations in 'French Political Parties: Ideological Myths and Social Realities' in Sigmund Neumann (ed.), *Modern Political Parties* (University of Chicago Press, Chicago, 1956).

9. Ernst Halperin, *Nationalism and Communism in Chile* (MIT Press, Cambridge, Mass., 1965) sustains this view.

PART II

PSCh under Military Rule (1973–85)
a Study in Fragmentation

6 Integration or Mobilization: A Socialist Dilemma

INTRODUCTION

The outstanding feature of the PSCh under the military rule is the malignant spreading of breakaway factions to the extent that there are now over twenty groups which claim to be Socialist offspring. How can this seemingly endless process of fragmentation be explained?

In contrast to the PCCh, whose history is cut through by long and intense periods of repression,[1] the PSCh had enjoyed in the past the leniency of the ruling élites, either because the 'costs of tolerance' were lower than the 'costs of suppression', or because the ruling élites envisaged that the PSCh could be 'bought over' into the political system as a kind of legitimate opposition. Riding on the crest of the big waves of popular unrest which have regularly swept Chile in the past forty years, the PSCh held cabinet posts in five administrations before taking up the reins of government in 1970. Most of them were disappointing experiences which brought about party strife, but this harsh, soul-searching exploration led to the commitment, clearly stated at the Twenty-Second Ordinary Congress of Chillán (1967), not to play into the hands of the oligarchy any longer. The political erruption of the masses during the Allende administration overstepped the 'tolerance mark' of the system, convincing the ruling élites that the old, highly sophisticated but ailing political system needed to be scrapped.

The replacement of the liberal democratic system by an authoritarian régime accounts for the state of fragmentation of the PSCh. Despite its anti-status-quo claims, the PSCh had lived in symbiosis with the political environment: it was the severance of this relationship which altered the chemical composition of the PSCh. What role has the PSCh played in Chile's political system? The party's own perception of itself was, of course, that of a "revolutionary vanguard", but such a view was contested from several quarters. James Petras has described the PSCh in terms of its integrating function: "the parties of the Left obtained the right to negotiate, their legitimacy was admitted by the political élites, and they became the mouthpiece of a strata of the organised industrial workers. By the same token, however, they relinquished their role as mouthpieces of all the working class'.[2] This was due, Petras says, to the fact that the PSCh was controlled by a parliamentary élite which replaced mass mobilization with low-grade parliamentary hokum.[3] More recently, Ian Roxborough *et al*. have argued that 'the Socialists have clearly been divided into a revolutionary current (usually with a bare majority of the party's supporters behind it) and a reformist current closely associated with the PCCh'.[4] Roxborough *et al*. sustain that even during the Allende administration the parties of the Left were unable 'to provide their supporters with the political means to erect a socialist order out of the resources of the bourgeois state'.[5] There is one common strand in Petras and Roxborough: it is the perception of a socialist party solidly incorporated into the bourgeois political system and incapable of leading a process of social mobilization towards the building of a socialist order. The PSCh could not be distinguished from the European socialist parties which, despite their working-class grass-roots, are geared to the bourgeois order and oppose all brands of the revolutionary ideology.

In the preceding chapters, the PSCh was described as a mass party, with a permanent organization, wide and stable electoral support and a nationally responsible leadership: this is the 'integrating' face of the PSCh. At the same time, there has been almost complete antagonism between what has been considered as society's goal and those considered party goals. The PSCh has never forsaken its Marxist ideology, and although there were occasions when it was willing to collaborate with bourgeois parties, these associations almost always led to party strife and splits. A more balanced perception would suggest the co-existence of two contrasting but dialetically linked tendencies: a mobilizing, radical, impulse, and an integrating function which might have facilitated the political control of the masses by the ruling élites but which did not necessarily make the masses well mannered.[6] It is the conflicting co-existence of both these tendencies that distinguishes the PSCh from 'the Socialist parties of Europe that rejected the parliamentary framework [but] were often ultimately socialized into the democratic constitutional order'.[7] The domestication of European socialism can be attributed to the lack of a basis for intense class conflict, while in Chile economic and social imbalances and the rigid, old-fashioned attitudes of the ruling élites contributed to make the class-cleavage pattern so apparent that the phrase 'expression of the democratic class struggle' is particularly apt to describe the Chilean political system.[8]

THE CHILEAN ROAD TO SOCIALISM (1970–73)

The Popular Unity experience is the only historical instance of a particular strategy, the 'peaceful road to socialism', whose goal was to build a socialist order within the framework of parliamentary democracy. Chile was, after all, one of the most solid, stable, modern democracies of Latin America. Could the resiliency of its political institutions be stretched beyond the boundaries of the capitalist system? At the Congress of La Serena (1971), a few months after Allende was inaugurated as Chile's president, the PSCh was aware of the limitations of the 'peaceful road': 'The proprietary classes still possess all the means of dominance of a ruling class. The actions of the Government are obstructed by bourgeois institutions and by the growing resistance displayed at all levels by the national and international reactionary forces'.[9]

Although the Congress made extolling references to the 'revolutionary impetus of the masses led by their working-class parties', it advised that this energy should not be set free but channelled through the institutional network. The immediate task facing the party was 'to create as soon as possible, during this government, the conditions for transforming the capitalist system into a socialist system'.[10] This statement reflected the dual nature of the PSCh, on the one hand socialized into the democratic constitutional order, on the other hand committed to erect a socialist régime. It is perhaps excusable that contemporary issues should be discussed in the light of past ideological debates: the old 'isms' (Trotskyism, Titoism, Maoism) don't die easily. However, although muddled with old ideological irrelevancies, the key issue for the PSCh (and indeed for the Popular Unity)—integration or mobilization—would still crop up. Some ideological trends were well disposed towards either one or the other. The Trotskyists, with their perennial warning of Thermidorian bureaucracies, were eager to see the masses solving their problems directly through self-organization as the setting for 'people's power'; for the Allendistas, it was the government who must take the lead in the building of the socialist order. In May 1971, President Allende urged the Members of Parliament:

not to obstruct the changes of the legal system. The replacement of the capitalist legal system by a socialist one, in accordance with the pace of the social and economic changes that we are making, depends on a realistic approach by the congress. A violent break with our institutions would open the doors to arbitrary acts and excesses which we want to avoid.[11]

In sharp contrast to this conception which conferred the leading role of building socialism upon the government, the mobilizing tendency argued that the government, encircled by bourgeois institutions, would be starved into submission if the masses did not push the revolutionary process beyond the boundaries of the democratic constitutional order. At the Plenary Session of Algarrobo (February 1973), Carlos Altamirano, Secretary-General of the PSCh, said that it was:

essential to build a true people's power. This power cannot be set up by fiat, it can only be achieved through the struggle of a grass-roots movement. Only those changes which are brought about by the masses are revolutionary. Reforms made by the government will distort the revolutionary process and the government itself will become reformist, bureaucratic and paternalistic.[12]

Altamirano, however, made certain qualifications to this acknowledge-ment of the leading role of the people, by stating that revolutionary changes would be the 'product of the common struggles of the government and the mobilization of the masses',[13] which in practice could only mean that the overall control of the revolutionary process lay in the hands of the govern-ment. The mobilizing tendency, which called itself the 'Revolutionary Tendency', was influential in the Trotskyist-minded *Cordillera* and *Centro* Regional Committees, who were committed to widening the bases of the people's power through the enlargement of workers' control, in the factories, on the farms, in the *poblaciones*, and the setting up of networks of popular organizations. Although the PCCh–PSCh alliance constituted the backbone of the Allende administration, the mobilizing tendency preferred to act in conjunction with the MAPU and the Christian Left (IC) (both left-wing breakaways from the Christian Democratic Party and members of the Popular Unity coalition) and the Movement of the Revolutionary Left (MIR) (an extreme left-wing split frm the PSCh which was not part of the Popular unity) in the *tomas de pobladores* (seizure of land by shanty-town dwellers), and the seizure of agricultural estates, mines and factories. In its extreme form, the mobilizing tendency argued for the creation of 'dual power'—an alterna-tive 'people's power' confronting the ruling élites outside the framework of capitalist institutions as opposed to the Popular Unity government, which had arisen as a power confronting that of the bourgeoisie within the bourgeois-democratic institutional system. The integrating current, on the other hand, held the view that revolutionary changes should be initiated and carried through by the government 'without failing to observe the capitalist rule of law'.[14] Joan Garces, one of Allende's political analysts, stated that 'people's power should not enter into conflict with the Popular Unity government and with the institutional system, but should be set up and work in harmony with the government apparatuses'.[15]

Mass organizations, which had made a first sporadic appearance in 1971 in the shape of workers assemblies in the factories, people's supply committees in poor and working-class suburbs, and peasants' councils in the rural areas, were to play a key role during the employers' strike of October 1972. The massive takeover of factories and distribution networks, and the creation of the *cordones industriales* (workers' committees co-ordinating a number of fac-tories), were largely responsible for the defeat of the employers lockout and paralysis of the country as the workers ran production, the transport of raw materials and finished products, and distribution in liaison with the *población* committees and peasants' councils. The *cordones* were promoted mainly by members of MIR, MAPU and the PSCh, but they were looked upon with suspicion by the Communist-controlled trade union federation (CUT), which saw in them a danger of 'parallelism'. The PSCh was now in favour of building and strengthening the *cordones* but, unwilling to collide with the PCCh, offered no concrete plan for organization beyond the spontaneity that had characterized their birth.

The PSCh had been a major agent of mass mobilization in Chile in the past precisely because of its integration into the liberal-bourgeois political system. It was through the PSCh that the working and low-middle classes had become aware of their distinctive class interests, and their demands had been channelled into the framework of parliamentary democracy. The fact that this integrating role had been performed without the party disavowing its revolutionary beliefs speaks well of the vitality and confident feeling of the PSCh. But now under the Popular Unity government these two modalities—integration and mobilization—were brought into a complex, contradictory relationship: on the one hand, mutual support; on the other, if not conflict, at least reciprocal obstruction. There can be little doubt that the Popular Unity government, without the watchful support of the masses, would have been compelled to compromise by the ruling élites, but, on the other hand, mass mobilization rendered the 'peaceful road to socialism' largely ineffectual since mass movements are not in the mood for all the parliamentary haggling and higgling. The 'peaceful road', for example, required careful negotiations with the Christian Democratic Party (PDC) to make sure that Allende's bills would be passed by Parliament, but, of course, during the bargaining process the government would have to give up something of its radical commitments and not come up to the masses' expectations precisely when the working class had developed a greater feeling of political competence. The Allende administration became embroiled in bitter arguments between those who accused the mobilizing tendency of obstructing the negotiations with the PDC, thereby isolating the working class and smoothing the opposition's path, and the mobilizing tendency who argued that the PDC, controlled by imperialism and the big bourgeoisie, would only enter into negotiations to suppress the revolutionary process. Under the growing influence of the mobilizing tendency, the PSCh refused to entangle itself with any sort of negotiation with the PDC despite Allende's requests, and in fact such talks collapsed over and over again as social antagonisms worked up to a climax.

In August 1973, on the eve of the military coup, a communiqué from ten PDC MPs stated that 'the Popular Unity government stands in open violation of the law and the constitution', and a week later the Chamber of Deputies declared in the same vein that the Allende administration had 'a regular pattern of behaviour' of transgressing the Constitution, addding that 'the

Armed forces cannot lend themselves to such partisan and minority politics'.[16] The foundations of the 'peaceful road to socialism' had been demolished by the opposition, and in the face of escalating right-wing violence, new employers' strikes and the imminence of a new military coup after the one which had been attempted in June 1973, it seemed to the mobilizing sector that the only possible way for the Allende administration to survive would be to resort to mass mobilization and armed struggle while the integrating sector saw a compromise as the only way forward.

The Congress of La Serena (1971) had recommended the creation of a 'defence committee' and the Central Committee had stated, in March 1972, that 'since 4 September 1970 the class struggle has reached a higher level of "permanent class confrontation" that is leading to a kind of armed struggle and which we must be prepared to face'.[17] But the PSCh, without any paramilitary experience, was unable to work out by itself any contingency plan of armed resistance, while Allende refused even to consider any suggestion of military arrangements for the defence of the government. After the idea of a 'single military leadership' put foward by the PSCh and MAPU in February 1973, had failed once again to make any impression on Allende, the PSCh made the attempt of turning 'people's power' into 'armed power', but it was too little and too late, and, in fact, it only gave the Armed Forces an excuse for raiding factories, rallying points, mass organizations' meeting places and political headquarters. Absurd as it may seem, the government had entrusted its own defence to the Armed Forces in spite of the unequivocal signs that a military plot was in the making.

As the 'institutional road' had been brought to a halt, suggesting that socialism could not be erected within capitalist institutionality, Allende decided that a plebiscite should be called to vote about the conflict between the government and the congress. But this decision—which the PSCh opposed on the grounds that it amounted to political surrender—would never become publicly known, as the military coup was to take place the very same day it was to be announced. In the early hours of 11 September 1973, as the news of the military takeover spread like wildfire, the Political Committee of the PSCh met only to conclude that a military defence of the government was impossible. Isolated points of resistance in factories and shanty-towns were easily overcome by the military. The 'peaceful road to socialism' had ended in a blood-bath.

THE CRISIS OF THE DEMOCRATIC CONSTITUTIONAL ORDER

It was already apparent by the 1960s that the ruling élites in Chile were going through a crisis of their economic and political capacities. Table 6.1 shows that in the period from 1960 to 1971 Chile's economic performance was consistently lower than the average for Latin America. And whilst in the 1940s the Liberal and Conservative parties managed to achieve 40 per cent of the vote, in 1965 they had to settle for less than 15 per cent. It is purely coincidental that the weakening political power of the right occurred as the economy grew increasingly ineffective? We may consider this 'coincidence' in the terms put forward by Anderson.[18] The roots of the crisis date back to the 1929 Great Crash, when the calm, tranquil neocolonial economy was rudely awoken by the world crisis and by the turbulent ideological conflicts which were storming the world. Urbanization, which rapidly increased in the 1930s, along with the ensuing growth and diversity of the economy, gave birth to new social forces. The urban masses and the middle class made their political debut with a bang. The PSCh is one element in this outburst, an outward sign that the ruling class's political power was crumbling. The middle classes, however, were gradually incorporated into the power system according to the pattern described by Anderson: newcomers pledged never to pursue redistributive policies at the expense of the old oligarchy; acceptance of the interests of all existing members was the price paid for admission to the club. In what Anderson calls a 'living museum', newcomers learned that admittance was dependent on rejecting 'forward strategies' of showdowns over basic allocations while traditional participants retained a veto power even though they could easily be outvoted by more modern actors. As a result of

Table 6.1 Economic performance of selected Latin American countries, 1960s (%)

1960–70	Chile	Brazil	Colombia	Region
GNP growth	66.5	99.0	76.0	83.0
GNP growth (per capita)	27.1	46.8	28.3	35.0
Exports growth	53.8	85.5	37.3	66.1
Imports growth	78.0	108.2	97.9	81.1
Manufacturing added value growth	93.2	119.3	92.7	110.0
Agricultural added value growth	33.7	70.8	44.7	49.7
Foreign public debt growth	262.7	166.5	346.5	199.4

Sources: Inter-American Bank of Development, *Economic and Social Progress in Latin America* (1976); *Cifras seleccionadas sobre America Latina* (1978).

these compromises, none of the élites had the necessary strength—or the will power—to reshape society in accordance with their exclusive interests.

A key point of the political foundations of Chile's liberal democratic system is apparent. The purpose of this submission to the institutional order was to render impossible any form of whimsical adventurism by any new élite. Every word of the Constitution, every piece of legislation, was intended to safeguard the 'sanctity' of the interests of those with power, and to block any attempt of reform by calling upon the abundant pool of politicians, bureaucrats and judges who were well and truly esconced within the institutional framework. On occasions, the up-and-coming élites tried to force their way into the 'oligarchy's club' using the threat of mobilizing the masses in order to gain entry; sometimes the right of entry was not due so much to the inner might of the élite but to their ability to manipulate and control the masses. In the 1960s it was precisely this skilful manipulation of mass politics which brought the PDC—the political expression of a new, modernizing élite—to power. The paralyzing effect of compromises within the power system resulted in an increasingly stagnant economy. Mamalakis has pointed out that the *desarrollista* policies in the 1960s led to a huge growth of the foreign debt, large outflows of much-needed hard currency, a chronic deficit in the balance of payments, and an impressive, although technologically backward, consumption industry.[19]

Regardless of the plausibility of this interpretation, it is significant that an analogous argument has been put forward by the military government. One military document has described Chile before September 1973 as 'one long period of decadence' which produced governments more vote-conscious than dedicated to the 'public interest'.[20] General Pinochet himself has pointed out that the 1973 military coup 'not only represents the destruction of an illegal and failed government but also provides a solution to the collapsing, ineffective political system by fulfilling the need to create a new order'.[21] His civilian advisers have put forward a more elaborated view:

The old institutional system was not only corrupted by demagogy and petty political interests, but had also become completely out of date and incapable of resolving contemporary problems which are of a social and economic nature. These problems must be studied and solved by a strong government with a capable and single vision which can provide a practical and efficient solution, and not by a system of weak political assemblies.[22]

During the period from 1973 to 1975, which García and Wells have called 'the years of the capitalist normalization',[23] the main objective of the junta was to eliminate all traces of the left and to re-establish the capitalist basis of the Chilean economy. All those benefiting from the capitalist normalization could, despite their differences, join the bandwagon of the faithful which supported the military dictatorship. However, in 1975 the first signs of dissent emerged quite dramatically. It became obvious that the military government was under the influence of a reactionary, quasi-fascistic right-wing and was not about to tolerate a return to the former system whereby all political and economic interests could be incorporated. The old democratic state, which was open to a whole range of pressures and was a willing arbitrator of conflicting interests, was now replaced by a bureaucratic-authoritarian state which abandoned all ideological and institutional pretensions of guaranteeing 'equal access' to influence government decisions. The state became impervious not only to the demands of the 'dangerous classes' but also to the needs of some sectors of the middle classes and the bourgeoisie.

The bureaucratic-authoritarian state set the foundations for a new economic model, inspired by Friedman's brand of monetarism and euphemistically called the *economía social de mercado* (the social market economy), which was based on (1) the 'subsidiary' role of the state and the privatization and deregulation of the economy, and (2) the opening of the economy to the international capitalist system—thereby transforming the country into an exports base. The model was aimed primarily against the import-substituting industry which had, politically and economically, reigned supreme for the previous two or three decades, and which was now accused of 'squandering' Chile's economic resources and distorting its productive capacities. The new 'export-led' model of development would 'rectify the inefficient, unproductive and artificial distribution of resources carried out during the import-substitution period'.[24] Domestic demand would be restricted, technologically backward industry would be eliminated, and resources would be transferred to dynamic, expanding exporters and high-tech entrepreneurs.

The attempt to restore capitalist profitability in Chile through radical surgery is now well known.[25] By 1979 five economic clans controlled 53 per cent of the assets of the 250 largest companies in the country.[26] It is one of the many ironies of history that the path to this reorganization of capital was smoothed by the existence of a public-ownership sector which had been widely enlarged by the Allende administration. The military junta not only returned the 259 companies which had been taken over by Popular Unity to their former owners but proceeded in earnest to denationalize all public corporations (except those which did not make profits that would attract private buyers), maintaining that privatization would increase competition and efficiency in the economy. The result was a changed balance in the ownership of Chilean industry in favour of monopolistic conglomerates. The state of the world economy played a substantial role as American banks were keen to lend much of the idle OPEC surpluses on deposit to voracious Third World countries. Huge profits were made by the conglomerates, which lent at extremely high interest rates in Chile what they had borrowed at low interest rates in the international market to credit-thirsty entrepreneurs who had suddenly found themselves exposed to foreign competition. Many of these entrepreneurs, however, went bankrupt as the government followed deflationary policies which shrunk the domestic market. In 1978, service industries like banking and insurance had expanded, but gross industrial output was lower than in 1974 and fixed-capital investment had been declining at an annual average rate of 1.3 per cent.[27]

The political realignments that became perceptible after 1975 must be seen in the light of this process of capital restructuring. The middle classes realized, with a feeling of mute impotence, that the control of the military government had fallen into the hands of an arch-conservative, money-grubbing élite which was not content with putting the clock back to 1970, as they had expected, but aimed at erecting an entirely new rigid, hierarchical and authoritarian social and economic order. By the end of 1974 the PDC protested that the extreme right was making every endeavour 'to impose a reactionary and dictatorial system upon Chile'.[28] And in December 1975 Eduardo Frei, the PDC leader, broke his cautious silence by writing a clear indictment of the violation of human rights, and the hardships of the working class and the middle classes. He denounced the fascist ideology of the élite which was mismanaging the government, causing an increasing concentration of power and wealth and he criticized the sale of public assets which had led to the appearance of 'colossal economic empires'.[29] The emergence of a kind of middle-class opposition made some dents in the steely armour of the military: eleven generals wrote to Pinochet requesting of him to put DINA—the Chilean secret police—under restraint and to moderate the 'shock treatment' which, in acquiescent obedience to the monetarist godfathers, was being experimented in Chile. Frei's strictures and the generals' requisition were not unconnected facts, but the Armed Forces remained fiercely faithful to Pinochet. The generals were forced to retire ahead of schedule, leaving Pinochet as the absolute master of the country and his civilian mentors free to indulge the sadistic fancies of monetarist discipline.

The nature of Pinochet's rule became a contentious issue among the socialist intellectuals. The discussion focused on whether the military dictatorship should be regarded as a 'fascist' régime or not. This may sound like another instance of the PSCh's taste for ideological verbosity (and, certainly, during the hotly contested debate nobody seemed aware that the concept of fascism was controversial in itself), but the real issue at stake was serious enough: the class nature of the bureaucratic-authoritarian state and the class alliance line which the party should pursue. In short, if Pinochet's autocratic régime was the brutal, blatant rule of the bourgeoisie, the Left could only rely on its own strength. But if it stood for the most reactionary sector of the monopolic grand bourgeoisie, the Left should set up a broad 'anti-fascist front' including all social and political forces opposed to the military dictatorship—in practical terms, the middle classes and the PDC. The 'blatant rule' argument seemed appropriate for the years of 'capitalist normalization' (1973-5) and the 'anti-fascist front' for the new capitalist scenario between 1975-9. By mid-1975 the editorial of *PS Informa*—the mouthpiece of the PSCh's 'Dirección Interior' (see Chapter 7)—stated that the fascist dictatorship 'is in contradiction not only with the working class and its historical goals but also with significant social sectors who had initially supported the overthrowing of the Popular Unity government'.[30] But the suggestion of an alliance between the Left and the PDC could not then be stomached either by the PSCh or the conservative PDC leadership. The 'Dirección Interior' maintained that the inclusion of the PDC in the anti-fascist front, was of course important, but it would not materialize 'as long as its leadership represent the interests of the monopolistic bourgeoisie and imperialism'.[31] The PDC repaid the PSCh's dismissive mood in kind. Patricio Aylwin, the PDC's chairman, turned down any hint of coming to terms with the 'Marxist Left' while pointing out that the party would make every endeavour to reach agreement with those who had opposed Allende and with the 'democratic' sectors of the Armed Forces. His successor, Andrés Zaldívar, followed the same path when he suggested forming 'a wide alliance of humanists' which would still exclude the Left, although it acknowledged a role for them once democracy had been restored. A left-wing minority in the PDC had denounced the military coup from the beginning and talked in favour of an alliance with the Left. In fact, a meeting between the PSCh, the Radical Party, the Christian Left, and the PDC's left wing took place in Colonia Tovar (Venezuela) in July 1975, but this meeting was dismissed with scorn both by the PSCh and the PDC. The PSCh affirmed that the meeting had been organized without proper consultation and that any 'bourgeois alternative' to Pinochet would be rejected,[32] while in April 1975 only 3 per cent of the PDC leadership voted on building a broad coalition with the Left.[33]

In 1977 the Chilean economy, having plunged the depths, seemed to take off. The military government spoke of the 'Chilean miracle', and in 1980 *The Economist*, which was in the peak of its flirtation with monetarism, reported, admiringly, that Chile's 'GDP which shrank some 12 per cent in 1974 has grown at an average rate of nearly 8 per cent over the past three years'.[34] It is sad that the good life does not last for ever. Two years later, the Chilean economy fell into a new slump, the price of copper (Chile's main export) dropped sharply, industrial output declined by 20 per cent, and GDP plummeted by 14 per cent, cancelling out the high growth rates of the previous three years.[35] As had happened before, the state of the world economy played the leading character. World-wide sluggishness, high rates of interest, the shrinking world trade, the protectionist mood of the industrial countries and the falling prices of primary raw materials were only some of the symptoms of a malaise in the world economy which could not spare Chile from entering into recession. American banks suddenly woke up to a reality consisting of bankrupted Latin American countries about to default. Chile's foreign debt had skyrocketed from $4,010 million in 1975 to $17,000 million in 1983. Most of these loans were pocketed by the economic clans which used them as 'hot money' or spent them on luxurious imports. The huge expansion of a short-term speculative economy was greatly encouraged by the government's policy in 1979 to peg the peso to the dollar and hence curb Chile's inflation. Since 1981, however, the peso became overvalued—partly because of the strength of the dollar—and the country's competitiveness fell dramatically. Once foreign bankers had refused to finance current-account deficits, large devaluations were unavoidable. The first devaluation took place in June 1982, prompting the bankruptcy of the entire private financial system. In November 1981 the government had already intervened in four defaulting banks, but matters were brought to a climax in early January 1983 when the management of most of the private financial system passed to the state. The two biggest conglomerates, those of Javier Vial and Fernando Larraín, were virtually terminated. Rolf Luders, the last of the 'Chicago boys', was fired from the cabinet.

Economic collapse was accompanied by a resurgence of open political activity. The devaluation of the peso in mid-1982 brought so much confusion and disillusionment—even among government supporters—that it can be said that Chile entered a new political phase characterized by a wider and more outspoken oppositon and where the socialist Left, despite its domestic quarrels, was increasingly accepted as a political actor. In September 1983, in the heat of massive demonstrations against Pinochet, a wide-ranging 'Democratic Alliance' (AD) was established, with the PDC playing the pivotal role and including a constellation of smaller parties ranging from the right (the Republican Right) to the left (splits from the PSCh). AD's goals was to achieve recognition as a kind of 'legitimate opposition' by the government in order to open negotiations for the re-establishment of political democracy in Chile. The PDC had finally realized that an agreement with the Left was desirable, but were still unwilling to include the PCCh or the extreme Left. AD's inimical actions propelled the PCCh to set up an alternative coalition—the 'Popular Democratic Movement' (MDP) with the 'residual' Left, which willy-nilly, took the role of the 'hard opposition'. The MDP advocated all forms of struggle against

Pinochet and refused to compromise over the immediate and unconditional departure of the military from the government.

It was appropriate for the PSCh—that is, for the various factions of the PSCh—to take part in both of these coalitions as it kept in line with the party's old dilemma: integration or mobilization. If in the past these conflicting tendencies (which reasserted themselves under different guises at each historical period) resulted in one single impulse towards growth and maturity, if these opposing currents flowed into a single mass party which was both integrated into the political system and committed to erecting a socialist order out of bourgeois institutions, now, in the new political scenario set up by the 1973 military coup, these impulses seemed to be increasingly drifting apart.

THE SOCIALIST DILEMMA

The PSCh's immediate reaction to the military coup was a scornful dismissal of the bourgeois political system:

For the urban bourgeoisie and the landed oligarchy in Latin America as well as for American imperialism, the rule of law is only good to the extent that it reinforces their power. But when they feel threatened by the strenght of the people, as happened in Chile, they are the first to raze democracy, freedom and pluralism to the ground and to set up a fascist dictatorship to preserve the substance of the capitalist régime.[36]

The PSCh was still committed to democracy, but it would be a new brand of democracy, a 'revolutionary democracy' which would ensure 'that the effective control of the state remains in the hands of the people'.[37] It seemed as if the PSCh's historical association with the liberal-democratic institutions had finally come to a conclusive end. And the party was quick to point out that 'those who killed democracy in Chile were not the Marxists'.[38]

The surfacing of a middle-class opposition to military rule, prepared to work with a 'reasonable' Left, seemed, however, to offer the PSCh a place in the sun which was too tempting (and too risky) to refuse. The socialist factions in the AD began to reassess the significance of democracy for the socialist utopia. To be sure, 'the main contradiction nowadays is between capitalism and socialism', but there are others, and notably among them is 'the contradiction between dictatorship and democracy'.[39] An important article published in *Pensamiento Socialista* in 1983 elaborates the political implications of this commitment to democracy. The socialist society will be 'a workers' democracy, not a dictatorship of the proletariat',[40] and not only 'dissidence within the ruling block of classes' will be permitted, but also 'the political organization of the old dominant classes'.[41] In the economic field, 'the socialist model distinguishes between public ownership over economic areas which are strategic for national development, and which will include co-operative societies and worker participation in ownership, and non-strategic economic areas under the control of private enterprise.[42]

The socialist factions in the AD were keen on giving the middle classes a definite assurance that the old socialist follies had been left behind for good. Socialism itself was not shelved but redefined in such terms as to render it harmless. Socialism, according to Ricardo Lagos, a distinguished intellectual, was 'a system which entrusts everyone with the task of organizing society and guarantees the independence of its intermediate organizations',[43] a definition of socialism so broad and vague that it could be endorsed by all members of the opposition. This was in sharp contrast to the resolutions which had been adopted in the Congress of Chillán (1967), when the party described itself as a 'Marxist–Leninist organization' aiming at 'establishing a Revolutionary State which will make Chile free from dependence and cultural and economic backwardness and will erect a socialist order'.[44] The 'National Agreement' of August 1985, sponsored by the Catholic Church and signed by the members of AD, stated that 'democratic values should rule our co-existence' and that 'the stability of the democratic system which is established demands the solemn commitment of all those who sign or support this document to carry out future political action with a spirit of loyalty to democracy, effective enforcement of the law and mutual respect, making it compatible with the institutional, economic and social principles mentioned herein'.[45] Democratic consensus, the document said, involves a basic agreement about social and economic structures. 'Democratic co-existence demands stability of the basic rules for the functioning of the economy, with the aim of ensuring social harmony and economic efficiency'.[46] The document laid out the picture of a mixed economy where 'state and private enterprise complement each other through a defined demarcation of roles and consequent division of tasks'.[47] The 'National Agreement', finally, emphasized that 'the right to private property, in terms of both material possessions and liquid assets, including the means of production, must be given constitutional guarantee'.[48] In short, the socialist factions who expressed their support of the 'National Agreement' had concluded that a stable democratic order required a basic consensus of values and structures which, in fact, amounted to the reconstruction of bourgeois hegemony.

Despite the apparent differences, the process of re-democratization which is now taking place in Latin America displays certain similarities which are worth considering. The political inability of the ruling classes to secure power within the framework of parliamentary democracy was of prime significance in bringing about the installation of bureaucratic-authoritarian régimes. The ruling classes, however, may now be re-establishing their hegemony—the military have 'softened' the masses, the ruling élites have persuaded the radical Left, using the method of violence and compromise, that democratic tolerance is the best deal they will get, and that they should keep themselves away from foolhardy plans of radical social and economic reform. The Left is taught that they themselves are the greatest losers when democracy is laid to waste, that the Left themselves are indeed to blame for their downfall because they induce social agitation to an unacceptable level, they encourage hopes for social change and they rock the political boat to such an extent that democracy is washed away and drowned.[49] The fact that bureaucratic-authoritarian régimes took the form of military dictatorships is particularly fortunate for the ruling élites. There is no doubt that the ruling classes were the mentors of the 'Southern Cone Model',[50] yet the tangible reality of military power was predominant in all spheres of society. Hence, the key role of the ruling classes in bringing about the bureaucratic-authoritarian régimes did not become apparent to everyone. This has allowed the ruling classes to disassociate themselves from a crumbling military rule and even to present themselves as the only alternative to military dictatorship. As Ricardo Lagos has put it:

The past ten years have enhanced the value of democracy as the answer to the dictatorship, and this common experience had led us to look at our past with an open mind and to spell out our mistakes which led to the downfall of our democratic system. In other words, we fell into the dictator's clutches because we were politically immature, because of the failure of many political sectors and the blindness of our ruling classes. If we want to rebuild the democratic system, we must seriously study the causes of its demise. Nobody can deny responsibility. It is true that there was foreign intervention, that many opposed necessary reforms, but it is also true that there was the attempt to carry on reforms which did not enjoy social support.[51]

A distinctive feature of all hegemonic projects is that they are never all-embracing, that all civilizations have their discontents. The PSCh factions who joined the MDP are unwilling to write off the mobilizing role of the party. Parliamentary democracy, they argue, cannot be considered in isolation from its social and economic framework. The old democratic system was made possible by the large post-war expansion of the world economy, but once Chile's process of substitutive industrialization met with unsurmountable obstacles, an intense struggle between classes for political control broke out. The attempts to resuscitate the democratic institutions, without questioning their capitalist foundations, are bound to fail: 'A radical option for democracy must be made. It is an option which does not envisage democracy as upkeeping the status quo . . . but as an impulse to convert a formal democracy into a real, socialist democracy'.[52] This impulse is the revolutionary transformation of capitalism into socialism. Although this tendency admits to 'the retreat in the Left to moderate opinions which have confined left-wing politics to pathetic appeals for the restoration of democracy',[53] the rising expectation of the masses will lead to 'the radicalization of the fundamental social forces who are carrying on the struggle against the dictatorship'.[54]

In his elegy for Allende's death, Gabriel García Marquez has written that fate granted Allende the privilege of dying 'defending all the moth-eaten paraphernalia of a dirty system he wanted to demolish without firing one single shot'.[55] Carlos Altamirano, the former secretary-general of the PSCh, on the contrary, argues that 'it is not the bourgeois democracy which has been honoured with Allende's death',[56] but the moral and revolutionary legitimacy of the peaceful road to socialism. This brief exchange of views sums up the complex role the PSCh has played in Chile's political system. Rephrasing García Marquez' words, it could be said that fate granted the PSCh the privilege (or perhaps the burden) both of acting as an engine for social mobilization and radical reform, and of becoming tightly integrated into the liberal bourgeois institutions to the paradoxical extent that Allende 'died defending with a gun the grotesque, obsolete bourgeois rule of the law'.[57]

OPTIONS FOR THE FUTURE

What role will the PSCh be expected to play in the post-Pinochet era? Wisdom advises that political analysts should confine themselves to predicting the past, but a summary account of the options which are open to the PSCh can be rapidly outlined here. An obvious option would be to resume the old historical role, that of a driving force for social mobilization and radical reform, on one hand, and that of an intermediate organization which links the social forces to the structures of the politic body, on the other hand. This may well be the PSCh leadership's secret dream, but, how could the PSCh take up this role in good faith when the Popular Unity experience seems to prove that 'the ruling classes will never tolerate a revolutionary process or consent to peaceful changes which might touch their class privileges'?[58] And it is safe to say that the ruling classes will never again admit a radical PSCh into the framework of parliamentary democracy.

What are the remaining options? If it is true, as Trotsky has asserted, that history takes the line of least resistance, it may be expected that the PSCh will come to terms with the past and the present, acknowledging that a brave new world requires a brave new socialist party, that certain roles are no longer available, and that playing the part of 'legitimate opposition' is as good as playing any other part. Such an option, however, requires as a condition that the system be able to deliver the goods which are wanted by all social groups, but it should be remembered that the political crisis was triggered off by the apparent failure of Chile's political and economic structures to meet competing demands from too many actors. It looks as if the only feasible option is to take up a mobilizing and firm anti-status-quo stand, but such a policy could condemn the party to the wilderness or to annihilation. The PSCh leadership will need all their ingenuity to overcome these dilemmas.

NOTES

1. Carmelo Furci, *The Chilean Communist Party and the Road to Socialism* (Zed Books, London, 1984).

2. James Petras, *Fuerzas Sociales y Politicas en el Desarrollo Chileno* (Amorrortu, Buenos Aires, 1971), p. 151.

3. Evidence, however, shows that the parliamentary élite has not played such a prominent role in the PSCh. See p. 113–14.

4. Ian Roxborough *et al.*, *Chile: The State and Revolution* (Macmillan, London, 1979), p. 9.

5. Roxborough *et al.* (*op. cit.*), p. 172.

6. The distinction between mobilizing functions and integrating functions have been succinctly expressed by Otto Kirchheimer when he writes that 'parties have functioned as channels for integrating individuals and groups into the existing political order, or as instruments for modifying or altogether replacing that order (integration–disintegration)'. Integrating functions are compatible with the process of social mobilization when the later generates an increasing volume and range of demands made upon the government. Their distinctive feature is that they ensure the integration of the clienteles into the political system. Mobilizing parties, on the contrary, serve as an instrument for effecting radical changes 'of' the political, social and economic order, and not 'within' that order, although they might as well be concerned with winning and maintaining support in the body politic. Ottor Kirchheimer, 'The Transformation of the Western European Party System', in La Palombara and Weiner (eds.), *Political Parties and Political Development* (Princeton University Press, Princeton, 1969), p. 188.

7. Joseph La Palombara and Myron Weiner, 'The Origin and Development of Political Parties', in La Palombara and Weiner (eds.), *Political Parties and Political Development* (Princeton University Press, Princeton, 1969), p. 11.

8. This phrase is used by Seymour Martin Lipset, *Political Man* (Heinemann, London, 1969), p. 220.

9. Quoted by Eliecer Carrasco, *Acerca del desarrollo histórico del PSCh* (Taller Orlando Letelier, Paris, 1980), pp. 84–5.

10. Ibid., p. 86.
11. Quoted by Carlos Altamirano, *Dialéctica de una Derrota* (Siglo XXI, Mexico, 1977), p. 66.
12. Ibid., p. 109.
13. Ibid.
14. Joan Garces, *El Estado y los Problemas Tácticos en el Gobierno de Allende* (Siglo XXI, Buenos Aires, 1974), p. 280.
15. Ibid., p. 267.
16. Quoted by Camilo Taufic, *Chile en la Hoguera* (Ed. Corregidor, Buenos Aires, 1974), pp. 28–9.
17. Quoted by Altamirano (*op. cit.*), pp. 67–8.
18. Charles W. Anderson, *Politics and Economic Change in Latin America* (Van Nostrand, New York, 1967).
19. Markos H. Mamalakis, *The Growth and Structure of the Chilean Economy* (Yale University Press, New Haven, 1967), p. 158.
20. Quoted by the *Washington Post*, 23 March 1974.
21. Quoted by *Los Angeles Times*, 17 August 1977.
22. Enrique Ortúzar, *La Nueva Institucionalidad Chilena* (Universidad Católica, Santiago, 1976), p. 2.
23. A. García and J. Wells, 'Chile: A Laboratory for Failed Experiments in Capitalist Political Economy', *Cambridge Journal of Economics*, 7, 1983, p. 290.
24. Sergio de Castro quoted by *Qué Pasa?*, 20 May 1975.
25. See Fernando Dahse, *Mapa de la Extrema Riqueza* (Edit. Aconcagua, Santiago, 1979) and Roberto Carri, 'Competencia poco libre', *Mensaje*, 283, October 1979, pp. 645–51.
26. Dahse (*op. cit.*), p. 146.
27. 'En la pista de las cifras', *Hoy* 109, 23 August 1979, pp. 53–4.
28. *Ercilla*, 16 November 1974.
29. Eduardo Frei, 'El mandato de la historia y las exigencias del porvenir', *Chile-América*, 14–15, January–February, 1976, p. 102.
30. *PS Informa*, 9 August–September 1975, p. 8.
31. Ibid., p. 18.
32. 'Una ofensiva por la unidad del partido', *PS Informa*, 10, October–November 1975, p. 20.
33. Altamirano, *Dialéctica de una Derrota* (*op. cit.*), p. 100.
34. *The Economist*, 2 February 1980.
35. Lucy Blackburn, 'The Current Economic Situation, Alternative Policy Choices and Future Perspectives', in David E. Hojman (ed.), *Chile After 1973* (Centre for Latin American Studies, Liverpool, 1985), p. 33.
36. Carlos Altamirano, 'En el Acto del PS Francés', *PS Informa* 10, *op. cit.*, p. 41.
37. *PS Informa*, 9, *op. cit.*, p. 9.
38. Altamirano, 'En el Acto del PS Francés', *op. cit.*, p. 44.
39. 'Editorial', *Pensamiento Socialista* 26–7 January–April 1983, p. 8.
40. Armando Arancibia *et al.*, 'El Socialismo por el que Luchamos', *Pensamiento Socialista* 29 July–September 1983, p. 11.

41. Ibid., p. 13.
42. Ibid., p. 15.
43. Ricardo Lagos, *Democracia para Chile: Proposiciones de un Socialista* (Ensayo, Santiago, 1985), p. 107.
44. Quoted by Eliecer Carrasco, *Acerca del desarrollo histórico del PSCh*, (*op. cit*.), p. 80.
45. 'National Agreement for the Transition to a Full Democracy', *Chile Update*, Bulletin of the Chile Committee for Human Rights 63, October–November 1985, p. 9.
46. Ibid., p. 11.
47. Ibid.
48. Ibid.
49. See Paul Cammack, 'Democratisation: a Review of the Issues', *Bull. Latin Am. Res.* (2), 1985, pp. 39–46.
50. For a more sceptical view, see Laurence Whitehead, 'Whatever Became of the "Southern Cone Model"?', in Hojman (*op. cit*.), pp. 9–30.
51. Lagos (*op. cit*.), pp. 114–15.
52. Clodomiro Almeyda, 'La salida democrático-revolucionaria a la crisis chilena', *Cuadernos de Orientación Socialista* 22, December 19895, p. 17.
53. Ibid., p. 28.
54. Ibid., p. 29.
55. 'Autopsia de un asesinato', *Postdata* 3, March–April 1974, p. 9.
56. Altamirano, *Dialéctica de una Derrota* (*op. cit*.), p. 199.
57. 'Autopsia de un asesinato', *op. cit*., p. 9.
58. Altamirano, *Dialéctica de una Derrota* (*op. cit*.), p. 199.

HOLOCAUST AND RESURRECTION

The dictatorship's initial policy towards the Left can succintly be described as the politics of holocaust. In March 1974 the State Department said that 20,000 people had been killed in Chile and that between twenty and fifty people were still being slain every week. By 1975 the Chilean government admitted having executed thirty-three trade union leaders and that sixty remained in prison, although ILO's figure on union leaders who had been shot dead by the firing squad was 110. Over 100,000 people representing 1 per cent of Chile's population, had been arrested during the first two years of military rule.

The PSCh was one of the main targets of the military. Five out of the forty-five members of the Central Committee were brutally assassinated, and twenty-six others were thrown into jails. Whole Regional Committees, such as those in Antofagasta, Atacama and Coquimbo, and Section Committees in Iquique, San Felipe, Barrancas, Talca, Valdivia and many others were brutally suppressed. Most of the PSCh's élite (MPs, councillors, trade union and peasant leaders, intellectuals, shanty town leaders and students) were dismissed from employment, expelled from universities, beaten and tortured, put in prison, executed, or 'disappeared' without trace.

But even the cold and mechanical efficiency of the military could not annihilate all the 1,000 *núcleos* or decimate the 120,000 members of the party. Of course, the bulk of those who survived were persuaded into political apathy, but a painful and slow process of reconstruction was perceptible by early 1974, when a self-appointed 'Dirección Interior', under the leadership of Exequiel Ponce, Ricardo Lagos (no relation to Ricardo Lagos, the PSCh representative at AD) and Carlos Lorca—all members of the Political Commission (COPOL)—emerged, claiming to be the highest authority of the party. Strictly speaking, however, the party's highest authority was the Central Committee, which had been duly appointed in the 1971 Congress of La Serena, but it could not be expected that such a decimated body could take over the leadership. Those who knew about the party's quarrelsome factions could deduce that the lack of constitutional legitimacy of the Dirección Interior might sow the seeds of discord in the future, not necessarily because Chileans were keen on legal niceties but because the Dirección Interior was closely identified with one of these factions, the Brigada Revolucionaria. The 'Brigada' (also known as the 'Elenos'—which was derived from the old name of the faction, 'Ejército de Liberación Nacional', or ELN) had surfaced in the late 1960s with the purpose of supporting Che's guerrilla work in Bolivia, but later on had come to advocate reorganizing the party as a tightly obedient structure of committed revolutionaries in the Leninist mould. The Socialist-Communist alliance was regarded by the Brigada as the Alpha and Omega of any attempt at radical politics in Chile. During the Allende administration, the Revolutionary Tendency tactics of widening the 'people's power' (see p. 172) had met with strong disapproval from the Brigada, who regarded such a line as blind extremism. The Direccion Interior set up a stringently centralized organization, restructuring party hierarchies with fellow-comrades and ignoring other factions (the so-called 'Cooptación')—which, of course, made some groups walk away in resentment.

In March 1974, the Dirección Interior issued a comprehensive analysis of Popular Unity's defeat, the weaknesses of the party and how to overcome them, and the tactical line to face the dictatorship under the clumsy title 'In the heat of the struggle against Fascism, let us build the leading force of the people to reach victory'—better known, more briefly, as the 'Documento de Marzo'. Its analysis of Popular Unity's defeat is condensed in the following statement: 'The UP was doomed to fail politically even before September 11 because of the isolation of the working class and the absence of a real leadership with the ability to make a successful use of the revolutionary energy of the masses and the institutional power of the government'.[1]

Although the bulk of the party's membership, the 'Documento de Marzo' says, was proletarian, real control laid in the hands 'of the intellectual and bureaucratic petit bourgeoisie' which was unable 'to transform the party into a truly Marxist-Leninist organization'.[2] The main responsibility for the lack of a single, unified leadership during the Popular Unity government lies with the PSCh since its 'diffuse and fluid' kind of structure made it impossible to 'establish working-class hegemony upon the revolutionary process'.[3] The 'Documento de Marzo' ends pledging that the party will be rebuilt as a disciplined and tightly Leninist organization, empowered with a 'strong organic unity, clear ideological unity and combatant unity of action'.[4]

The 'Documento de Marzo' met with strong criticism from many party quarters. That the PSCh should bear the blame for the Popular Unity's failure disturbed many party members; to be branded as petit bourgeois mortified the former party leaders; the commitment to build a party with strong discipline, tight organization and monolithic ideology displeased those who had been attracted to the party by its open, pluralistic nature. The 'Documento de Marzo' had also suggested building an 'Anti-fascist Front' which would include 'all classes and groups who are in objective contradiction with our fundamental enemies',[5] that is, the middle classes—an unpalatable proposal to those who blamed the middle class for the military coup and regarded

Pinochet's dictatorship as the blatant rule of the bourgeoisie. Carlos Altamirano, the secretary-general of the PSCh who had miraculously escaped from the clutches of the junta, had his own misgivings since the 'Documento de Marzo' categorically affirmed that 'the party's leadership rests with the Dirección Interior in Chile; the Secretariado Exterior [external leadership], headed by the secretary-general, Carlos Altamirano, must follow the revolutionary line set up by the Dirección Interior'.[6] It was, of course, hard to question the moral legitimacy of the Dirección Interior, who, under Pinochet's iron-clad rule, had undertaken the gruelling task of reconstructing the party with its few survivors; but it was still harder for Altamirano and other members of the Central Committee to surrender their authority to the self-appointed internal leadership. The rift between Altamirano and the Dirección Interior would repeatedly crop up despite the attempts to put on a facade of unity.

Unhappy with the 'Documento de Marzo', some sectors who had been excluded from the Dirección Interior—in particular, members of the Revolutionary Tendency with strong influence in the Cordillera and Centro Regional Committees—broke away to constitute the so-called Coordinadora Nacional de Regionales (CNR), the first significant schism since Ampuero's breakaway in 1967. By early 1975 the CNR had already appointed a 'Dirección Transitoria', issued a political manifesto and gained some support at the grass-roots level, but after this auspicious starting it met with a number of frustrating difficulties. Altamirano, cautious not to give offence to the Dirección Interior, did not either endorse it nor dismiss it, but in any event, the CNR suffered from the lack of legitimacy, which could have been provided by Altamirano. The CNR was plagued with petty quarrels, and its open structure made it vulnerable to government repression to such an extent that the Norte Regional Committee was completely annihilated. Benjamín Cares, the CNR's controversial leader, did not have the political skills to patch up quarrels between factions, and serious differences between the Centro Regional Committee, headed by Cares himself, and the Cordillera Regional Committee broke out, with neither prepared to meet the other halfway. Funding was scarce, and the party did not have external support. When in 1978 the CNR organized in Europe a 'First World Meeting', appointing an external leadership, Cares declared them without authority since his political line had been defeated. Such an action struck party members with dismay, and eventually a splinter group broke off from the CNR in 1980.

What were the main political differences between the CNR and the Dirección Interior? The CNR agreed with the 'Documento de Marzo'—although perhaps meaning something different—that during Allende's administration the PSCh had been impaired by 'ideological, political and organic incoherence' and by the malign influence of 'ideologies which were diametrically opposed to proletarian ideology'.[7] The CNR, however, rebutted the representation of the dictatorship as a fascist régime; the military rule as was in fact the brutal, blatant rule of imperialism and the bourgeoisie. Whereas the Dirección Interior maintained that 'the first thing to do is to overthrow the dictatorship, and later on we shall establish the bases for the political and ideological confrontation between the various anti-fascist forces',[8] the CNR argued that 'the dictatorship will be defeated by the masses led by the proletariat under the guidance of the Revolutionary Party and through a process of armed insurrection aiming at the capture of total power'.[9]

In April 1976 the Dirección Interior had issued a widely circulated document, 'The Political Situation and the Road of the People', which stated that 'the most urgent task is to build an anti-fascist front at grass-roots level', and which would include the PDC, 'whose party members share our eagerness for freedom, bread and democracy'.[10] In sharp contrast, the CNR affirmed that 'the PDC has not yet yielded an inch as a bourgeois party and as an utterly uncompromising stronghold of the capitalist system'.[11] So any compromise between the Left and the PDC would 'imperil the strategic goals of the proletariat and the masses'.[12] For the Dirección Interior, finally, the PCCh–PSCh alliance was accepted as a dogma; for the CNR, a new revolutionary alliance with the MAPU, MIR and the IC— a 'Polo Revolucionario'— should replace the obsolete association with the ineffective and 'reformist' PCCh.

The Dirección Interior had arrogated to themselves the right to appoint the Secretariado Exterior, whose members met for the first time in August 1974 and established themselves in East Berlin. Where did the funding come from? A PSCh document gave thanks to 'the generous solidarity of the socialist world and the democratic and revolutionary movements in the capitalist countries',[13] but it seems certain that the bulk of the PSCh's funding was coming from East Germany. This helps to explain the predominance of the Dirección Interior over the money-starved CNR and Altamirano's wariness of colliding with the Dirección Interior. East Germany, furthermore, had offered Altamirano sanctuary at a time when the Chilean junta was pleged to kill him wherever he was to be found. Altamirano, however, felt increasingly discontented with the inconsequential role the Dirección Interior was trying to corral him into. On the other hand, Altamirano's unwillingness to grant full recognition to the Dirección Interior had now become a substantial issue. After a round of talks, it was agreed that these questions would be raised in a new party plenum.

The plenum took place in Habana from 23 April to 5 May 1975, with exiled members of the Central Committee, delegates from Chile, party personalities and, curiously enough, representatives of the CNR. The atmosphere was amicable, but the problems were put off rather than settled. That the Central Committee who had been appointed in the La Serena Congress in 1971 was still the highest authority was acknowledged, but the practical implications of such a recognition were doubtful. What was significant was that it was accepted that the Central Committee comprised two sections, an internal leadership—the Dirección Interior—and a nine-strong external leadership—the Secretariado Exterior—headed by Carlos Altamirano. The new composition of the Secretariado Exterior was transparently the result of a compromise: four members were staunch supporters of the Dirección Interior while the four others did not hide their sympathies for the CNR. Decisions by the Secretariado Exterior would be carried out by a three-member executive which comprised of Altamirano, Adonis Sepulveda and Clodomiro Almeyda, a distinguished intellectual who had just been set free by the junta. Later on Altamirano would argue that the majority of the participants in the plenum had objected to the 'Documento de Marzo', but, if this was so, the objections were not made public.

In June 1975 the junta struck the PSCh a heavy blow when Lorca, Ponce and Lagos, the leaders of the Dirección Interior, were captured and disappeared without trace. The party's strength is demonstrated by the fact that such a blow did not, however, lead to the party's extinction. By late 1975 the first issue of a sporadic party bulletin *Unidad y Lucha*, came out, and by 1979, the bulletin had a circulation of more than 7,000. The PSCh held clandestine conferences in Chile in 1976, 1977 and 1979—the latter attended, according to party reports, by delegates from thirty-two regional committees representing 5,000 party members.[14] Starting in 1976, the party began to spread its forces out into any political space which happened to be available; it helped to rebuild the militant Ranquil peasant trade union; to set up the Committee of Democratic Lawyers and the National Trade Union Co-ordinating Body (CNS); to take part in the work done by the Catholic Church human rights organization, the Vicariate of Solidarity; to create the Group of Relatives of Disappeared Prisoners, the Chilean Commission on Human Rights, the Committee for the Defence of the Rights of the People (CODEPU), the National Commission for Young People's Rights, the 'Group of the 24', the University Cultural Group, and, in general, to rebuild old and create new popular organizations. The dictatorship's politics of holocaust had failed to extirpate the PSCh from the Chilean body politic.

Despite these accomplishments, new dissensions in the party had cropped up. The disappearance of Lorca, Ponce and Lagos meant that the legitimacy of the new Dirección Interior could be put into question. Altamirano was again reluctant to recognize a leadership which he disliked and which had reciprocated by criticizing his role during the Allende administration. But Altamirano's options had become restricted. The CNR had lost ground to the Dirección Interior, was split into petty factions and resented Altamirano's evasive tactics. Furthermore, Clodomiro Almeyda had been successfully campaigning for the Dirección Interior.

Altamirano was finally persuaded to issue a letter, 'Mensaje a los Socialistas del Interior de Chile', in June 1977, which disowned the CNR for its erroneous political line—that is, its attempt to replace the PSCh–PCCh alliance with a 'Polo Revolucionario' with the MIR—and asserted the legitimacy of the Dirección Interior. Pedro Vuskovic, the radical CNR spokesman, was expelled from the party. The Mensaje, on the other hand, held out the olive-branch to two splinter groups, the Comisión para el Consenso and the MR2, suggesting the creation of a single unified leadership, the Dirección Unica. In return for his recognition of the Dirección Interior, Altamirano demanded that he should be accorded the leadership of the party. Following the party's tradition of giving official status to behind-the-scenes negotiations by holding a congress, party members were summoned to another plenum in Algeria in March 1978.

DIFFICULT RECONCILIATION: FROM THE PLENUM IN ALGERIA (1978) TO THE THIRD CLANDESTINE PLENUM IN CHILE (1979)

Questions of leadership were not the only ones which required attention. The differences between Altamirano and the Dirección Interior had hindered the party from making a comprehensive plan of action to face the dictatorship. Revealing a traumatic fixation on the past, most of the political discussion had been concerned with the political and military defeat of Popular Unity. But the 'tasks of the present' could no longer be ignored now that the emergence of a kind of middle-class opposition, led by the PDC, was apparent and the continuous violations of human rights had made the Catholic Church a vocal critic of the government.

In some socialist circles the feeling was that the party should enter into conversations with the MIR and other extreme left-wing groups to constitute a Polo Revolucionario—this view, held by the CNR, was indeed widespread among the party's left-wing affiliates. Intense repression had, however, softened up the MIR. In 1974, Miguel Enríquez, MIR's secretary-general, had died in an armed confrontation with the security forces in Santiago, and in

1975 four members of MIR's Central Committee, urging their comrades to give up the struggle against the military, had been displayed on TV by the dictatorship. Exhausted by its efforts to survive, the MIR could no longer aim at becoming a Polo Revolucionario in opposition to the PCCh's 'reformist' line. But if the party's left wing had been weakened by military repression, a sudden burst of right-wing views had broken out into a confusing kaleidoscope of loose groups. The Movimiento de Acción Socialistat (MAS), formally launched in April 1978, described itself as 'democratic socialist', and rejected 'Leninism'; the Tendencia Humanista Socialista was loyal to Aniceto Rodríguez, a former social democratic secretary-general living in exile in Venezuela; the Comisión para el Consenso avowed itself to be Marxist but not Leninist; a Movimiento Recuperacionista (MR) was set up by Eduardo Long, whose social democratic ideas were well known. On the 19 April 1979 all these groups, prompted by the acute state of conflict between Altamirano and the Dirección Unica (see below), issued a political manifesto, the 'Declaration of Socialist Unity', calling a halt to party strife but denouncing the sectarian politics of the party's leadership. In 1980 the party's right wing had widened to include the Suizos (a tiny group of socialist intellectuals), the Iniciativa Regional Europa (a group of socialists in exile in Europe, most concentrated in Belgium), and the Unión Socialista Popular (USP), Raúl Ampnero's minuscule political machine which had broken away from the PSCh in 1967, having evolved from the extreme left to the moderate right. These groups agreed that military dictatorship in Chile could only be brought to an end by opening negotiations with the PDC, the 'democratic' Right and the 'democratic' sections of the Armed Forces (if they could be found), excluding the PCCh and the extreme left wing and putting socialist goals off for an undefined period of time.

The plenum in Algeria was attended by the members of the Central Committee in exile and still politically active, and a delegation from the Dirección Interior. The delegation took overall control of the plenum, as its request for a vote block of 51 per cent was, against Altamirano's wishes, granted. The legitimacy of the Dirección Interior was reasserted, but the old Central Committee appointed in 1971, was replaced by a Dirección Unica consisting of thirty members in Chile and nine members in exile, putting an end, at least in theory, to the submission of the external leadership to the internal authorities. The Dirección Unica would last three years and meet every four months. Altamirano would continue to be the party's secretary-general, but would be excluded from the three-strong external executive which was now presided over by Clodomiro Almeyda, also the new under-secretary-general. As a concession to Altamirano, it was agreed that the secretary-general would be a member of the COPOL, the highest policy-making body in the party, but the practicality of this arrangement was doubtful, as the COPOL was placed in Chile.

Although the plenum in Algeria was pronounced a success in eliminating party strife, very soon dissent started up again. Altamirano argued that the Secretariado Exterior was still confining him to a subordinate position, and described himself as 'a queen of England who reigns but does not govern'.[15] If this was so, why had he become the target of so much animosity? As PSCh's secretary-general during the Allende administration, he could be held responsible for the undisciplined and diffuse nature of the party, but, on the other hand, it could be argued that such features went back to the very inception of the party in 1933 and were found in most mass parties in the world. Altamirano could be reproached for his extravagant bouts of left-wing extremism, but extreme leftist rhetoric had been a persistent stamp of each successive leadership. It could be held against him that his inflammatory speech of 9 September 1973 triggered off the military coup, but, in fact, plans for a military putsch had been hatched since April 1972. He could be blamed for abandoning President Allende to his fate on the 11 September, but it was the party's COPOL who had concluded that the government could not be militarily defended. Perhaps a charismatic figure such as Altamirano was bound to become the scapegoat for all the failures of a political experiment which had brought about so much tragedy and bitterness. Furthermore, the Dirección Unica was unhappy with Altamirano's growing links with the European social democratic parties and his critical remarks about the 'socialismos reales'. Party members in exile in Western Europe, such as Erick Schnake, Oscar Waiss and Jorge Arrate, who stood close to Altamirano, had been able to establish a dense network of relationships with socialist and social democratic leaders whose influential parties were already, or were about to be, in office. The idea of replacing the embarrassing ties with the Eastern block with the companionship of Mitterand and his like in Spain, West Germany, Holland, Sweden and Great Britain, appealed to Altamirano and those who had been exposed to the influence of fashionable ideologies, such as Euro-communism, the rediscovery of Gramsci, or the anti-communist Marxism of Claudin, which were reinterpreting Marx in the 1970s. But it would be wrong to judge this interest in democratic socialism as mere opportunism or intellectual affectation. PSCh's perception of socialism had historically been interpreted as a kind of democracy, and party members in Chile had come to reappraise the significance of democratic values in a progressive society.

Once the brotherly feelings of revolutionary comradeship, stirred up by the plenum in Algeria, passed away, Altamirano found himself in the minority in the Secretariado Exterior. Not only was there no practical way he could take part in the meetings of COPOL, but the identity of most of the COPOL's members was unknown to him. Altamirano wrote to the Dirección Interior saying that the resolutions of the plenum had been ignored and suggesting that the whole Dirección Unica, including the secretary-general, be placed in Chile. This proposal was turned down, as the Dirección Unica argued that such an arrangement would eventually raise doubts about who was the true secretary-general since the secretary-general in Chile would remain unknown to party members, friendly governments, parties and movements abroad for security reasons while Carlos Altamirano, who everyone knew as our secretary-general, would in practice continue holding the post'.[16] A round of conversations between Altamirano and the Secretariado Exterior failed to patch up the quarrel, and a delegate from Chile listened to their mutual complaints but did not make comments. In February 1979 Altamirano received a letter from Chile signed by thirty-six party members accusing the Dirección Interior of 'Stalinism' and asking him to call a party congress. The Dirección Interior said that the letter was a fraudulent device engineered by Altamirano himself, who, funded by the Italian Socialist Party and the German Social Democracy, had sent two envoys to Chile to stir up trouble among party members. Unexpectedly, a new delegate from Chile came in February 1979 to announce that an extraordinary plenum to settle the dispute would take place in Chile between February and April 1979. It was of course, difficult for Altamirano to get adequate support in the plenum at such a short notice. At the end of the plenum, the Dirección Interior resolved, apparently by a unanimous vote, that Altamirano be replaced by Almeyda as the party's secretary-general. The majority of the Secretariado Exterior espoused the decision. Altamirano's stalwart supporters would argue later on that the party's rank-and-file were quite ignorant of this manoeuvre since it was not discussed in the plenum itself.

Altamirano's reaction was drastic: he called for a reorganization of the party, affirming that both the plenum in Algeria and the extraordinary plenum were illegitimate as the various tendencies of the party had not been democratically represented. Such a reaction made Berlin too hot for him. Altamirano and his entourage were compelled to leave East Germany and take shelter in sympathetic West European countries.

How should this political cataclysm be interpreted? On the surface it looked like a question of leadership, of a struggle for the control of the party. Below the surface, however, more substantial issues were at stake. The PSCh (Almeyda) charged Altamirano with representing a 'rightist deviation' aimed at compromising with the PDC and playing into the hands of the bourgeoisie. They also accused him of entering into negotiations with the party's social democratic factions to serve his own purposes, and castigated him for attempting to replace democratic centralism with a 'federal' structure where all ideological shades would be represented. Finally, the PSCh (Almeyda) affirmed that Altamirano's self-indulgence reflected petit-bourgeois habits of lapsing into irrelevant power struggles which would encumber the party with unnecessary strains.[17] Altamirano retorted that a 'Stalinist faction' had taken over the party and shaped it into a sectarian, bureaucratic organization, submitted to the will and pleasure of the PCCh.[18]

It may be more promising, however, to study the meaning of this conflict from the context of political roles played by the PSCh in Chile. After spending six years in the political wilderness, the 'integrating tendencies' had come to the surface in the hope that the party would regain its footing as a legitimate mass party in Chile's parliamentary system. For these tendencies, the party's 'special relationship' with the PCCh was more of a liability than an asset—and it must be admitted that the PSCh's association with the Communists had so far borne little fruit. Altamirano's amazing shift in politics from the left to the right—or rather from 'mobilizing' currents to the 'integrating' tendencies—pointed not to political inconsistency but to a shrewd flexibility to set off on a different tack when events were taking a radical turn.

The schism threw the party's rank-and-file into great confusion. Most of the socialists in exile followed Altamirano, but in Chile the bulk remained loyal to Almeyda. It would take time before a better perception of the true nature of the conflict prompted a more coherent realignment of the various factions. Ideological misrepresentations would in the meantime, set off an extravagant process of fragmentation as bewildered party members found out that they had apparently taken sides with the wrong leaders.

THE CRISIS CONTINUES: I

As Altamirano's base in Chile was weak, he began to seek support from the factions which had kept the Dirección Interior at a distance. These groups ranged from the right, like the Recuperacionistas, to the left, such as the MR2 (also known as La Chispa, the name of its clandestine newspaper). The groups which had just signed the 'Declaration of Socialist Unity' (see p. 194), former members of the CNR, and the Sur and the San Miguel Regional Committees had already stated that they would side with him. At this difficult time Altamirano was prepared to set aside ideological prudery in the belief that his charismatic personality would be enough to unite the most disparate factions. After hasty preparations, Altamirano appointed a Commission for the Unity of the Socialist Party, which met in Paris in September 1979 and in Habana in

November 1979. Altamirano himself held a round of conversations with Aniceto Rodríguez, Jorge Arrate, Erick Schnake, Jaime Suarez and other party personalities. An ordinary party congress was scheduled to take place at the beginning of 1980.

In March 1979 Raúl Ampuero, the USP's leader who had in the past played a crucial role in shaping the special character of the PSCh, organized, with the sponsorship of the Lelio Basso Foundation, a Conference in Ariccia, Italy, to discuss the political role of socialist ideology in Chile, and which was attended by 'personalities' from the PSCh, the MAPU and the IC. In the course of the conference, the idea of a massive convergence of all the socialist forces found an enthusiastic welcome. According to the press release: 'everyone agreed on the need to build a kind of socialist project which would be internationally independent and lead to the building of a new popular bloc. This project should represent not only the interests of the proletariat but the interests of all the workers, i.e. the oppressed majority of the country including the middle stratas'.[19] It was also emphasized that 'the need for a gradual process of political and organic convergence of all the socialist tendencies which will create the basis for a new kind of political organization. This new type of organization will go beyond the traditional concept of the party which has bureaucratically and rigidly distorted the Marxist thesis regarding how a party should be related to the masses'.[20]

In the following months, a 'Comité de Iniciativa' (later renamed the 'Comité de Enlace'), made of twelve members representing the Suizos, the PSCh (Almeyda), the PSCh (Twenty-Fourth Congress), the MAPU, the MAPU (OC) and the IC, was set up to study the materialization of a wide socialist bloc which 'should include all shades of socialism which are democratic, national and popular'.[21] In May 1980 the Comité de Enlace issued a document, 'Convergencia Socialista: Fundamentos de una Propuesta', which affirmed that the Chilean Left had become worn out and could only be revitalized by 'the coming together of all the parties which proclaimed themselves socialists'. The 'Convergencia Socialista' affirmed its allegiance to Marxism, but it was a Marxism 'pervious to other cultural and theoretical contributions' and, above all, receptive to 'Christian revolutionary values which play such a key role in the new socialist project for Chile'. How should this 'Convergencia' be envisaged? Would it be a new, reborn socialist party, made of the debris of the PSCh, the MAPU and the IC? Or was it only a new left-wing coalition which would substitute for the ineffective Popular Unity? The document was ambiguous. The MAPU favoured creating a new socialist party; the IC and the MAPU (OC) preferred to confine the 'Convergencia' to the role of a loose coalition of left-wing parties. What was unambiguous was that the notion of a 'special relationship' between the socialist forces and the

PCCh would be shelved; any negotiation between the Left and the PCCh should be conducted 'on the bases of a fair discussion about our tactical and strategic discrepancies, without attempting to impose one's thoughts on the others'.[22] In June 1980 a 'Secretariado de Convergencia', made of delegates from the PSCh (Twenty-Fourth Congress), the MAPU, the MAPU (OC) and the IC was established.

Altamirano's congress (called the Twenty-Fourth Congress) took place in Paris in August 1980. Its purpose was to build a single party out of a hotch-potch of tendencies which ranged from the extreme left—the MR2—to the kaleidoscopic jumble of self-styled 'altamiranista' groups, including those who had signed the 'Letter of the 36', and which had been hastily assembled by the 'Commission for the Unity'.[23] After arduous negotiations, the factions consented to the proposal of melting together into a single central committee which would be constituted by twenty-one members in Chile and ten members in exile. The COPOL would in turn be composed by seven people in Chile and three abroad. Both the Secretary-General and the under-secretary-general would be placed in Chile, but there would also be two under-secretary-generals in exile, one for Europe and Africa and the other for the Americas. Altamirano's controversial leadership had come to an end, but there was no doubt that he was still expecting to be the power behind the throne. He presented a political document, '8 Tesis sobre una Estrategia Socialista para Chile', putting forward his views about what the party's politics should be. Thesis I said that 'the broadest and strongest unity against the dictatorship'[24] must be established. Thesis II described the PSCh as a national, revolutionary, proletarian, not dogmatic, liberating and Latin-Americanist organization. Thesis III said that the party should aim at being both a cadre party and a mass party and follow the principle of democratic centralism. Thesis IV stated, in a Gramsci-like style, that the party should organize and lead a broad historic bloc of political, social and cultural forces to build a socialist order. Thesis V suggested that 'convergence with progressive Christian sectors on socialism is a first priority for the party'.[25] Thesis VI affirmed that the party should discuss how to create an army which is democratic. Thesis VII rejected any claim to hegemony by a socialist big power, reasserted the party's support for national liberation movements, stressed that the PSCh would remain internationally non-aligned, reaffirmed the party's 'close and deep relations with the Cuban Revolution and the Cuban Communist Party',[26] suggested 'strengthening our links to European socialist and social democratic parties'[27] and regretted that in the past 'there was little understanding of the origin, purpose and role of these parties'[28] despite the fact that 'they showed a genuine sympathy for the Chilean revolutionary experience and, in particular, for Salvador Allende'.[29] Thesis

VII also suggested three main lines for political action: (1) the defence of Chile's interests; (2) to contribute to Latin America's political and economic unity and 'to improve the degree of co-ordination of all the democratic, anti-imperialist and revolutionary forces',[30] and (3) the re-establishment and deepening of democratic principles in Chile. Thesis VIII, finally, advocated strengthening the party's role in the Convergencia Socialista.

The resolutions which were taken at the Twenty-Fourth Congress echoed most of Altamirano's recommendations. The party's traditional stance of non-alignment was reasserted, and fierce criticism was made not only of 'Yankee imperialism' but also of 'Soviet military intervention in Afghanistan' and of the Chinese leadership, 'which has taken sides with the main enemy of the people' (i.e. the USA). The party's commitment to the 'Worker's Democratic Republic' was, of course, restated, but it was also qualified by the *realpolitik* remark that 'the achievement of the party's democratic and socialist goals requires the overthrow of the dictatorship. The party is prepared to make agreements with all social forces which are committed to this main purpose'.[31] New alliances with other socialist forces, such as the Convergencia, should be forged, but links with the PCCh, despite strategic differences, would still be maintained. Finally, the resolutions advised that the party teach the masses 'all forms of struggle', which was supposed to mean that the PSCh might endorse some kind of armed struggle in Chile.

There is no doubt that there was a deliberate vagueness in the resolutions about immediate tactics since the purpose of the Twenty-Fourth Congress had been to bring together factions of different sorts. The Left, however, which was the minority in the leadership, felt increasingly uneasy at the party's steady turn to the right. In February 1981, Erick Schnake, the party's under-secretary-general for Europe and Africa, disapproved of a recent declaration for the need of armed insurrection in Chile made by the PSCh (Almeyda), the PCCh and the MIR, saying that it was 'Utopian to claim that armed insurrection is feasible at the moment'.[32] Such a statement dismayed the Left, which was expecting that the PSCh (Twenty-Fourth Congress) would at some stage be prepared to embark on paramilitary operations against the dictatorship. Neither was the Left happy with the party's close identification with the Convergencia Socialista, which was seen as a pot-pourri of parties characterized by political blandness and willing to ingratiate itself with the 'bourgeois opposition'. The Left's anger exploded in October 1981 at the first meeting of the Central Committee. The Left charged the leadership with 'social democratic beliefs' which were distorting the party's historical heritage. The leadership answered saying that a lunatic fringe was trying to replace the party with a piece of military apparatus. The Left broke off from the PSCh (Twenty-Fourth Congress) and proclaimed itself to be the genuine party, but for the sake of the narrative this new faction will be referred to as the PSCh (Alzate Chile)–'Alzate Chile' being the title of the document where the Left presented its account of what had happened.

The departure of the Left prepared the ground for the complete control of the PSCh (Twenty-Fourth Congress) by the 'integrating tendencies'. A letter signed together by Carlos Altamirano, Raúl Ampuero and Aniceto Rodríguez stated that the party would never again submit itself to the whims of the PCCh, and that the goal of the socialist forces would be 'to build a type of national consensus for change where the historic traits of Chilean socialism— its national, democratic, popular and revolutionary features—and the mobilizing capabilities and humanist values of the Christian movement would come together'.[33] The idea of 'consensus for change' implied a succession of stages and strategic priorities: consensus first, changes later; achieve integration before attempting mobilization, this was the underlying moral to be drawn from the politics of socialist consensus.

THE CRISIS CONTINUES: II

The extraordinary plenum which took place in Chile from February to April 1979 (see p. 196) described the military dictatorship not only as the response of the bourgeoisie to the 'popular threat' but also as a new scheme of capitalist accumulation under the control of imperialism and the monopolistic bourgeoisie, and as a new political régime where 'democratic-bourgeois fantasies' had been wiped out. The socialist revolution, said the plenum, was still the strategic objective of the party, but the main enemy at the present was the fascist military dictatorship. According to the plenum, Chile's early processes of urbanization and industrialization had brought about social diversification and the mushrooming of intermediate organizations between the state and civil society. It could be inferred from this picture that 'the final confrontation between the bourgeois state and us requires, as a previous stage, the conquest of these social and political bastions of power in civil society'.[34] In other words, the party's struggle against military rule should be seen as 'a movement of encirclement of Chile's capitalist state, based on the growing strengthening of the working class and the masses, which will allow us to attract a larger number of social sectors to our fight for democracy and socialism. The working class will lead this broad social alliance to the final conquest of power'.[35]

Gramsci's theses about the 'war of positions' can be recognized in this sweeping picture of the party's line. The PSCh, said the plenum, was bound to play a key role in the building of 'a broad bloc for socialism, an historic alliance of the working class, the popular masses and the middle classes coming together around a democratic, socialist programme'.[36] When the time came, the party would trigger off a rupturing crisis, 'a general political crisis when all the contradictions of the Chilean dependent capitalist society will crop up'.[37] A key element in this strategy was the mobilization of the masses and the accumulation of forces which would eventually lead to an armed uprising of the people.

This analysis pleased both the Left and the right of the PSCh (Almeyda). The emphasis could be either put on 'the need for the unity of all the forces against the military dictatorship around a Democratic Programme',[38] or on the mobilization of the masses which would conclude with the military defeat of Pinochet's rule; and different emphases would give rise to different political readings. A 'Mensaje del Comité Central a los militantes en el exilio' summed up the plenum's resolutions in the following four points: (1) the need to strengthen Popular Unity as the nucleus of a bloc where 'Marxist-Leninist forces, the forces associated with the radicalized democratic and liberal parties, and the Christian popular progressive forces'[39] would come together; (2) the party's commitment to establish a 'Worker's Democratic Republic'; (3) the party would elaborate a 'National Democratic Programme', stating that both Popular Unity and the PDC should take part in a wide democratic consensus; and (4) the plenum finally reiterated the 'Marxist-Leninist' character of the party. The recent triumph of the Sandinist Revolution in Nicaragua impressed on the party the importance of armed struggle. By December 1980 the MIR, the PCCh and the PSCh (Almeyda) reached an agreement on the need to start armed resistance in Chile,[40] and in October 1981 Almeyda was loudly applauded in the Conference of the Socialist Young People in Berlin when he described the party's line as focused on 'the insurgent mass struggle with an insurrectional perspective'. The party's theoretical magazine published lengthy articles on 'the insurgent mass struggle' tactics.[41]

In September 1981 the PSCh (Twenty-Fourth Congress) had set up a Comité de Enlace Permanente (CEP) with the purpose of bringing all socialist factions together. Although the PSCh (Almeyda) had refused to join, many party members felt that the split between 'altamiranistas' and 'almeydistas' had been created by personal power struggles, that the party should proceed without indulging in personalities and that differences between the PSCh (Almeyda) and the PSCh (Twenty-Fourth Congress) should be patched up. By early 1982 *Unidad y Lucha* —the PSCh (Almeyda)'s clandestine bulletin— suggested 'opening negotiations about the party's unity at all levels' since 'the unity of Chilean socialism can become the catalytic factor, the key political fact to speed up the struggle against the military dictatorship'.[42] After a long debate, the PSCh (Almeyda) decided in favour of joining the CEP; this was done by issuing a joint announcement with the MAS–USP–MR coalition.[43] A substantial proportion of the PSCh (Almeyda) leadership, however, were dissatisfied with the decision. The dissatisfaction increased when in August 1982 the CEP entered into negotiations with Tomás Reyes, the PDC's new leftist chairman, despite the fact that the party had stated that the Popular Unity and the PDC should come together in a democratic programme: the PDC was still envisaged as an enemy, not as an ally. Those who were unhappy with the party's role in the CEP had the chance they had been waiting for when in December 1982 a plenum was held to reorganize the Central Committee, which had been scaled down by government repression. The new leadership decided that the party should withdraw from the CEP but a sector of the Central Committee, headed by Julio Stuardo and Carlos Briones, refused to obey. It seems that the quarrel became extremely rancorous because the Stuardo–Briones group complained about 'open persecution against those of us who are trying to keep the party on the path of socialist unification'.[44] Stuardo and Briones contacted the Secretariado Exterior in Berlin and suggested that all members of the Central Committee resign their posts so as to give Almeyda a free hand to appoint a new COPOL which would, in turn, choose the members of a new Central Committee; this suggestion, however, was turned down by the Central Committee. Meanwhile, the CEP had made substantial progress. In March 1983 the CEP and the PDC made public a manifesto, the 'Manifiesto Democratico', calling for the re-establishment of democracy in Chile—the first substantial expression of the emergence of a solid, broad-based opposition to Pinochet's rule. In April 1983 the CEP was transformed into the Comité Político de Unidad Socialista (CPUS), with the purpose of welding the socialist factions together into a grand socialist party.

Almeyda was apparently hesitant about leaving the CPUS. A plenum with members of the Central Committee in Chile and abroad took place in Buenos Aires in June 1983 to get round the difficulties. Stuardo and Briones had said that their participation was conditional on (1) the members of the Central Committee in Chile resigning their posts, and (2) the acceptance of the process of reunification. In the event the resignation did not take place, but the party's involvement with the CEP was not questioned either. However, Almedya himself was now the target of bitter criticism from the Left, who accused him of selling out the party's line. The Stuardo–Briones group characterized the conflict in the following terms: the leftist faction 'thinks that the struggle of the masses will lead to an armed insurrection to bring down the dictatorship',[45] whilst their own position was 'that the seriousness of the crisis which the dictatorship has brought upon the country, affecting all social classes, indicates that a realistic strategy to overthrow the military and rebuild democracy makes it necessary to set up a National Opposition made of the widest range of democratic political forces and the broader spectrum of social forces'.[46]

The intensity that the dispute between the Stuardo–Briones group and the Left had reached after the plenum in Buenos Aires was particularly unfortunate since Almeyda had, in April 1983, called a congress to take place in August or September 1983. Fearing that this congress would be used as an opportunity to trigger off another split, Almeyda substituted it with a meeting of the Central Committee which would take place in Buenos Aires in August. The leftist faction, made up of five members of the Central Committee in exile, put forward a series of accusations against Almeyda, including that he 'had gone over to the right' and that the 'revolutionary sectors' were being persecuted, adding that the calling for a Central Committee meeting was illegal. The meeting was one of compromise: on the one hand, 'it reaffirmed the political line based on the insurgent mass struggle with an insurrectional prospect',[47] and on the other 'the party resolved to become part of the unifying socialist process'[48] and to participate in 'the coalition of all the anti-dictatorial democratic forces which will make the downfall of Pinochet's régime possible'.[49] The problem brought about by the leftist faction was eliminated with one blow by a resolution that all the members of the Central Committee that resided out of the country would be suspended, consequently stripping the left of legitimate representation abroad and leaving Almeyda as the only authorized spokesman. The leftist faction was reduced to a small, isolated group called 'PS Insurrección de Bruselas'—so called because Belgium was its most staunch stronghold in Europe.

In August 1983 the agreements between the PDC and the CPUS had crystallised to the point of establishing an official opposition front called 'Democratic Alliance' (AD). This was the materialization of the anti-fascist front that for a long time sections of the Left, including the PCCh, had tried to set up. The problem was that the PDC and other right-wing parties were adamant in opposing the inclusion of the PCCh. It was only now, with its hopes dashed, that the PCCh decided to launch another opposition front in conjunction with the PSCh (Almeyda), the 'Popular Democratic Movement' (MDP), officially launched on 21 September 1983. The PSCh (Almeyda) found itself participating in two coalitions which, in certain ways, were rivals. Thge PSCh (Almeyda) declared itself profoundly committed to the MDP, 'which represents the unity of the Left',[50] on the one hand, and on the other, insinuated that it would attempt to enlarge the AD 'so as to include the remaining democratic popular forces, introducing the popular democratic programme in the debates'.[51] Regarding the CPUS, the PSCh (Almeyda) declared that it supported every effort for the unity of socialism and that it expected 'the majority, if not all the members of the CPUS, to become part of the MDP'.[52]

However, the PSCh (Almeyda) pointed out that its participation in the CPUS should not be regarded as accepting joining a grand socialist party. Nevertheless, in September the CPUS announced that from that moment it had transformed itself into the direction of a 'Unified Socialist Party'. The PSCh (Almeyda) left the CPUS, claiming that this 'premature' unification obeyed 'the desire of the most right-wing sectors of the CPUS to prevent all socialists from joining the MDP'.[53] The Stuardo–Briones sector, however, refused to heed the party's decision, thus provoking another split.

According to the PSCh (Almeyda)'s understanding of the situation, there was a plan to 'destabilize and dismantle the PSCh, distancing it as much as possible from where it stands and has always stood ... in order to rebuild from it an *ad hoc* "socialism" with regard to the various plans for Pinochet's removal which would not pose any real threat to the survival of the capitalist régime'.[54] Within the idea of building a democratic socialism—an aim encouraged by the political Right and Centre with strong backing from the international social democracy—was the intention of submitting the PSCh to the hegemony of the bourgeois classes, divorcing it from the anti-capitalist content which had guided its historical course, dimming 'its distinctive aspiration to power as the vanguard of the exploited sectors'.[55] The PSCh (Almeyda) did not deny the need for understanding amongst all currents opposed to the military régime, but the party had to maintain its position as a 'radical wing', rejecting the political hegemony of the middle-of-the-road bourgeoisie.

NEW CRISES, NEW OPPORTUNITIES

Early in 1983, after the tortuous and secessionist course followed by the PSCh since the military coup, two basic poles of agglutination had emerged. On the one hand, there was the CEP, embracing the PSCh (Twenty-Fourth Congress), the MAS–USP–MR coalition, the group of intellectuals and professionals known as the Suizos, the 'Consenso 19 de Abril',[56] the Stuardo–Briones group, and a sector of the CNR.[57] Factions grouped in the CEP favoured on the whole the articulation of a wide range of democratic forces, which should include the PDC, and which, on concentrating a vast spectrum of political and social sectors, would have sufficient strength for the negotiation of a gradual return to democracy. A more ambitious project associated with the CEP was the creation of a Gramsci-type socialist historico-cultural bloc, an idea originated by the Convergencia Socialista. On the other hand, there was the position represented by the PSCh (Almeyda) and the PSCh (Alzate Chile), who presented an approach based on the 'struggle of the masses', emphasizing its paramilitary, insurrectional character and its class basis, since, although not unwilling to reach an agreement with the PDC, they wanted to maintain their autonomy with regard to the hegemonic aspirations of the bourgeoisie. The Comité Coordinador de la Izquierda Chilena had been set up in January 1983 in reply to the Convergencia Socialista, with the participation of the PSCh (Almeyda), PSCh (Alzate Chile), MIR, PCCh, the Radical Party and MAPU (OC).

Meanwhile, it should be remembered that the severe economic crisis which began in 1982, referred to above (see p. 179), had shaken the apparent solidity of the military régime, opening up new spaces to the opposition and instilling a new breath of life into the 'mass struggle'. Suddenly the mass struggle had acquired vitality in a way which surprised even the Left who had exploited it as a rhetorical artifact. Trade unions had gradually roused themselves from their apathy to take on a more independent and critical position with respect to the government. Early in 1978, sectors of the Left and the PDC had set up a more combative trade union federation, the National Trade Union Co-ordinating Body (CNS), which at the end of 1981 published a 'Pliego de Chile', asking for the implementation of far-reaching political and economic changes. The dictatorship imprisoned the leaders of the CNS, but the 'Pliego' raised the morale of the rest of the trade union movement. Increasing trade union co-ordination and activism was doubtless the motive for the murder in February 1982 of Tucapel Jiménez, the influential president of the National Association of Public Employees (ANEF) and vice-president of the Democratic Union of Workers (UDT), controlled by the PDC, who, a week earlier, had proposed the formation of a 'common front' against the government's economic policies. In July 1982, 623 trade union leaders presented a new petition to Pinochet and, following this, the unions of the Copper Workers' Confederation (CTC) took the surprising initiative of calling for a general strike for 11 May and 17 June 1983.[58] In terms of concrete results, these attempts were not successful: the government imposed strict censorship of the press and the mines were militarized, and virtually the whole of the leadership of the CTC and some members of the CNS were arrested and sent into internal exile. But its powerful effects on social mobilization were undeniable. Various popular and trade union organizations began to organize regular Days of National Protest which escalated to surprising proportions. At the end of 1983 some of the largest political demonstrations in Chilean history had taken place. The UDT, CTC and CNS united to launch the National Workers' Command (CNT), which was to play a crucial role on the re-emergence of the mass movement. One significant result is the appearance of what could be termed the 'visibility' of the opposition, which until then had been incoherent, clandestine or limited to taking forms which were tolerated by the dictatorship, but which now re-emerged much more publicly, offering convincing alternatives to the military régime.

The first popular demonstrations surprised the PSCh—and, in fact, the whole of the opposition—more enmeshed in its own problems than in those of the mobilization of the masses. On 19 April 1983, as mentioned above, the CEP had become the CPUS, giving rise to heated debates within the PSCh (Almeyda), and the eventual departure of the CNR, who argued that it would not be right to rebuild the party from factions which were marginal to the bases, and that the socialist sectors of the CEP had abandoned 'revolutionary and Leninist principles'. The CPUS resumed talks with the PDC within the Multipartidaria, which had been created for the launching of the 'Manifesto Democratico' in March 1983. After arduous negotiations, a three-point pro- gramme was agreed, consisting of: (1) Pinochet's resignation; (2) the estab- lishment of a provisional government, and (3) the election of a constituent assembly. A fourth point proposed by Gabriel Valdes, the PDC's new chair- man, that of a first constitutional government of national unity comprising all shades of opposition against Pinochet, was rejected by the CPUS. This was the programme of the Democratic Alliance launched in August 1983, and headed by Valdés, with the participation of the PDC, CPUS and some centre and right-wing parties (the Republican Party, the Social Democrats, the Radical Party). The AD immediately entered talks with the new minister of the interior, Onofre Jarpa, who seemed to favour a policy of 'opening up' regarding a future transition to democracy. The only group not represented at the talks (although one member attended in a personal capacity as an observer) were the socialists, who argued that the dictatorship's repressive methods made any dialogue impossible. The régime, in effect, rejected any concessions at all, and talks were suspended after the national protest on 8 September.

In September 1983 the formation of the Popular Democratic Movement was announced, integrated by the PSCh (Almeyda), the PCCh, the MIR, MOC Tendencia Proletaria and MAPU (Lautaro). Later, the affiliation of MAPU (OC), the CNR (Vuskovic and Palestro) and the PSCh (Alzate Chile), took place. The MDP did not see itself as a rival to the AD. On the contrary, its manifesto stated that 'the constitution of the Democratic Alliance is with- out doubt an initiative we welcome' and that 'like the MDP, the AD should contribute to the development of the National Democratic Accord to which we aspire'.[59]

The impact on political life caused by the appearance of two opposition platforms was considerable, as revealed by the poll undertaken by the weekly magazine *Hoy* (Table 7.1). In spite of the restrictive political conditions imposed by the government, the existence of two opposition forces could not

Table 7.1 Degree of knowledge of the existence of five political blocs

Political blocs	Respondent knows it exists (%)
AD	82.8
MDP	45.5
MUN*	22.8
UDI*	32.7
MAN*	20.1

Note: * Pro-government blocs.
Source: *Hoy*, 7 December 1983, p. 13.

pass unnoticed at a moment when support for Pinochet was reduced to 29 per cent (see Table 7.2).[60] The opposition had finally managed to raise itself high on the political scene, and the PSCh, in spite of the politics of holocaust from the military, its fragmentation, its endless internal quarrels and its incapability to hegemonize any political coalition, had nevertheless jumped into prominence to become one of the largest opposition forces in Chile.

Notwithstanding the favourable political perspectives for the opposition by the late 1983, the party's maladies were, alas, not yet over. The CPUS had constituted a Central Committee consisting of thirty-six members, and a Political Commission of six members, postponing the designation of a secretary-general. The lack of agreement between the various factions paralysed the Central Committee, which only held its first plenum in April 1984 when a new split took place between, on the one side, the Suizos, the PSCh (Twenty-Fourth Congress), the MR and the Stuardo–Briones group, who appointed Carlos Briones as secretary-general, and, on the other side, the MAS, USP, the Tendencia Humanista Socialista and the Consenso 19 de Abril, who elected Manuel Mandujano as secretary-general. The reasons for this split are obscure, and observers interpreted it as more of a power struggle than a difference in political strategy.

If the MDP and the AP could have agreed on acting together, the prospects of the opposition would have been good, but such an accord did not materialize. Strong resistance was put up by the PDC's rightist sectors and the conservative parties which had joined the AD. During the course of 1984 it became clear that the MDP and the AD acted more in the sense of rivalry than in cooperation, even more so when, at the end of May, a member of the conservative Republican Party, Hugo Zepeda, became chairman of the AD and publicly declared that the opposition should adopt a more pragmatic stance towards Pinochet's Constitution of 1980 (that the AD had originally declared illegitimate) as it was the only existing institutional model, and that Pino-

Table 7.2 Support for General Pinochet (%)

1983 (a)		1985 (b)	
Do you support him?		Pinochet's government has been:	
Yes	29.0	Good or average	15
No	59.8	Bad	27
Don't know or no reply	11.0	Terrible	59

Sources: (a) *Hoy*, 7 December 1983, p. 14; (b) *The Economist*, 11 September 1985, p. 16.

chet's resignation was not a precondition for reopening conversations on the return to democracy. Zepeda held conversations with the 'Group of Eight', a conglomerate of right-wing parties, organized by Jarpa, the minister of the interior, but very quickly the Group of Eight collapsed following the departure of the National Party, the only one with any significant social support, which was evolving towards a position of growing autonomy and criticism towards the military government.

Meanwhile, Manuel Almeyda, chairman of the MDP, at the First National Assembly had put forward the 'minimum bases for any real national democratic agreement'. The programme, although calling for the AD to work together with them, included points that went much further than the AD platform, such as agrarian reform, and the complete removal of the Armed Forces high command, at the same time as proposing the staging of a national strike and declaring that 'the people repressed, subdued and broken day in, day out, have the right to defend themselves and to use every means possible within their grasp to fight back and to put an end to oppression now'.[61] The MDP played a substantial role in the numerous mass protests in 1984 and more especially in the massive demonstrations that took place in September and October.

Therefore two great opposition alliances had emerged and different factions of the PSCh participated in both. Little by little the AD, in which the dominant force was the PDC, was abandoning their more radical positions in order to be recognized as a legitimate opposition within the system, using mass mobilization to obtain a better bargaining standing. The MDP, under the hegemony of the PCCh, proposed more strategic goals in the transformation of Chilean society and played an essential role as a driving force in the process of mass mobilization, even though it was subjected to intense repression.

At the beginning of September 1983, the Convergencia Socialista was replaced by the Bloque Socialista, which included the PSCh (Twenty-Fourth Congress), the MAPU, the MAPU (OC), the IC and professional and university groups known as the 'Grupo por la Convergencia Socialista' and the 'Movimiento de Convergencia Universitaria'. The Bloque was defined as 'a channel for political participation and organization for the wide populace who call themselves socialists'.[62] The Bloque's aim was to become an autonomous political actor representing all socialist shades. Like the Convergencia Socialista, the Bloque argued that a Socialist–Communist front was unable to reflect 'the whole of the radical forces in Chile'.[63] The Bloque would include 'the historic socialists' (i.e. the PSCh), 'the popular Christian movement' and 'the socialist forces which were born in the 1970s' (i.e. the MAPU and the IC), and 'the socialist groups and organizations which in the universities and schools, in the women's movement, in the workshops and in the factories, stand up to the historical need of renewing and enriching the socialist ideology'.[64] The Bloque's platform was condensed in three points: (1) the strengthening of the people's organizations and the practice of civil disobedience against the dictatorship; (2) the development of the unity of all socialist forces and the fight against sectarianism; and (3) the end of the military régime and the establishment of democracy now and without preconditions.[65]

The Bloque's attempts to become an influential political actor and the locus of all the socialist factions have, so far, not succeeded. The Bloque wanted to serve as a bridge between the AD and the MDP, but contrasting political interests seem to have more weight than the efforts to build a single, unified opposition. In 1984 the Bloque suggested a 'Constitutional Pact' to be signed by all the opposition forces, but the conservative parties did not want the MDP. By the end of 1985 the paralysis of the Bloque was so plain that even its stalwart supporters spoke of a 'positive overcoming' of the Bloque towards 'a wider socialist consensus'—although the ways to achieve this positive overcoming were obscure. By early 1986 the more radical sectors of the opposition were still asking for the creation of a 'wide co-ordinating body for mass mobilization' and meeting strong resistance from the AD's right-wing groups.

In October 1985, while the Bloque Socialista was entangled in the weed of contrasting political interests, the PSCh (Almeyda), the CNR and the PSCh (Alzate Chile) established a 'Comité Coordinador por la Unidad Socialista y la Lucha Popular' to bring all these brands of socialism together into a single socialist party. By the end of 1985, therefore, Chilean socialism was still split between two magnetic fields which, in the last analysis, expressed disparate views, not only about political alliances and tactics, but, above all, about the role the PSCh should fulfil in Chile's political system.

NOTES

1. PSCh, *Al calor de la lucha contra el fascismo, construir la fuerza dirigente del pueblo para asegurar la victoria*, n.d., p. 19.
2. Ibid., p. 64.
3. Ibid., p. 63.
4. Ibid., p. 69.
5. Ibid., pp. 44–5.
6. Ibid., p. 70.
7. CNR, 'Carta al Secretario General del PS, Carlos Altamirano', *Chile-América*, 31–32, May–June 1977, p. 118.
8. Hernán del Canto, 'Discurso', *Chile-América* 31–32, *op. cit.*, p. 102.
9. CNR, *op. cit.*, p. 121.
10. Dirección Interior, *La situación política y el camino del pueblo*, n.d., p. 3.
11. CNR, *op. cit.*, p. 122.
12. Ibid., p. 121.
13. PSCh, 'Una ofensiva por la unidad del partido', *PS Informa* 10, October 1975, p. 11.
14. Manuel Almeyda, 'Partido Socialista de Chile a sus militantes y al pueblo chileno', speech, 25 October 1983.
15. PSCh (Almeyda), *Salida de Carlos Altamirano Orrego: Las razones de su relevo y expulsión*, Chile, 8 May 1979, p. 11.
16. Ibid., p. 2.
17. For PSCh (Almeyda)'s interpretation of the 1979 crisis, see ibid.
18. For Altamirano's interpretation of the 1979 crisis, see Secretariado Local Holanda, *Boletín Informativo* 1, n.d.; PSCh (Twenty-Fourth Congress), *La estrategia de simulación de la fracción*, Santiago, July 1979; *Itinerario de una crisis*, Rotterdam, May 1979.
19. Raúl Ampuero, 'Comunicado de Prensa', in La Liga por los Derechos y la Liberación de los Pueblos y el Seminario de Ariccia, *Una propuesta para el area socialista chilena* (Rome, 1980), p. 16.
20. Ibid.
21. Interview with Oscar Garretón, *Convergencia*, 5–6, 1981, p. 96.
22. Comité de Enlace, *Convergencia Socialista: Fundamentos de una propuesta*, n.d., p. 7.
23. Long's 'Movimiento Recuperacionista' and a 'Frente Socialista', led by Juan Carlos Moraga, had their invitations to the Twenty-Fourth Congress withdrawn after being charged with embezzling party funds.
24. Carlos Altamirano, *8 tesis sobre una estrategia socialista para Chile*, Paris, August 1980, p. 13.
25. ibid., p. 49.
26. Ibid., p. 67.
27. Ibid.
28. Ibid., p. 66.
29. Ibid.

30. Ibid., p. 70.
31. PSCh (Twenty-Fourth Congress), 'Resoluciones políticas XXIV Congreso Nacional (Resumen)', *Pensamiento Socialista*, 22 February 1981, p. 58.
32. Erick Schnake, 'Reflexiones para aunar criterios', *Pensamiento Socialista*, 22 February 1981, p. 32.
33. Carlos Altamirano, Raúl Ampuero and Aniceto Rodríguez, *Mensaje a los socialistas chilenos*, n.d., p. 4.
34. PSCh (Almeyda), Secretariado Exterior, *Resoluciones del Pleno del Comité Central*, April 1979, p. 46.
35. Ibid., p. 48.
36. Ibid., p. 51.
37. Ibid., p. 60.
38. Ibid., p. 61.
39. PSCh (Almeyda), *Mensaje del Comité Central a los militantes en el exilio*, Santiago, June 1979, p. 3.
40. The PCCh, for the first time, adopted a line of armed struggle which brought it close to the MIR. See Carmelo Furci, 'The Chilean Communist Party (PCCh) and Its Third Underground Period, 1973–1980', *Bulletin of Latin American Research* II, 1, October 1982, p. 90; Jean-Pierre Clerc, 'Chile: A Second Wind from the Dictatorship', *Guardian–Le Monde Weekly*, 29 March 1981, pp. 12–13.
41. See Juan Carvajal, 'Acerca de la perspectiva insurreccional', *Cuadernos de Orientación Socialista* 9, November 1981, pp. 39–56; Ernesto Rauchit, 'Movilización rupturista de masas', *Cuadernos de Orientación Socialista*, 11–12, July–September 1982, pp. 37–51. According to the PSCh (Almeyda), about 170 armed actions against the dictatorship took place in 1981, following this new line of 'rupturing mass struggle'.
42. PSCh (Almeyda), 'El momento político y la necesidad de la unidad del socialismo chileno', reproduced in PSCh (Twenty-Fourth Congress), Subsecretaría Europa–Africa, *Boletín Informativo*, April 1982, p. 20.
43. In December 1979 the Iniciativa Regional Europa and the MAS merged. In March 1980 the MAS, the USP and the MR agreed to act together as a coalition.
44. Stuardo–Briones group, *Síntesis de un conflicto: dos facetas de la reunificación socialista*, n.d., p. 5.
45. Ibid., p. 6.
46. Ibid.
47. PSCh (Almeyda), 'Unidad y lucha: el Partido Socialista en la coyuntura', *Cuadernos de Orientación Socialista* 16, October 1983, p. 21.
48. Ibid.
49. Ibid, p. 16.
50. Ibid, p. 15.
51. Ibid, p. 16.
52. Ibid.
53. Ibid.
54. PSCh (Almeyda), 'El problema socialista', *Cuadernos de Orientación Socialista* 16, October 1983, p. 3.

55. Ibid.
56. The Consenso 19 de Abril was made up of the Comisión para el Consenso and the Regional Venezuela.
57. After the 1978 crisis (see p. 190), the CNR also found itself faced with divisions, giving rise to four different factions, one headed by Benjamín Cares, another by Pedro Vuskovic and Mario Palestro, and two tiny groups on the far left. The sector referred to here is that of Vuskovic and Palestro.
58. Originally the CTC, and the El Teniente branch, which had played an important part against Allende in 1973, were led by Bernardino Castillo and Guillermo Medina, respectively, both collaborators with Pinochet's régime. The growing dissatisfaction amongst the workers, and the Left's strategy of unification paved the way in trade union elections first for the displacement of Medina, and following this, to manage to get an extraordinary meeting to elect Seguel as president of the CTC, causing a U-turn in the position of this organization with regard to the government.
59. Manuel Almeyda, 'Manifiesto del MDP al pueblo de Chile', *Cuadernos de Orientación Socialista* 16, October 1983, p. 30.
60. If this figure is accurate, Pinochet's support in 1983 was quite significant, although not sufficient enough to justify his being in power. No president has ever governed constitutionally in Chile with less than 30 per cent of the votes. Pinochet's support in 1985 had dwindled to 15 per cent.
61. Manual Almeyda, 'Discurso de clausura de la primera Asamblea Nacional del MDP', *Cuadernos de Orientación Socialista* , 17, April 1984, p. 77.
62. *Orientaciones para construir el Bloque Socialista* , Santiago, 24 May 1984, p. 1.
63. Ricardo Nuñez, *Discurso en el Acto de Homenaje al Compañero Salvador Allende* , 23 March 1984.
64. Ibid.
65. Bloque Socialista, *Movilización y unidad para poner fin a la dictadura* , n.d.

8 Conclusion: What Kind of Party?

Split as it was between two opposite goals, integration and mobilization, the PSCh was nevertheless able to gather significant electoral support to the extent of having its leader, Salvador Allende, inaugurated as the first self-professing Marxist head of state in the Western hemisphere in 1970. It is this inner dialectic which explains both the political impetus and the severe failures and weaknesses of the PSCh.

Although from its very inception the party declared itself Marxist, Marxism appeared more as a general ideological background than as an exclusive set of beliefs, and this is why it was so often relegated to the rear of fashionable isms like Peronism, Titoism or Nasserism. Latin American nationalism and Third World stands on a variety of issues have always been salient features of the party's ideology which, together with its multi-class base and its successful efforts to become an influential mass party, have brought it nearer to Latin America's populist parties, like Peronismo, Aprismo or the MNR, than to the classical Marxist–Leninist model of a party of committed revolutionaries. But this resemblance ends here, not only because the PSCh is missing some of the most characteristic traits of populist parties, such as the charismatic leader or the corporatist ideology, but, above all, because it never forsook its mobilizing tasks, its purpose of replacing capitalism with a socialist régime.

This anti-status-quo impulse assumed the shape of extreme leftism. In terms of ideology at least, the party showed itself as well to the left of any other political organization in Chile (with the only exception, perhaps, of the MIR, which declared itself apart from the political establishment). The party was always proud of its mass base and resolutely adverse to multi-class alliances. But here again the paradox and the ambiguity spring up. The party was also multi-classist, and both the working and middle classes had significant proportion of both the leadership and the membership. In the late 1960s, even a 2 per cent bourgeois element could be traced in the Central Committee. And even when the party disapproved of any attempt at class collaboration and denied the progressive character attributed to the national bourgeoisie, it never refused in practice to take part in broad electoral coalitions which included the middle sectors and 'progressive' factions of the national bourgeoisie. The party was able to project both an extremely radical image on political issues as well as an extremely liberal, flexible image on matters of internal structure and ideology which were quite appealing to workers, intellectuals and professionals. Despite its radical image and its vocal commitment to Marxism, the party was clearly structured and worked along mass-type lines, although its leadership erroneously believed they were in charge of a genuine cadre party of the Leninist model.

Ambiguities and misperceptions sprang up time and again. The party's organization was described by the leadership and party members as a Leninist structure based on democratic centralism. This perception is not founded on facts. Its structure was open and loose, discipline was weak, implementation of policies inefficient, and its diffuse and fluid character was in sharp contrast to the strong discipline, tight organization and monolithic ideology of the PCCh. Instead of the authoritarian and hierarchical structure which is typical of parties based on democratic centralism, the PSCh has been aptly described as 'a federation of ideological tendencies and groups'.[1] Beside the formal structure and the official leadership, a complex network of party personalities and factions receptive to ideological fashions were found, bringing up *asambleísmo* (long discursive discussions) and lack of implementation of policies and instructions, but also a sense of vibrant energy and liveliness which attracted workers and intellectuals disenchanted with the rigidity and the dull, conventional leftism of the PCCh. This weak general articulation found it difficult to withstand military repression after 1973. The history of the party between 1973 and 1985 is the history of a seemingly endless process of fragmentation, although by the 1980s two basic poles of conglomeration had emerged, one which stressed the need to establish a broad socialist and democratic consensus, and the other one which put emphasis on the revolutionary purpose of the party.

Lukacs has suggested that 'organisation is the form of mediation between theory and practice'.[2] If this is so, the PSCh is the exception. The PSCh is the extreme example of a divorce between theory and practice which has often dragged the party into ineffectiveness and factious quarrels. The PSCh cultivated an anti-parliamentarian tradition, a deep distrust of the democratic parliamentarian framework and an ideology which affirmed the line of mass struggle and direct action. Lukacs' motto implies a close connection between organization and tactics. Despite the party's anti-parliamentarian tradition and extreme leftism, its loose, open, liberal type of structure was at odds with armed, revolutionary struggles, but appropriate to the parliamentarian tactics which in practice the party employed since its birth, taking part in elections at every level of Chilean society—presidential, parliamentary, student bodies, trade unions—and entering into compromises with other political parties in order to get legislation passed. And in this long list of ambivalences it should be noted that the PSCh, despite its anti-status-quo stand, played a key role in the development of the liberal, bourgeois, parliamentary framework, modernizing Chile's political institutions and, like the European socialist parties, exercising an important socializing function of the emergent urban masses and facilitating the transition from agrarian to industrial society.

There is, however, a significant difference between the European socialist parties and the PSCh. European socialism was ultimately socialized into the democratic constitutional order, but the PSCh never gave up its mobilizing, radical goals. It is this distinctive dialectic between an anti-integrative tendency and a true integrative function which constitutes the singleness of the PSCh. The so-called 'peaceful road to socialism' was the only strategy in tune with the party's Janus-like face, although the party itself—and this is but another expression of its paradoxical nature—always denied the feasibility of the peaceful road in Chile. The PCCh, on the contrary, undauntedly pursued since 1952 a strategy based on the building of a broad class coalition and on the conviction that the attainment of power within the framework of parliamentary democracy was the only viable option for the left in Chile.[3]

The 1973 military coup, by destroying the PSCh's symbiotic relation with the liberal, democratic system, triggered off a malignant process of breakaway factionalism where power struggles combined with the questioning of many aspects of the historical tradition of the party, but whose ultimate sense can be grasped only if we realize that the historic bonds between the mobilizing and integrating functions lost their living interrelation and interdependence and assumed an independent form. Any discussion about future scenarios for the PSCh must be situated within this framework.

The PSCh is now committed to rebuilding a broad democratic consensus which will restore parliamentary democracy in Chile. The issue at stake is whether behind the reconstruction of the democratic system does not lay in fact a plan for the re-establishment of bourgeois hegemony and the taming of the Left, which is persuaded, in the name of consensus, moderation and parliamentarism, to abstain from advocating radical social and economic reform. The PSCh might evolve into a social democratic party which even the monopolistic bourgeoisie might smile on. The idea of building a historic socialist bloc, a broad arc of social forces which will guarantee that socialism becomes an hegemonical cultural and political movement which will not abjure its revolutionary tradition, as suggested by Gramsci, has made a strong impression in some socialist circles, but such a bloc looks more like a metaphysical myth than realistic politics. Perhaps the only feasible alternative is a type of 'second best' tactics, based on the creation of a modernizing, progressive coalition made of the PSCh, the PCCh and the PDC—not a government coalition, which is unlikely, but a basic consensus of values and attitudes which imply, on the one hand, the recognition of the economic and political expectations of the masses which require a more integrated, responsive and democratized political system, and, on the other hand, the undertaking that the demands of the masses will be limited to more immediate short-term goals within the existing socio-economic order.

Chile's unequal, dependent and unbalanced economic development is, however, unsuitable for 'second best' tactics. As Weber suggested, modern democracy can occur only under capitalist industrialization. Both main economic strategies applied in Chile—substitutive industrialization and export-led growth—failed to create a self-expanding, modern economy, which would be the condition of the PSCh's capacity to become an agency for the political integration of the masses, as was the case in Western Europe. The economic system is one of the elements which help to understand the role played by mass parties in Chile. The structural weakness of Chile's economy provides the basis for class conflict and the party's mobilizing impulse. It is true, however, that the historical PSCh, with its open and pluralistic structure, its lack of a centralized, firm organization and discipline, has been a far cry from the Leninist cadre party which seems necessary to produce a revolution. Does the party need to be reformed? Will the party ultimately choose mobilization rather than integration? The PSCh faces baffling dilemmas whose resolution nobody would dare predict. It can, however, be safely stated that if in the past the PSCh played a crucial role in the development of democracy and the sense of political efficiency in the masses, in the future there can be no genuine democracy without the PSCh. Both democracy and socialism have been honoured by Allende's death.

NOTES

1. Carmelo Furci, *The Crisis of the Chilean Socialist Party (PSCh) in 1979*, (London, Institute of Latin American Studies, n.d.), p. 1.
2. Georg Lukacs, *History and Class Consciousness* (London, Merlin Press, 1971), p. 299.
3. Carmelo Furci, *The Chilean Communist Party and the Road to Socialism* (Zed Books, London, 1984).

Bibliography (Parts I and II)

1. **Party and other archives**

Official PSCh headquarters in Santiago
Regional Headquarters in Antofagasta, Concepción and Chillán
Party Members' private libraries
National Library of Chile's Central Library
Library of the Institute of Political Science of the Catholic University of Chile
Library of the Department of Political Science of the University of Chile
    (a) Official records (acts, voting)
    (b) Official documents (reports, instructions and others)

2. **Manuscripts, letters and unofficial reports and statements** (private libraries)

3. **Periodicals and newspapers** (private libraries)

4. **Reference works**

National Library of Chile
University of Chile's Central Library
Library of the Institute of Political Science of the Catholic University of Chile
Library of the Department of Political Science of the University of Chile
Library of the University of Essex
Library of the University of London
Library of the University of Liverpool
    (a) General and Historical background
    (b) PSCh
    (c) Political parties:
        (i) General
        (ii) In the Latin American context
        (iii) Structures and organization
        (iv) Oligarchies
        (v) Finance

5. **Others**

Interviews with five former leaders, three Regional Committees and a sample of the
Political Commission of the Central Committee of the PSCh.

PART I

1. Party and other archives

(*a*) *Official records*

Dirección Nacional del Registro Electoral, *Estadísticas oficiales* (Statistical Abstracts), Santiago, Chile.

Ministerio de Economía, Fomento y Reconstrucción, Chile, *Estadísticas de la Dirección Nacional de Estadísticas y Censos de la República de Chile*, Santiago, 1971.

Ministerio de Educación Pública, Chile, *Estadísticas sobre Desorrollo Educacional*, Santiago, 1952.

Senado de la República de Chile, 'Discursos', 1933–48 (in *Anales del Senado Chileno*, Santiago, 1949).

Senado de la República de Chile, 'Discursos', 1949–59 (in *Anales del Senado Chileno*, Santiago, 1960).

Senado de la República de Chile, 'Discursos', 1960–70 (in *Anales del Senado Chileno*, Santiago, 1970).

Universidad de Chile, *Estadísticas Oficiales*, 1972.

Universidad Católica de Chile, *Estadísticas Oficiales*, 1972.

Partido Socialista, Comité Central, *Archivos oficiales*, 1937–73.

Partido Socialista, Comité Central, *Archivos confidenciales del Comité Central*, 1947–70 (confidential).

Partido Socialista, *Actas de las Sesiones del Comité Central*, 1943–70 (confidential and reserved).

Partido Socialista, Comité Central, Cartas (from and to the Central Committee), 1933–70 (confidential and reserved).

(*b*) *Official Documents*

Acta de la sesión de fundación del Partido Socialista (Act of foundation of the Socialist party), internal document, July 1933.

Ampuero, Raúl, *Sobre el Uso y Abuso del Poder Político*, mimeographed, internal and confidential, Santiago, 1942.

Estatutos orgánicos del Partido Socialista, internal document, 1933, 1939–40, 1953, 1954 and 1967.

González Videla ante la Historia, mimeographed, internal, Santiago, 1951.

Manifiesto Socialista, Santiago, Chile, mimeographed, 1934.

Resolutions of the following ordinary and extraordinary congresses of the PSCh (internal documents, mimeographed):

X   Ordinary National Congress, Talca, July 1944

V   Extraordinary Congress, Santiago, July 1945

XI   Ordinary National Congress, October 1946, Concepción; National Conference on Program, Santiago, November 1947

XII Ordinary National Congress, June 1948, Valparaíso

XIII Ordinary National Congress, June 1950, Santiago

XIV   Ordinary National Congress, May 1952, Chillán
XV   Ordinary National Congress, October 1953, San Antonio
XVI   Ordinary National Congress, October–November 1955, Valparaíso
XVII Ordinary National Congress, July 1957, Santiago
XVIII Ordinary National Congress, October 1959, Valparaíso
XIX   Ordinary National Congress, December 1961, Los Andes
XX   Ordinary National Congress, Concepción, February 1964
XXI   Ordinary National Congress, June 1965, Linares
XXII Ordinary National Congress, November 1967, Chillán
XXIII Ordinary National Congress, November 1970, La Serena

Party Congresses' Resolutions 1935-1943, mimeographed, internal document, Santiago, 1946.

Un Parlamento para Ibáñez, mimeographed, 1953.

Un Programa para Ibáñez, mimeographed, 1953.

Raúl Ampuero (secretary-general), *Boletín del Partido Socialista Popular*, mimeographed, internal, Santiago, August 1956.

Informes Políticos del Comité Central del Partido Socialista a los Plenos Nacionales (1946-73), mimeographed, internal, Santiago, 1973.

Partido Socialista, *Memoranda*, collection from the Political Commission and the Central Committee, 1934–70 (total of 2,348 memoranda distributed among five different private libraries and several party medium- and top-level bodies, internal, confidential and restricted use).

Partido Socialista, *Circulares internas* (1935–70), mimeographed, internal, confidential and restricted documents (a total of 3,843 texts, distributed among the various party bodies).

Partido Socialista, Departamento de Difusión Interna, *Organización del Partido*, mimeographed, internal, confidential and restricted, Santiago, 1933, 1939 and 1953.

Partido Socialista, Comité Central, *Nuestros defectos en organización interna* mimeographed, confidential and restricted, Santiago, 1956.

Partido Socialista, Comité Central, *Informe al Comité Central*, internal, mimeographed, confidential and restricted, Santiago, 1966.

Partido Socialista, Comité Central, *Porqué Estamos por la Centralización* (*informe especial al Comité Central*), internal, mimeographed, confidential and restricted, Santiago, 1934).

A. Pezoa, *Informe sobre el comportamiento indisciplinado de algunos núcleos* (Comité Central, reserved documents for discussion) internal, mimeographed, confidential and restricted, Santiago, 1957.

Partido Comunista de Chile, *Documentos del XI Congreso Nacional realizado en Noviembre de 1958*, Lautaro, Santiago, 1959.

Partido Socialista, Departamento Técnico, *Encuesta internas*, 1961–73, mimeographed, internal, confidential and reserved document.

Partido Socialista, Departamento de Prensa, *Boletines* (numbers 34 to 786, from 1939 to 1969), mimeographed, internal and confidential.

Marmarduke Grove, *La crisis en los núcleos* (confidential report to the Central Committee), internal, mimeographed, Santiago, 1938.

Néstor Maturana, *Discurso a la Primera Conferencia de Organización*, internal, mimeographed, November 1939.

Partido Socialista, *Nuestro Nuevo Partido* (letter from the Central Committee to party members), internal, mimeographed, 1941.

2. **Manuscripts, letters and unofficial reports and declarations**

César Godoy Urrutia, Natalio Berman, Oscar Waiss and others *Porqué Fundamos el Partido Socialista de Trabajadores*, mimeographed, (internal circulation only), Santiago, 1940.

Clodomiro Almeyda, *Caso por el Tercer mundo*, mimeographed, Santiago, 1964 (internal).

Salomón Corbalán, *Letters* (private) to Socialist leaders and members, 1943–53 (1,357 in total).

Alejandro Chelén, *Los problemas del frente-populismo*, pamphlet, internal, Santiago, 1941.

Salvador Allende, *Porqué dejamos el partido* (letter to the members), mimeographed, Santiago, 1952.

Unofficial proceedings from the *Tercera Conferencia Nacional de Organización* (manuscript), Santiago (private library).

Unofficial party records, manuscripts, Santiago (covering 1936–1970) (manuscripts, archives, letters, diaries, etc.), (private libraries).

Partido Socialista, Comité Central, *Informe oficial: los resultados del plan organizativo de Chillán*, mimeographed, confidential and reserved, Santiago, 1970.

Conversations with Central Committee members E. Serani, Erick Schnake, Juan Valenzuela, Arsenio Poupin, Ariel Ulloa, Víctor Barberis, Eduardo Paredes and Leonardo Hagel.

Conversations with five former PSCh leaders.

Interview (survey) with three Regional Committees and the majority of the Political Commission.

3. **Periodicals and newspapers**

Periodicals and newspapers

Núcleo Valparaíso (monthly) from 1934 up to 1936

Acción 1933, Santiago

Acción Socialista Santiago, 1934

Jornada Santiago, 1934–5

Consigna Santiago, (weekly), 1934–40

Espartaco Santiago, 1947–8

La Calle Santiago (weekly), 1949–55

Izquierda Santiago (weekly), 1958–61

Arauco Santiago (monthly), 1959–67
Combate 1939–40
Ultima Hora Daily, 1950–73
El Mercurio 1900–73 (especially 1920–25), Santiago (daily)
Principios (PCCh official journal) 1958–70
El Siglo Daily, 1950–73
La Tercera de la Hora Daily, 1950–73
La Patria Daily, 1972–3

4. Reference works

(a) General and historical background

Allende, Salvador, *Cuba, un camino*, PLA, Santiago, 1960.

Amunategui, Gabriel, *Manual de Derecho Constitucional*, Editorial Jurídica de Chile, Santiago, 1950.

Andrade, carlos, *Elementos de Derecho Constitucional Chileno*, Editorial Jurídica, Santiago, 1971.

Angell, Alan, *Politics and the Labour Movement in Chile*, Oxford University Press, London, 1972.

Atria, Raúl, 'Tensiones políticas y crisis económica: el caso chileno (1920–1938)', *Revista de Estudios Sociales*, Santiago, No. 1, March 1973.

Barría, Jorge, *El Movimiento obrero en Chile*, UTE, Santiago, 1971.

Basso, Lelio, 'The Italian Left', in *The Socialist Register*, Merlin Press, London, 1966.

Bernaschina, Mario, *Constitución Política y Leyes Complementarias*, Editorial Jurídica de Chile, Santiago, 1958.

Calvert, Peter, *Latin America: Social Structures and Political Institutions*, University of California Press, Berkeley, 1971.

Cammet, John M., *Antonio Gramsci and the Origins of Italian Communism*, Stanford University Press, Stanford, 1969.

Cardoso, Fernando, H., *Ideologías de la burguesía industrial en sociedades dependientes*, Siglo XXI, México, 1971.

Cardoso, F. H. and Faletto, Enzo, *Dependencia y Desarrollo en América Latina*, Siglo XXI, México, 1970.

Catalán, Elmo, *La Propaganda, Instrumento de presión política*, PLA, Santiago, 1970.

Christensen, M. *et al.*, *Ideologies and Modern Politics*, Thomas Nelson, London, 1962.

Constitución Chilena de 1925, Editorial Andrés Bello, Santiago, 1970.

Corvalán, Luis, *Chile y el nuevo Panorama mundial* (speeches), Lautaro, Santiago, 1959.

Cravenne, Theo, *La Clase Media*, Unión Panamericana, Washington, 1950.

Djilas, Milovan, *The New Class*, Unwin Books, London, 1966.

Draper, Theodore, *Castroism, Theory and Practice*, Praeger, London, 1965.

Estévez, Carlos, *Reformas que la Constitución de 1925 introdujo a la de 1833*, Cuadernos jurídicos y Sociales de la Universidad de Chile, Santiago, 1942.

Faletto, Enzo *et al.*, *Génesis Histórica del Proceso Político Chileno*, Quimantú, Santiago, 1972.

Frank, Andre Gunder, 'Chile, el Desarrollo del Sub-Desarrollo', *Monthly Review*, Santiago, Enero–Febrero, 1968.

Friedrich, Carl J., *Man and His Government: An Empirical Theory of Politics*, McGraw-Hill, New York, 1968.

Frühling, Hugo, 'Capas medias en Chile (1920–1938)', unpublished Social Science thesis at the University of Chile, Santiago, 1973.

Furtado, Celso, 'Hacia una ideologia del desarrollo', *El Trimestre Económico*, No. 131, México, 1966.

Gramsci, Antonio, *Macquiavelo y Lenin*, Biblioteca Popular Nascimento, Santiago, 1968.

Halperin, Ernst, *Proletarian Class Parties in Europe and Latin America*, MIT Press, Cambridge, 1967.

Heisse, Julio, *Historia Constitucional de Chile*, Editorial Juridica de Chile, Santiago, 1950.

Jaguaribe, H. *et al.*, *La dominación en América Latina*, Moncloa, Lima, Perú, 1968.

Jobet, Julio César, *Ensayo Crítico del Desarrollo Económico Social de Chile*, América Nuestra/Editorial Universitaria, Santiago, 1969.

Joxe, Alain, *Los Fuerzas Armadas en el sistema político Chileno*, Edit. Universitaria, Santiago, 1970.

Klugman, James, *From Trotsky to Tito*, Lawrence & Wishart, London, 1951.

Kardelj, Eduard, *La Democracia Socialista en la prática*, Yugoeslavia, PLA, Santiago, 1960.

Lagarrigue, Fernando Pinto, *Crónica Política del Siglo XX*, Orbe, Santiago, 1972.

Lagos, Ricardo, *La Industria en Chile antecedentes estructurales*, Instituto de Economía, Santiago, Chile, 1966.

Lacquer, Walter (ed.), *Polycentrism*, Praeger, New York, 1962.

Bureau Sudamericano de la Internacional Comunista, *Las grandes luchas revolucionarias del proletariado Chileno*, Editorial Marx-Lenin, Santiago, 1931.

Lebovitz, Herman, *Social Conservatism and the Middle Classes in Germany (1914-33)*, Princeton University Press, NJ, 1969.

Lechner, Norbert, *La Democracia en Chile*, Signos, Santiago, 1971.

Lehman, David (ed.), *Agrarian Reform and Agrarian Reformism (Studies of Peru, Chile, China and India)*, Faber & Faber, London, 1973.

Lichtheim, George, *The Origins of Socialism*, Weidenfeld & Nicolson, London, 1968.

Mchan, Jitendra, 'Varieties of African Socialism' in *The Socialist Register*, Merlin Press, London, 1966.

McVicker, Charles P., *Titoism*, Macmillan, London, 1957.

Marx and Engels, *The Communist Manifesto*, ed. S. P. Taylor, Penguin, London, 1967.

Muñoz, Oscar, *Crecimiento Industrial de Chile, 1914-1965*, Universidad de Chile, 1967.

Pinto, Anibal, 'Desarrollo y Relaciones Sociales', in *Chile Hoy*, Siglo XXI, México, 1971.

Poulantzas, Nikos, *Poder Político y Clases Sociales en el Estado Capitalista*, Siglo XXI, México, 1972.

Ramírez, Hérnán, *Historia del Imperialismo en Chile*, Austral, Santiago, 1970.
   El Movimiento Obrero en Chile, Austral, Santiago, 1966.
   Orígenes y Fundación del Partido Comunista de Chile, Austral, Santiago, 1962.
Raynor, John, *The Middle Classes*, Penguin, London, 1969.
Roméro, Réne, *Confesiones Políticas*, Orbe, Santiago.
Stein, Stanley, J. and Stein, Barbara H., *The Colonial Heritage of Latin America*, Oxford University Press, New York, 1970.
Sunkel, Osvaldo, 'El trasfondo estructural de los problemas del desarrollo, latino-americano', in *El Trimestre Económico*, México, Enero–Merzo, 1967.
Vergara, Ximena and Barros, Luis, 'Las ideologias de la clase dominante' in *Escuela Latinoamericana de Sociologia* ed. Vergara and Luis, Santiago, 1972.
Waiss, Oscar, *Amanecer en Belgrado*, PLA, Santiago, 1956.
Zetlin, Maurice, 'Determinantes Sociales de la Democracia Política en Chile', *Revista Latinoamericana de Sociología*, Vol. 11, July 1966.

(b) PSch

Almeyda, Clodomiro, *Hacia una concepción marxista del Estado*, Ercilla, Santiago, 1949.
Alvarez, Agustín, *Objetivos del socialismo en Chile*, Gutenberg, Santiago, 1946.
Ampuero, Raúl, *La Izquierda en punto muerto*, Orbe, Santiago, 1966.
Casanueva, Valencia, F. and Fernández, M., *El Partido Socialista y la lucha de clases en Chile*, Quimantú, Santiago, 1973.
Chelén, Alejandro, *Trayectoria del socialismo*, Austral, Santiago, 1966.
Flujo y reflujo del socialismo chileno, Austral, Santiago, 1961.
Chelén, Alejandro, and Jobet, Julio César, *Pensamiento Teórico y Político del Partido Socialista*, Quimantú, Santiago, 1972.
—— and ——), *El socialismo chileno a través de sus Congresos*, Quimantú, Santiago, 1972 (revised and enlarged edition).
Jobet, Julio César, *Tres ensayos históricos*, Austral, Santiago, 1950.
——, *Recabarren, los orígenes del movimiento obrero y del socialismo chileno*, PLA, Santiago, 1955.
——, *El socialismo en Chile*, PLA, Santiago, 1956.
——, *La realidad chilena y la fundación del Partido Socialista*, ARAUCO, Santiago, March 1967.
——, *El socialismo chilena a través de sus congresos*, PLA, Santiago, 1965.
——, *El Partido Socialista de Chile*, PLA, 2 vols., Santiago, 1971.
Millas, Orlando, 'El Senador Raúl Ampuero y los tópicos anti-communistas', in *La Pólémica Socialista Comunista*, PLA, Santiago, 1962.
B. Pollack and G. Geisse, *Aportes al Estudio del Partido Socialista* Chileno-I, *Revista de Ciencia Politica y Derecho Publico*, Universidad de Chile, No. 13, año 1972, pp. 31–48.
B. Pollack, 'The Chilean Socialist Party: Prolegomena to Its Ideology and Organisation', *Journal of Latin American Studies*, 10, I, 117–52.
B. Pollack (ed), *Mobilization and Socialist Politics in Chile*, Centre for Latin American Studies of the University of Liverpool, Monograph Series No. 9, 1980.
Waiss, Oscar, *El Drama Socialista*, Santiago, 1948.

(*c*) *Political Parties*

(*i*) *General*

Basso, Lelio, 'The Italian Left', in *The Socialist Register 1966*, pp. 27–45.

Blondel, Jean, *An Introduction to Comparative Government*, Weidenfeld & Nicolson, London, 1965.

—, *Comparative Government* (a reader), Macmillan, London, 1969.

Charlesworth, James C. (ed.), *Contemporary Political Analysis*, Free Press, New York, 1967.

Dahl, Robert, *Modern Political Analysis*, Prentice Hall, Englewood Cliffs, NH, 1970.

Dahl, Robert and Neubauer, Deane, E., *Readings in Modern Political Analysis*, Prentice Hall, Englewood Cliffs, NJ, 1968.

Davies, Ian and de Miranda, Shakuntale, 'The Working Class in Latin America: Some Theoretical Problems' in *The Socialist Register 1967*, pp. 239–56.

Duverger, Maurice, *Political Parties*, Methuen, London, 1972.

Eldersvold, Samuel, J., *Political Parties: A Behavioural Analysis*, MacNally, Chicago, 1964.

Field, C. Lowell, *Comparative Political Development*, Alden Press, Oxford, 1968.

Jupp, James, *Political Parties*, Routledge & Kegan Paul, London, 1968.

Kim, Young, C., 'The Concept of Political Culture in Comparative Politics', *The Journal of Politics*, Vol. 26, pp. 335–6.

La Palombara, Joseph, 'Political Party Systems and Crisis Government: French and Italian Contrasts', *Midwest Journal of Political Science*, Vol. 11, No. 2, May 1958, pp. 117–42.

Leys, Colin, 'Models, Theories and the Theory of Political Parties', *Political Studies*, Vol. VII, No. 2, 1959, pp. 127–46.

Liebman, Marcel, 'The Crisis of the Belgian Social Democracy', in *The socialist Register 1966*, pp. 44–65.

McDonald, Neil, A., *The Study of Political Parties*, Random House, New York, 1967.

Michels, Robert, *Political Parties*, Dover, New York, 1959.

Neumann, Sigmund (ed.), *Modern Political Parties: Approaches to Comparative Politics*, Chicago, University of Chicago Press, 1956.

Scarrow, Howard, A., 'The Function of Political Parties: A Critique of the Literature and the Approach', *The Journal of Politics*, Vol. 29, 1967, pp. 770–89.

Simmons, Harvey G., 'The French Opposition in 1969', *Government and Opposition*, Vol. 4, 1969, pp. 757–76.

Smith, Gordon, 'What Is a Party System?' *Parliamentary Affairs* 19 (3), 1966, pp. 551–62.

Soares, Glaucio and Hamblin, Robert L., 'Socio-economic Variables and Voting for the Radical Left: Chile, 1952', *APSR*, Vol. 61, 1967, pp. 1055–65.

Tomasson, Richard F., 'The Extraordinary Success of the Swedish Social Democrats', *The Journal of Politics*, Vol. 31, 1969, pp. 772–93.

Wildawsky, A., 'A Methodological Critique of Duverger's *Political Parties*', *The Journal of Politics*, Vol. 21, 1959.

(*ii*) *In the Latin American context*

Aguilar, Luis E. (ed.), *Marxism in Latin America*, Knopf, New York, 1968.

Angell, Alan, 'Chile: From Christian Democracy to Marxism?' in *The World Today*, Chatham House, November 1970.

Anglade, Christian, 'Party Finance Models and the Classification of Latin American Parties', in *Comparative Political Finance. The Financing of Party Oragnizations and Election Campaigns*, ed. Arnold J. Heidenheimer, Heath, Lexington, Mass., 1970, pp. 163–89.

Blackburn, Robin, *Strategy for Revolution: Essays on Latin America*, (ed.), Regis Debray, Trinity Press, London, 1970.

Dinerstein, Herbert S., 'Soviet Policy in Latin America', *APSR*, Vol. 61, 1967, pp. 80–90.

Huberman, Leo and Sweezy, Paul, H., *Regis Debray and the Latin American Revolution*, MR Press, London, 1968.

Izaguirre, Inés, 'Imagen de clase en los partidos políticos argentinos', *Revista Latinoamericana de Sociologíca*, Diciembre 1967, no. 2.

Martz, John D., 'Dilemmas in the Study of Latin American Political Parties', *The Journal of Politics*, Vol. 26, 1964, pp. 509–31.

Petras, James, 'Negocia dores Políticos en Chile: Los Empresarios, la clase media, la burocracia', in *Monthly Review* (in Spanish), Año VII, nos. 70, 71, 1970 (Special number).

(*iii*) *Structure and organization*

Blondel, Jean, *An Introduction to Comparative Government*, Weidenfeld & Nicholson, London, 1969.

—, *Comparative Government* (a reader), Macmillan, London, 1969.

—, *Comparing Political Systems*, Weidenfeld & Nicolson, London, 1973.

Beck, Carl, 'Party Control and Bureaucratization in Czechoslovakia', *The Journal of Politics*, Vol. 23, 1961, pp. 279–94.

Djilas, Milovan, *The New Class*, Unwin Books, London, 1966.

Duverger, Maurice, *Political Parties*, Lowe & Brydone, London, 1969.

Gramsci, Antonio, *Soviets in Italy*, Pamphlet Series No. 11. (Institute for Workers Control, London, 1970).

Hallas, Duncan, Cliff, Tony, Harman, Chris and Trotsky, Leon, *Party and Class* (essays), Pluto Press, London, 1970.

Johnstone, Monty, 'Marx, Engels and the Concept of the Party', in *The Socialist Register 1967*, pp. 725–58.

Lenin, Ilych Vladimir, *Selected Works*, London, 1947, Vol. 1.

—, *What Is to Be Done?* Progress Publishers, Moscow, 1968.

Luxemburg, Rosa, *Leninism or Marxism? The Russian Revolution*, ed. Bertram D. Wolfe (Ann Arbor, University of Michigan Press, 1961).

McKenzie, Robert, *British Political Parties*, William Heinemann, London, 1955.

Magri, Lucio, 'What Is a Revolutionary Party?', *New Left Review*, No. 60, March–April 1970, pp. 97–128.

May, John D., 'Democracy, Organization, Michels', *APSR*, Vol. 59, 1965, pp. 417–25.

Rossanda, Rossana, 'Class and Party', in *The Socialist Register*, 1970, pp. 217–31.

Soligman, Lester C., 'Political Recruitment and Party Structures: A Case Study', *APSR*, Vol. 55, 1961, pp. 77–86.

Zariski, Raphael, 'Intra-Party Conflict in a Dominant Party: The Experience of the Italian Christian-Democracy', *The Journal of Politics*, Vol. 27, pp. 3–34.

—, 'The Italian Socialist Party: A Case Study in Factional Conflict', *APSR*, June 1962.

—, 'Party Factions and Comparative Politics: Some Preliminary Observations', *Midwest Journal of Political Science*, Vol. 4, No. 1, February 1966, pp. 27–51.

(*iv*) *Oligarchies*

Blondel, Jean, *Comparative Government*, Macmillan, London, 1969.

—, *An Introduction to Comparative Government*, Weidenfeld & Nicolson, London, 1969.

Duverger, Maurice, *Political Parties*, Lowe & Brydone, London, 1969.

Gehlen, Michael P. and McBride, Michael, 'The Soviet Central Committee: An Elite Analysis', *APSR*, Vol. 62, 1968, pp. 1232–41.

Lodge, Milton, *'Grappovshina' in the Post-Italian Period*, The Laboratory for Political Research, Department of Political Science, the University of Iowa, Iowa City, 1968.

McCloskey, Herbert and Dahlgrea, Harold E., 'Primary Group Influence on Party Loyalty', *APSR*, Vol. 53, 1959, pp. 757–76.

McCloskey, Herbert, Hoffman, Paul and O'Hara, Rosemary, 'Issue Conflict and Consensus Among Party Leaders and Followers', *APSR*, 1960, Vol. 52, pp. 406–27.

Mosca, Gaetano, *The Ruling Class*, McGraw-Hill, New York (n.d.).

Parry, Geraint, *Political Elites*, Allen & Unwin, London, 1969.

Walker, Jack L., 'A Critique of the Elitist Theory of Democracy', *APSR*, Vol. 60, June 1968, pp. 285–305.

Wright, Mills, C., *The Power Elite*, Oxford University Press, Oxford, 1965.

(*v*) *Finances*

Blondel, Jean, *Comparative Government* (a reader), Macmillan, London, 1969.

—, *An Introduction to Comparative Government*, Weidenfeld & Nicolson, London, 1969.

Duverger, Maurice, *Political Parties*, Lowe & Brydone, London, 1969.

Heidenheimer, Arnold J., 'Comparative Party Finance: Notes on Practices and Towards a Theory', *The Journal of Politics*, Vol. 25, 1963, pp. 750, 811.

Heidenheimer, Arnold J. (ed.), *Comparative Political Finance, the Financing of Party Organisations and Election Campaigns*, Heath, Lexington, Mass., 1970.

PART II

1. Party and Other Archives

Official documents

Clodomiro Almeyda (secretary-general), 'La salida democrático-revolucionaria a la crisis chilena', *Cuadernos de Orientación Socialista* 22, December 1985.

Manual Almeyda, 'Partido Socialista de Chile a sus militantes y al pueblo chileno', speech, 25 October 1983.

——, 'Manifiesto del MDP al pueblo de Chile', *Cuadernos de Orientación Socialista*, 16, October 1983.

——, 'Discurso de clausura de la primera Asamblea Nacional del MDP', *Cuadernos de Orientación Socialista*, 17, April 1984.

Carlos Altamirano (secretary-general), 'En el acto del Partido Socialista Francés', *PS Informa* 10, October–November 1975.

——, 'Reflexiones críticas sobre el proceso revolucionario chileno', *Boletín Informativo* 4, September–October 1974.

——, *8 tesis sobre una estrategia socialista para Chile*, Paris, 1 August 1980.

Carlos Altamirano, Raúl Ampuero and Aniceto Rodríguez, *Mensaje a los socialistas chilenos*, n.d.

Raúl Ampuero, 'Comunicado de Prensa', in La Liga por los Derechos y la Liberación de los Pueblos y el Seminario de Ariccia, *Una propuesta para el Area Socialista chilena*, 1980.

Armando Arancibia *et al*., 'El socialismo por el que luchamos', *Pensamiento Socialista*, 29, July–September 1983.

Bloque Socialista, *Orientaciones para construir el Bloque Socialista*, Santiago, 24 May 1984.

——, *Movilización y unidad para poner fin a la dictadura*, n.d.

Juan Carvajal, 'Acerca de la perspectiva insurreccional', *Cuadernos de Orientación Socialista* 9, November 1981.

Comité de Enlace, *Convergencia Socialista: fundamentos de una propuesta*, n.d.

CNR, 'Carta al Secretario General del PS, Carlos Altamirano', *Chile-América* 31–2, May–June 1977.

Oscar Garretón, 'Interview', *Convergencia*, 5–6, 1981.

Ricardo Nuñez, *Discurso en el Acto de Homenaje al Compañero Salvador Allende*, speech, 23 March 1984.

Partido Socialista, 'Una ofensiva por la unidad del partido', *PS Informa* 10, October–November, 1975.

——, *Al calor de la lucha contra el fascismo, construir la fuerza dirigente del pueblo para asegurar la victoria*, Santiago, March 1974.

Partido Socialista (Almeyda), *Resoluciones del Pleno del Comité Central*, 1979.

——, *Mensaje del Comité Central a los militantes en el exilio*, Santiago, June 1979.

——, 'El momento político y la necesidad de la unidad del socialismo chileno', reproduced in PS (XXIV Congreso), *Boletín Informativo*, April 1982.

——, 'Unidad y lucha: el Partido Socialista en la coyuntura', *Cuadernos de Orientación Socialista* 16, October 1983.

——, 'El problema socialista', *Cuadernos de Orientación Socialista* 16, October 1983.

Partido Socialista (XXIV Congreso), 'Resoluciones políticas XXIV Congreso nacional (Resumen)', *Pensamiento Socialista* 22, February 1981.

——, *Nuestros 46 años de vida*, 1979.

Ernesto Rauchit, 'Movilización rupturista de masas', *Cuadernos de Orientación Socialista*, 11–12, July–September 1982.

Erick Schnake, 'Reflexiones para aunar criterios', *Pensamiento Socialista*, 22 February 1981.

2. Manuscripts, Letters and Unofficial Reports and Declarations

CNR, *Conversando con el Partido Socialista (CNR)*, mimeographed (internal circulation only), n.d.

Partido Socialista (Almeyda), *Salida de Carlos Altamirano Orrego: las razones de su relevo y expulsión*, mimeographed (internal circulation only), Chile, 8 May 1979.

Partido Socialista (XXIV Congreso), *La estrategia de simulación de la fracción*, mimeographed (internal circulation only), Santiago, 1979.

——, *Itinerario de una crisis*, mimeographed (internal circulation only), Rotterdam, 1979.

Stuardo–Briones Group, *Síntesis de un conflicto: dos facetas de la reunificación socialista*, mimeographed (internal circulation only), n.d.

Anonym, *Facciones del partido Socialista chileno*, mimeographed (internal circulation only), n.d.

Vera, Hector and Poblete, Carlos, *El Partido de Allende en la clandestinidad y en el exilio*, mimeographed (internal circulation only), Brussels, June 1980.

3. Periodicals and Newspapers

Alzate Chile PSCh (Alzate Chile) official journal; from 1980 up to 1984.

Boletín Informativo PSCh (XXIV Congress), 1979.

Bulletin of the Chile Committee for Human Rights Bimonthly, from 1978 up to 1985.

Chile-América Bimonthly, from 1976 up to 1980.

Cuadernos de Orientación Socialista PSCh (Almeyda) official journal; from 1980 up to 1985.

Pensamiento Socialista PSCh (XXIV Congress) official journal; from 1979 up to 1985.

PS Informa PSCh official journal; from 1974 up to 1976.

Hoy Weekly current-affairs magazine, from 1979 up to 1985.

Ercilla Weekly current-affairs magazine, from 1973 up to 1983.

Qué Pasa? Weekly current-affairs magazine, from 1973 up to 1980.

4. **Reference Works**

(*a*) *General and Historical Background*

Altamirano, Carlos, *Dialéctica de una derrota*, Siglo XXI, México, 1977.

Anderson, Charles W., *Politics and Economic Change in Latin America*, Van Nostrand, New York, 1967.

Blackburn, Lucy, 'The Current Economic Situation: Alternative Policy, Choices, and Future Perspectives', in David Hojman (ed.), *Chile After 1973*.

Cammack, Paul, 'Democratization: A Review of the Issues', *Bull. Lat. Am. Res.*, 4 (2), 1983.

Carrasco, Eliecer, *Acerca del desarrollo histórico del Partido Socialista chileno*, n.d.

Cerri, Roberto, 'Competencia poco libre', *Mensaje* 283, October 1979.

Clerc, Jean Piere, 'Chile: a second wind from the dictatorship', *Guardian-Le Monde Weekly*, 29 March 1981.

Dahse, Fernando, *Mapa de la extrema riqueza*, Aconcagua, Santiago, 1979.

Frei, Eduardo, 'El mandato de la historia y las exigencias del porvenir', *Chile-América* 14–15, January–February 1976.

Furci, Carmelo, *The Chilean Communist Party and the Road to Socialism*, Zed Books, London, 1984.

Garces, Joan, *El Estado y los problemas tácticos en el gobierno de Allende*, Siglo XXI, Buenos Aires, 1974.

García, A. and Wells, J., 'Chile: A Laboratory for Failed Experiments in Capitalist Political Economy', *Cambridge Journal of Economics* 7, 1983.

García Marquez, Gabriel, 'Autopsia de un asesinato', *Postdata* 3, March–April 1974.

Hojman, David E. (ed.), *Chile After 1973: Elements for the Analysis of Military Rule*, University of Liverpool, Centre for Latin American Studies, Monograph Series, No. 12, 1985.

Lagos, Ricardo, *Democracia para Chile: proposiciones de un socialista*, Ensayo, Santiago, 1985.

Lipset, Seymour Martin, *Political Man*, Heinemann, London, 1969.

Mamalakis, Markos M., *The Growth and Structure of the Chilean Economy*, Yale University Press, New Haven, 1976.

Ortuzar, Enrique, *La nueva institucionalidad chilena*, Universidad Católica, Santiago, 1976.

Petras, James, *Política y fuerzas sociales en el desarrollo chileno*, Amorrortu, Buenos Aires, 1971.

Roxborough, Ian *et al*., *Chile: The State and Revolution*, Macmillan, London, 1979.

Taufic, Camilo, *Chile en la hoguera*, Corregidor, Buenos Aires, 1974.

Whitehead, Lawrence, 'Whatever Became of the "Southern Cone Model"?' in David Hojman (ed.), *Chile After 1973*.

(*b*) *PSCh*

Furci, Carmelo, *The Crisis of the Chilean Socialist Party (PSCh) in 1979*, University of London, Institute of Latin American Studies, Working Papers 11, n.d.

(c) *Political parties*

La Palòmbara, Joseph and Weiner, Myron, 'The Origin and Development of Political Parties', in La Palombara and Weiner (eds.), *Political Parties and Political Development*, Princeton University Press, Princeton, NJ, 1969.

Lukacs, Georg, *History and Class Consciousness*, Merlin Press, 1971.

Kirchheimer, Otto, 'The Transformation of the Western European Party System', in La Palombara and Weiner (eds.), *Political Parties and Political Development*.

5. Others

Acción Democrática, 'National Agreement for the Transition to a Full Democracy', *Chile Update*, Bulletin of the Chile Committe for Human Rights 63, October–November 1985.

Inter-American Bank of Development, *Economic and Social Progress in Latin America* (1976).

——, *Cifras seleccionadas sobre América Latina*, (1978).

Index